REVEALING JESUS

Dear friend,

I thank God that you have found yourself with this devotional in your hand, and with all my heart I pray it is a great blessing to your life.

Revealing Jesus came about after many conversations with friends and even more conversations with God . . . asking about the finished work of Christ and what victory the Bible declares is available to us in Jesus' name. To say that I am desperate for the power of the cross and the power of the blood of Jesus to be worked out in greater measure in my life is an understatement. His presence beckons me. . . .

You will hear that the songs on the companion album of the same name are filled with declaration of Scripture to ensure that it is truly woven within the fabric of your heart. This devotional was written to give you food for thought each day about how Jesus is revealed in our everyday lives, to give you courage and strength for each day.

So I pray you are fueled for service as you read, and that your hearts yearn for more of Jesus as you worship Him with every fiber of your being.

Your friend,
Darlene Zschech

Jesus Be Revealed

REVEAL

BETHANY HOUSE PUBLISHERS
a division of Baker Publishing Group
Minneapolis, Minnesota

DARLENE ZSCHECH

ING
JESUS

A 365-DAY DEVOTIONAL

FAITHFUL

JESUS IS CALLED FAITHFUL.
JESUS IS CALLED TRUE.

JANUARY

GREAT is thy faithfulness!
GREAT is thy faithfulness!
Morning by morning
new mercies I see;
All I have needed
thy hand hath provided—
GREAT is thy faithfulness,
Lord, unto me!

Jesus, you are my
Faithful One!

IT BEGINS WITH JOY

*Blessed is the person who does not follow the advice of wicked people,
take the path of sinners, or join the company of mockers.*

PSALM 1:1, GOD'S WORD

The first promise we find in the Psalms is one of blessing, of a joy that resides deep inside the heart. What a marvelous place to start the year—the incredible joy found when we truly know Jesus. In fact, all the fruit of the Spirit—love, joy, peace, patience, kindness, goodness, faithfulness, gentleness, and self-control (see Galatians 5:22)—is available to every one of us who makes a decision to walk with Christ as our Lord and Savior, flourishing under godly counsel and walking away from ungodly influence.

When we follow God, our hearts and minds become alert and awake, shaken from our slumber. We experience the joy of God's ways. We are likewise warned of the enemy's deceptive plans to diminish us and hold us back from God's best for us. Is it any wonder he seeks to surround and distract us with ungodly thoughts and environments that are all too easily accepted as the norm?

Every time I read the Psalms, my thoughts turn to Jesus and my joy is renewed. I learn again how to pray and how to praise, in any circumstance of my life.

My prayer is that you will experience the truth that life in Christ is above and greater and more joyful than anything else you might be living for at the moment.

*Thank you, God, for the joy of knowing Jesus—and for
sending the Holy Spirit to guide and teach us your ways.*

GOD'S WAY OR YOUR WAY?

But my people didn't listen, Israel paid no attention;
so I let go of the reins and told them, "Run! Do it your own way!"

PSALM 81:11–12, THE MESSAGE

*I*f you've ever wondered about the wisdom of doing things God's way, of the power and joy found in obedience, then read Psalm 81 over and over until it settles in your heart.

The lessons on the blessings of obedience, love, and service are rich. We learn of the magnificent protective hand of our God. His heart toward us is indescribable. But in the end, He does not force what is continually rejected, for He is the ultimate gentleman.

When God declares, "Do it your own way!" there is a palpable sense of divine frustration and hurt. A recent personal experience, where a ministry team member lied to many of us who loved and trusted him, gave me a glimpse of God's sorrow when we demand to do things our way, in defiance of His good plans for our lives.

What is it about us that still wants to do things our own way? Why do we fight the hand that created us? The mystery of the great love of God is still so unfathomable, yet this is the journey of faith and trust.

I find tremendous encouragement and comfort in the prayer of Jesus in the garden of Gethsemane: "Father, if you are willing, take this cup from me; yet not my will, but yours be done" (Luke 22:42, NIV).

Even though our sin nature fights us, if we choose to serve God and do things as He has set out for us, then His covenant protects us not only from our enemies but from ourselves. Then we experience His plans and purpose for our lives fully.

God, sometimes obedience is hard. But not my will, but yours be done in my life.

HE IS PRESENT

They have seen Your procession, O God, the procession
of my God, my King, into the sanctuary.

PSALM 68:24, NKJV

When we come to the sanctuary of God, when we gather as His church, what is our posture and attitude?

The psalmist doesn't just see a ragtag army returning from a victory God delivered; he sees God in front, leading the procession.

I love meeting with God's people—coming together to celebrate, give, and be fueled for service—but if there is one thing that I truly treasure whenever I enter the house of God, it is His presence. Not a symbolic presence, but the knowledge that God himself is with us. What a constant source of strength and hope for you and me, for all His people. In Psalm 68 we are reminded that Yahweh is not an aloof, austere King who stands afar and is unconcerned for the needs of His people. Rather, He daily bears our burdens, providing us a way of escape from enemies and troubles.

Is it any wonder Jesus was called Immanuel, which literally means "God is with us"?

Do you feel defeated, overwhelmed by troubles on every side? Do you feel there is no way of escape? Does victory seem beyond your grasp? The good news is God is beside you, and even if you aren't strong enough to prevail, He will do for you what you don't have the human power to do yourself.

As you enter God's sanctuary, never forget He himself marches in ahead of you. He is present! Our very present help in times of need.

God, renew my spiritual eyes to see you walk before me and beside me as I turn to you in every situation of life. Thank you for being truly present in my worship of you!

AN ANGRY LOVE

Scatter the peoples who delight in war.

PSALM 68:30, ESV

*R*ead through Psalm 68:23–35, and you will quickly discover that God's love for the world is not always gentle. Just as Jesus fashioned a whip and drove out those who made mockery of God's temple (see John 2:15), so God's plans and mercies are revealed in His anger.

When we get angry, it often shows a lack of discipline or is based on self-interest. But God loves the world so much that He will rise up and "scatter the people who delight in war."

I love the picture painted here of nations that were once in rebellion, witnessing the glory of God and unable thereafter to resist joining in with the multitudes of those who worship and praise God.

We are seeing this before our very eyes even today. On a recent trip to Rwanda, a nation that has been ravaged by war and genocide, what joy I felt to discover that in recent days hundreds of thousands of people have accepted Jesus Christ as Lord. I genuinely pray daily that we will see this and other nations come alive from the inside out through the power and kindness of God.

When does anger show love? When it is godly anger that fulfills His plans to redeem the world: "That at the name of Jesus every knee should bow, in heaven and on earth and under the earth, and every tongue should acknowledge that Jesus Christ is Lord, to the glory of God the Father" (Philippians 2:9–10, NIV).

I pray today for the salvation of individuals and entire nations
that have previously lived in strife and war.

THROUGH THE FIRE

My lips will praise you because your mercy is better than life itself.

PSALM 63:3, GOD'S WORD

*S*uffering is a reality. Read through Hebrews 11 and you will discover that God's chosen and beloved at times walk through the fire. I can't read through the Psalms without feeling the emotional distress and pain that David suffered at the hands of his enemies.

But pain is never the last word. "Then I will make music to praise your name forever" (61:8). "I will lift up my hands to pray in your name" (63:4). "The [uncompromisingly] righteous shall be glad in the Lord and shall trust and take refuge in Him; and all the upright in heart shall glory and offer praise" (64:10, AMP).

In Psalm 64 we hear the jubilant reminder that despite present sufferings, all mankind will fear, proclaim, ponder, rejoice in, and ultimately praise the one true God.

How powerful, how beautiful is the praise that erupts from a life that has gone through the fire and comes out with a truthful, courageous new understanding of the faithfulness of God himself.

That kind of faithfulness must be fed by the Word of God, not just as casual reading, but where we bring our inner pursuits in line with Scripture; not just a source of comfort, but the priority of your heart.

*Father, thank you for the gift of your Son. Jesus experienced
the ultimate suffering to ultimately deliver us from any suffering
we experience in this world. I embrace that reality today.*

FROM THE DEPTHS

My God, my God, why have you abandoned me?

MATTHEW 27:46, GOD'S WORD

*I*n the anguish of the cross, Jesus called to His Father with the prayer recorded in Psalm 22:1: "My God, my God, why have you abandoned me?"

How wonderful, how astonishing it is to discover that the Psalms not only uniquely express the depths of the human soul, but they also convey the heart and soul of Jesus Christ.

I've always been grateful that the Psalms have helped shape my response to God in the joys and trials of life. But to then learn that I can know more of the inner depths of Jesus' heart in response to His Father brings me to tears. Is it any wonder I turn to the Psalms to know Jesus better and worship Him at a deeper level?

The rest of Psalm 22:1 reads, "Why are you so far away from helping me, so far away from the words of my groaning?"

For me to pray like that might have once given me pangs of guilt that I was not being faithful and giving honor to my redeemer God. But knowing Jesus felt and prayed this way has taught me that God wants me to come to Him in complete honesty, not holding anything back but expressing even my raw pain to Him.

Thank you, Jesus, for giving me a glimpse into the depths of your soul.
Thank you, heavenly Father, for allowing me to cry out to you
from the depths of my heart.

GOD SPEAKS

When you were in trouble, you called out to me, and I rescued you.
I was hidden in thunder, but I answered you.

PSALM 81:7, GOD'S WORD

Psalm 81 begins with the command that we are to sing joyfully and shout happily to the Lord. The psalmist doesn't stop with us just using our voices. He was a musician and worship leader. He tells us to sound the tambourine and drums in our song, to add some sweet sounding strings, and then to blow the horn boldly. None of this is to be timid. We are to make a joyful noise.

Just as God told Joseph to never forget what He did for him in Egypt, worship in music is our time to celebrate the marvelous acts of God in our lives.

To take the gift of music and use it for the reason God gave it to us is nothing short of miraculous, no matter how simple or how elaborate the offering is. As long as it proclaims truth and comes from a heart of praise, our singing delights the heart of God.

But what amazes me and causes me to tremble is that when we sing to the Lord, He speaks back to us. The psalmist tells us he hears God's voice in the midst of the sound of thunder. He receives a word of revelation and instruction from the One he never guessed would speak to him.

Don't let that truth slip by you. Savor the thought that the Maker of heaven and earth cares enough to bow down and speak with us. To me. To you.

In my words and my music
I will listen for your voice, O God.

HIS VICTORY IS OURS

With God on our side like this, how can we lose?

ROMANS 8:31, THE MESSAGE

Throughout Scripture, God's people called to Him for deliverance and He saved them. When you think all is lost and suddenly find yourself a victor—against all odds—how can you not celebrate our mighty God?

In Psalm 68:19, the psalmist declares, "Blessed be the Lord—day after day he carries us along. He's our Savior, our God, oh yes!"

What a tremendous cry of praise. But these words are also a reminder that God is our Savior and our strength. It is not by our might and cunning that we are saved; victory is a gift from God. His presence literally imparts power and strength to His people.

He knew our temptation to exalt ourselves and take credit for what God has done on our behalf. Have you ever cried to God for deliverance, received it, and then forgotten to give Him thanks? You are not alone.

After any victory in your life, great or small, always take time to express thanksgiving. Don't just move on as if it is business as usual, lest you lose the blessing of learning to trust Him more and more, becoming better able to face bigger and greater things with grace and faith.

My prayer for us today is that we always take time to celebrate the unfathomable power and the simple kindnesses of God in our lives. We will never truly know this side of heaven all that He has rescued us from.

I praise you as my Savior and thank you
for delivering me again and again, O God!

THE POWER OF WORDS

If a person thinks that he is religious but can't control his tongue,
he is fooling himself. That person's religion is worthless.

JAMES 1:26, GOD'S WORD

*I*n Psalm 64 David calls to God for deliverance, not from those who would do him bodily harm but from those conspiring against him and speaking ill of him. In verse 3 he says, "They sharpen their tongues like swords. They aim bitter words like arrows."

The tongue is a powerful and creative force. Through His words, Jesus forgave sins, healed the sick, and even raised the dead to life. In the very same moment, we can use our words to build others up or to bring about their destruction. David speaks of those who conspired against him as a "noisy crowd of evil doers" (64:2, NIV1984). It is possible it was only a few people, but I find that when evil words are spoken against me, even if by only a couple of voices, it feels like a crowd.

One of the reasons words do so much damage is that all of us have the need to belong, to know we are loved and approved of. I hope you will be surrounded by that affirmation. But approval addiction can be dangerous too. There will be many times when the choices we need to make are not going to make us popular.

Maybe you have been damaged to the core by the blade of unjust talk. Or maybe you have been the one who wielded the sword. The only way to move on in either case is forgiveness. You might need to offer it or seek it.

Dear God, you created the world with a word.
I pray that my words will always be creative and never be destructive.

IN THIS INSTANT

You rabble—how long do I put up with your scorn? How long will you lust after lies?
How long will you live crazed by illusion? Look at this: look who got picked by God!
He listens the split second I call to Him.

PSALM 4:2–3, THE MESSAGE

rayer is critical, and central to a vibrant relationship with Jesus Christ. As the Psalms have been designed to give us a language adequate for response to the God who speaks worlds into being and who speaks directly to us, then we must take note of the incredible confidence that David displayed in these two short verses to empower our own prayer life.

It's not as if everything is going David's way. He is surrounded by skeptics and cynics. They aren't respectful of David as king, but what slays him to the core is their disregard and disrespect for God. Sound familiar?

But that doesn't quench David's faith as he declares this about the God who answers prayer: "He listens the split second I call to him." David knew that everything he had just uttered before heaven—every need, every question, every hurt, every concern—not only had been heard but, in that instant, had been fulfilled! This is the kind of faith you can build your life upon. It becomes an immovable rock against the storms of life, held together by a childlike simplicity, a knowing deep inside, a trust that if God has said He will answer your petitions, then He will!

Just a thought to remind you: Your answer may not come about how you thought it should and when you thought it should. But God, the great Yahweh, is in control.

Father, thank you that you hear and answer me in this very moment,
that you respond as a loving Father to my every prayer.

KEEP THEM SAFE

I am coming to you; I will not stay in the world any longer.
But they are still in the world. Holy Father, keep them safe
by the power of your name, the name you gave me,
so that they will be one, just as you and I are one.

JOHN 17:11, NCV

*I*n the gospel of John we find rich detail of Jesus' last days and moments with His disciples. A passage I will come back to throughout this year of devotions that reveal Jesus is His prayer for the disciples—present then and present now—found in chapter 17.

All of Jesus' words are precious and powerful for the believer, but as He experiences His final earthly moments and shares from His heart with those closest to Him, we know what is urgent in His heart and mind. Isn't it amazing that He called together His followers, His closest friends, so He could pray for them? He went to His gracious Father and asked Him to keep them safe.

If you've ever experienced a moment when you felt uncared for or alone in the world, come back to the heart of the Savior. Read—and experience—again His innermost love and desire for you. In His Father's name, He has prayed for your safety, for your connection and oneness with those who will support you on the sometimes precarious journey of life.

Jesus loves you, my friend, always and forever.

Thank you that as I pray to you, Father God,
your Son has already prayed on my behalf for my safety and wholeness.

MY JEWEL

"On the day when I act," says the Lord Almighty, "they will be my treasured possession. I will spare them, just as a father has compassion and spares his son who serves him. And you will again see the distinction between the righteous and the wicked, between those who serve God and those who do not.

MALACHI 3:17–18, NIV

In Psalm 4:2, a heartbroken King David asks on behalf of God: "How long will you people turn my glory into shame? How long will you love delusions and seek false gods?"

Throughout the Psalms and Prophets, you will hear a familiar lament. Why did God's own children reject Him so? Was it for lack of love? Never. Were they mistreated in some way? Of course not.

Somehow the ungodly let their hearts and minds become delusional as they seek after vanities in life—false gods, false teachings, false riches, false security. They fall in love with sin and reap the reward of death and destruction.

What a stark contrast are those who love God. Something miraculous happens when we open our hearts to God's love. Our hope is in the name of the Lord. Our glory is that we finally stopped to hear Jesus' call to us and recognized in that moment the voice of the Good Shepherd (see John 10:3).

God calls us His precious jewels! When I read this verse I couldn't help but name my youngest child Zoe Jewel—I wanted her to know she is God's beloved treasure.

When is the last time you realized you are God's treasure?

Thank you, Father, for the true riches of your love for us.

ALL MY SINS

Look on my affliction and my distress and take away all my sins.

PSALM 25:18, NIV

Psalm 25 finds David gearing up spiritually for what is ahead of him. He spends significant time looking backward, admitting to his own inadequacies and past mistakes. But he doesn't keep his gaze backward for long.

Without ever making excuses for his past, David looks forward because he knows God is for us, not against us. When we realize this, we too are able to spend our lives growing in God's friendship instead of desperately and furtively trying to avoid His notice.

The enemy has always had a great way of trying to keep each of us tied to past sin, weighing us down with sorrow or pain and regret. Feeling heavy under the weight of knowing you made stupid mistakes will, if you allow it, cripple you for life. We have all fallen short. There is no one on earth who has not made mistakes.

But walking in the miracle of forgiveness gives God much glory. The ability to live life without the snares and chains of the past is one of the most glorious surprises you discover after asking our ever patient Lord for forgiveness. Do you remember feeling almost light when you were first saved? It's the literal removal of the weightiness of sin. What a glorious Savior!

Take a moment to look backward, asking for forgiveness if you need to. But then step forward to face whatever task God has laid before you, knowing you are whole and free.

Heavenly Father, saturate us in the love and forgiveness of your Son as we discover who we truly are, ready to serve you like we never have before.

ONLY ONE FEAR

The fear of the Lord is the beginning of knowledge,
but fools despise wisdom and instruction.

PROVERBS 1:7, NKJV

I learned many years ago that those who fear the Lord have nothing to fear, for the fear—and the respect and the awe—of the Lord is the beginning of all wisdom. Those who have no fear of God, however, continue to make incredibly unwise choices, consumed with caring for immediate wants and needs rather than caring for matters of eternal value. What does this kind of decision making create? Many fears, of course, as one thing after the other goes wrong.

What will it be for you and me? One fear or many fears? Only a fool would answer "many fears."

I love that Jesus is our Friend and desires an intimacy with us. My heart's prayer for you today is that you never lose that sense of holy fear in the presence of Jesus—at His majesty, His strength, His greatness.

Fear of God is the beginning of wisdom. A lack of respect inevitably shows up in the wisdom of your choices and will literally keep you out of walking in the fullness of God's promise over your life. Disrespect for God turns incredibly smart and once-wise men and women into fools.

In Psalm 25:14 David tells us, "The Lord confides in those who fear him; he makes his covenant known to them" (NIV). If we truly know our God and fear Him, He will trust us as confidants with His mysteries. What an absolute treasure.

God of majesty and glory, I come to you with all fear, all respect, all awe today.
Thank you for letting me partake in the wisdom of your counsel.

Victor's Crown ♡

You are always fighting for us
Heaven's angels all around
My delight is found in knowing
That YOU wear the VICTOR'S crown

You're my Help & my Defender
My Savior & my friend... by YOUR
grace I live & breathe to worship
YOU

THOSE IN NEED

Blessed (happy, fortunate, to be envied) is he who considers the weak and the poor; the Lord will deliver him in the time of evil and trouble.

PSALM 41:1, AMP

To be generous is to reflect the heart of God himself. Not a token generosity, but a stance that is central to who we are as Christ followers. Psalm 41:1 is another reminder of the responsibility we have to look after those in need. We are not to just carelessly throw a few dollars their way, but to consider them, to be mindful, to allow the plight of the poor to affect our hearts in a way that brings change both to them and to us.

The Lord promises that He will deliver those who care for the poor. God is so very kind. He is always rewarding faithfulness. But I pray in my heart of hearts that I'll never do to be seen or give to get. I want to do because I love; to give because I care.

God delights in a joyful giver (see 2 Corinthians 9:7), and I pray that I will always be that person. Will you join me in finding delight in giving and serving?

Because God blesses us so abundantly, it is easy to stop there. But have you stopped to consider that true success as a Christian is not in being blessed but in what we do with that blessing?

Jesus reminds us that when we bless the needy with the blessings we have received from God, what we ultimately do is bless the very heart of Jesus. He says in a story, "The King will reply, 'Truly I tell you, whatever you did for one of the least of these brothers and sisters of mine, you did for me'" (Matthew 25:40, NIV).

Father, all I do and give, I do and give for Jesus.

VULNERABLE

I said, Lord, be merciful and gracious to me;
heal my inner self, for I have sinned against You.

PSALM 41:4, AMP

King David was a man well acquainted with warfare of every kind—from the battlefield to the recesses of his heart. We know David didn't win all of his battles. And as he pleads for the health of his soul in Psalm 41, we learn once again that absolute honesty and transparency before God is our only hope for renewal. Repentance begins with honest confession.

But as our heart aches with David in his brokenness, we also learn that over time we must begin to understand our own vulnerabilities. There are times when we are more vulnerable to the attacks of the enemy. Places. Times. Conditions. When you are weak in your soul, you truly do leave your life open to all of your own weaknesses, whatever they may be. Do you know your own areas of vulnerability? Do you have healthy safety barriers in place to protect you?

For my own soul to be strong, I need God time, family time, thinking time, and creative time. When my soul becomes weary, I find myself vulnerable to waves of depression and insecurity. That's the moment—the second—when I know I need to go and care for my soul with all urgency.

Put plans in place to keep the enemy of your soul at bay. Love yourself enough to do whatever is needed to care for your soul. Ask God to show you when you are vulnerable. Ask Him to show how you personally need to care for your inner being.

Mighty God, protect us from the enemy.
In our time of battle, may we stand.

WORDS AND WALK

*But to the wicked person, God says: "What right have you
to recite my laws or take my covenant on your lips?
You hate my instruction and cast my words behind you."*

PSALM 50:16–17, NIV

What does God think of people who speak the Word with their lips but live an entirely different life with their actions? When He says "I will tear you to pieces" (v. 22), the answer to that question is emphatic.

Today is not so different from biblical days. So many live a life where their seen and unseen lives do not remotely look like each other. People complain that God has failed them and hasn't come through as He promised, but the excuse rings hollow. We've always known that defeat is the fruit of hypocrisy.

God reminds the ungodly what happens when they ignore wisdom, when they throw the Word of God behind them as if it holds no worth. He challenges every word that comes out of the mouths of the wicked, reminding them that they can fool some people some of the time, but they will never fool God.

God's heart for us is not only to proclaim truth but to walk in the power of truth, not living as we please but living to please God. And when it comes to worship, God doesn't accept the offerings of those who go through the motions, with not even a thought to a heart encounter with God. To live in victory, ask the Lord to continue to strengthen you in your pursuit of truth, that your words and actions would be as one. The joy, peace, and freedom that reign on the other side of obedience are incomparable.

*Father, may my thoughts, my words,
and my actions all proclaim your truth.*

FIRST THING IN THE MORNING

Listen to my voice in the morning, Lord. Each morning
I bring my requests to you and wait expectantly.

PSALM 5:3, NLT

*D*oes an athlete wake up a few minutes before an important competition, throw on a uniform, bounce into the parking lot moments before the meet or match is to begin, and then secure a victory? Well, not the successful ones, I'm sure. Watching swimmers and runners and other great athletes in the Olympics, I was reminded of their commitment to training, to constant preparation.

How about our spiritual lives? Do we share this same commitment to preparation? What comes first each day? Morning. When must our preparation to face the daily challenges and battles of life begin? Morning.

Even at the moment, in one of the busiest and somewhat challenging seasons of my own life, I'm so aware of His grace being sufficient for every day. The only time I find myself overwhelmed is when I have gone into the day without "looking up." To continually be aware of God's favor and presence in your every moment is one of the greatest treasures you'll ever discover. That discovery happens when you "look up" in the morning and throughout the day, your attitude and expectations attuned to hearing God's voice because that's how you started your day.

Prepare for life first thing in the morning. Open your eyes, take a breath, and then thank God for it. With outstretched arms, ask God for wisdom, direction, and courage, that your life would be one of blessing, living as you were designed. I would love to think that the enemy gets nervous when he knows I am waking up!

In the morning I will look up to you for guidance and strength,
to express my love and gratitude to you, my Lord.

LIFT UP YOUR VOICE

Arise, Lord! Lift up your hand, O God. Do not forget the helpless.
PSALM 10:18, NIV

I love the way the psalmist has such a great relationship with God that he cries in anguish on behalf of a hurting humanity, to awaken the answer of heaven.

We know God never sleeps. We know He knows every detail of every situation. But do we know He has invited us to bring the needs of others before Him? So I pray with the psalmist, my Father God, do not forsake these children who are being persecuted and crushed, sold and abused. Oh, God, we need you.

I believe in the potential of every human being, because we are all made in the image of God, even those who have been part of the most cruel acts against humanity. The problem is that everyone has a story, a reason for their hardness of heart. The enemy strolls around seeking whom he may devour, using hearts destroyed by experience to see evil plans executed.

The evil man referred to in Psalm 10 is a classic example of a disillusioned, prideful, selfish, exploitative heart. The man firmly believes his sin will be left without any repercussions. What a lie. God himself declares that He hates sin, and His compassion upon the downtrodden is too vast to let the perpetrator go unpunished.

Many blame God for the inhumane treatment millions suffer daily. But we must always remember, everyone has a will, and when it is unyielded to the power of the Holy Spirit, well, we know too well the results.

The real question is what you and I will do. Any worthwhile action begins with prayer, so today I lift my voice. In His presence He will instruct me.

Father, defender of the fatherless, act on behalf of your children today.
Show me where I may serve in delivering your salvation.

GREAT IS THY FAITHFULNESS

Because of the Lord's great love we are not consumed, for his compassions never fail.
They are new every morning; but great is your faithfulness.

LAMENTATIONS 3:22–23, NIV

*D*o you ever sing your prayers and worship? In Psalm 33:1 David urges us: "Sing joyfully to the Lord, you righteous; it is fitting for the upright to praise him." What a glorious hymn to sing to God as you begin your day in worship!

Great is thy faithfulness, O God my Father;
There is no shadow of turning with thee;
Thou changest not, thy compassions, they fail not;
As thou hast been thou forever wilt be.

Refrain
Great is thy faithfulness! Great is thy faithfulness!
Morning by morning new mercies I see;
All I have needed thy hand hath provided—
Great is thy faithfulness, Lord, unto me!

Pardon for sin and a peace that endureth,
Thy own dear presence to cheer and to guide;
Strength for today and bright hope for tomorrow,
Blessings all mine, with ten thousand beside!

Thank you, Father, for your faithfulness to me.
I will sing of your goodness now and for all of eternity. My heart is full!

HE EATS WITH SINNERS

*Now all the tax collectors and the sinners were coming near Him
to listen to Him. Both the Pharisees and the scribes began to grumble, saying,
"This man receives sinners and eats with them."*

LUKE 15:1–2, NASB

What was it that caused the religious readers to grumble and criticize about Jesus eating with sinners? Was it from pure motives and righteousness? Jesus makes it clear in numerous passages that they really didn't have a heart for God, but they liked the attention and honor that was theirs through their religious duties. It would seem their grumbling and criticisms were more a matter of insecurity and jealousy than any sense of righteousness.

Our motives to bring glory and honor to God can easily be corrupted when our flesh starts to desire glory and honor for ourselves. And when this starts to happen, our purpose on the earth is muddied, those within God's family are not properly cared for—and those outside of God's family are ignored. The agenda of our hearts is the one thing we must continually keep watch over. Proverbs 4:23 says we must keep our hearts with all diligence, as from here spring the issues of life. Jesus came to seek and save the lost, but these pharisees and scribes had become hardhearted and prideful, and were content to let the destitute remain in their pain.

When searching our own hearts before God, we can ask ourselves two questions to help us know where we stand: Do our actions bring glory to God or are they to bring glory to us? Do we have a burning desire to see sinners come to know Jesus, or are we indifferent and even hostile toward those who have not yet met our Savior?

———∞———

*Father God, let all my words and deeds be expressed for your glory.
May I have wisdom in regard to the state of my heart before you. Amen.*

THE ONE WHICH IS LOST

What man among you, if he has a hundred sheep and has lost one of them, does not leave the ninety-nine in the open pasture and go after the one which is lost until he finds it?

LUKE 15:4, NASB

Has there ever been a storyteller like Jesus? He had such a simple and lovely way of expressing truth in everyday word pictures.

In the parable of the lost sheep, He confronts those who are proud of their religion and consider it a small exclusive club for only special people—and they are, of course, special, better than others. Could anything be further from the nature of our loving heavenly Father? He doesn't play favorites. He doesn't love some people and hate others. He loves the entire world.

This parable reminds me that if my Savior dined with sinners, if He is the Good Shepherd who braves hardship and danger to find the one lost sheep, then so must I—not out of cold duty, but in response to the gracious love Jesus showed to me when I was the lost sheep. All of us have been there.

So we step out of our comfort zone and seek out those who are lost. Nothing was more valuable than a sheep in the eyes of a shepherd. Nothing is more urgent than a lost soul in the eyes of our Lord. Let's continue to be brave enough to ask God to give us eyes to see like He does and the courage to step out and bring resolve whenever we can.

Thank you, Lord, for seeking until you found when I was lost and far away from the safety of your flock. Help me to see the lost in my world with the same love and urgency you showed me.

HIS SHOULDERS

When he has found it, he lays it on his shoulders, rejoicing.

LUKE 15:5, NASB

The sheep is weak, unable to return to the flock under its own power. Perhaps injured and near starvation, the sheep is at the mercy of the elements. He has no strength to flee from predators that lurk in the shadows. But hallelujah, there is One who is merciful who never gives up on the sheep that went astray. He fights His way through thick forests, climbs hills and mountains, and crosses streams and rivers. And when He finds His lost sheep, He has shoulders that are strong enough to carry it all the way home.

Our Jesus is loving and gentle, but let's never forget His strength. He is the Lamb of sacrifice, but He is also the Lamb that conquers the power of sin and death. Every knee shall bow to the Victor. He is mighty in battle and mighty to save. His shoulders are strong enough to carry the weight of all the sins of the world.

Do you remember your state when Jesus found you? Have you stopped to thank Him for His persistence in finding you and then carrying you to safety? I am so thankful for the way Jesus picked me up and turned my life around, how I have found strength and joy in His presence that has overwhelmed and healed any past hurts that used to try to choke my soul and destroy my future. I pray we will always remember our BC life, the state we were in before we accepted Christ's love into our hearts. And remain ever grateful that His mercies are new every morning.

*I am forever grateful to you, my Lord and Savior, for rescuing me
in my state of despair and hopelessness. Thank you for carrying me to the safety
of your salvation and the fellowship of your fold.*

REJOICE WITH ME

And when he comes home, he calls together his friends and his neighbors,
saying to them, "Rejoice with me, for I have found my sheep which was lost!"

LUKE 15:6, NASB

The Good Shepherd finds the lost sheep and brings it home. The next thing He does is scold and punish the sheep for its carelessness and rebelliousness. Right? After all, the sheep knew the Shepherd's voice and should have listened. It was its own fault that it got into such a mess.

That is what the sheep—what you and I—deserve. But that's not how God treats us. In this parable from Jesus, He shows us what He and the Father are really like: "I tell you that in the same way, there will be more joy in heaven over one sinner who repents than over ninety-nine righteous persons who need no repentance" (v. 7). It is so comforting to realize today that we are now part of the redeemed, that we know how much He delights in us. We are His beloved children whom He cares for in every way. But the picture He paints for us is that all of heaven breaks out in a joyful, spontaneous celebration that the lost, the one who was so close to death, has been found.

Who is the lost sheep in your life? A child? A brother or sister? A parent? A longtime friend? A neighbor? Who has God put on your heart? And what will you do about it? Ask God to show you how to reach out to that person in the exact place, that depth of heart, where they know the truth that they need a Savior. Don't give up if you feel rebuffed. Be gentle and persistent. And be prepared to begin a most joyful celebration that reaches up to heaven!

Thank you, heavenly Father, for helping me to recognize my need for you.
Grow in me a heart of love that reaches others with the truth of your love for them.
Keep me sensitive to your leading when the time is right and hearts are ready.

LIGHT A LAMP

*Or what woman, if she has ten silver coins and loses one coin,
does not light a lamp and sweep the house and search carefully until she finds it?*

LUKE 15:8, NASB

For those in His audience who didn't relate as well to the cost and importance of a sheep to a shepherd, Jesus made sure they understood how important the lost are to His heavenly Father by telling a new story, this one about a woman who lost a silver coin.

We don't know if she was young or old, a widow or married, but we do know that the coin was valuable to her present and future financial condition. But let's be sure we understand that Jesus isn't putting a monetary value on the human soul. In fact, He assumes those present would know how much more valuable life is to silver. So if a woman would stop everything she was doing, light every corner of the house, sweep, and get down on hands and knees to sort through the dust and dirt to find the lost coin, then how much more should we be ready to do to find the lost soul?

Remember the context for these parables: Religious leaders were grumbling that He ate with sinners. We all know the importance of the company we keep. But we are never to turn our back on the lost of the world. Our purpose must be the same as God's: to seek and save those who are lost. We can't do the saving, as it is the Holy Spirit's job to reveal Jesus and His salvation plan, but we can turn on the lights, sweep the floors, and search carefully until we find the precious silver coin that means so much to God that He laid down the life of His Son for its redemption.

*Help me to never lose sight of how precious each and every person in the world is to you,
creator God. Give me a steadfast desire and passion to help find those who are lost!*

THE YOUNGER SON

The younger of them said to his father, "Father, give me the share of the estate that falls to me." So he divided his wealth between them.

LUKE 15:12, NASB

What a familiar picture. All of us know a younger son. He is someone who is loved and properly raised by parents, yet he insists on rejecting this love in order to make his own way in life. This younger son is not one who is showing maturity and responsibility for his own actions; he is purposely heading in the opposite direction of how he has been raised. He is rebellious.

Rebelliousness is part of our makeup since the fall of Adam and Eve. Embedded in our nature is a desire to say to God that we will do things the way we want to. We won't listen to Him or anyone else, even if doing things our own way is obviously foolish. So the younger son's demand to give him his share of the family wealth—even though he really didn't do anything to create that wealth—is not so surprising. What is so surprising is that the father listens to him and lets him have his way. He didn't force him into obedience; he gave him the choice to love or reject him.

Our gracious heavenly Father loves us so much that He too wants us to love Him freely. That means He will never force us to love and obey Him. He puts the choice into our hands, even if we squander all He has given us in the riches of His grace.

I would say to any parent who is suffering the heartbreak of a rebellious child to read on. There is always hope. I would say to all of us, let's never forget how much God loves us. He loves us so much that His desire is for us to love Him freely back.

Thank you for the spiritual wealth you have given me, O Father.
May I never squander or waste it. Thank you for your love for me, your child.

A SQUANDERED ESTATE

*And not many days later, the younger son gathered everything together and went on
a journey into a distant country, and there he squandered his estate with loose living.*

LUKE 15:13, NASB

God loves us so much that He does not demand our love and obedience in
return. Even if we choose to be foolish and run far away from Him, He
allows it. This younger son demanded and received his share of the family's wealth
and burned through it as fast as he could. He squandered it in a distant country. His
situation turned so desperate that this Jewish young man who was to abstain from
pork ended up in a pigsty: "He went and hired himself out to one of the citizens of
that country, and he sent him into his fields to feed swine. And he would have gladly
filled his stomach with the pods that the swine were eating, and no one was giving
anything to him" (vv. 14–16).

What a mess we make of our lives when we run from God. It's not just the young
son, it's all of us. The good news is that the story is not finished. As long as we have
breath we have hope, no matter what we've done or how low we've sunk. Even when
we are working in a pigsty and jealous of what the swine have to eat. Never forget that
there is still hope for you and for the prodigal sons that you meet in life. It is so easy
to judge and give up on others: "They've messed up too badly this time. They'll never
change. There is no hope for them."

As long as there is a loving father—and in God, we certainly have a loving
Father—the story is not finished. There is hope.

❧

*Thank you for not giving up on me, O Father. Thank you that when I was
rebellious and intent on doing things my own way, you waited patiently for me.
Thank you that there is hope for all who draw breath.*

THE RETURN HOME

But when he came to his senses, he said, "How many of my father's hired men have more than enough bread, but I am dying here with hunger! I will get up and go to my father, and will say to him, 'Father, I have sinned against heaven, and in your sight; I am no longer worthy to be called your son; make me as one of your hired men.'"

LUKE 15:17–19, NASB

The younger son was starving and knew that he needed to get back home if he was to survive with his life. He rightfully knew that he was not worthy to be called his father's son. He had squandered every last bit of his share in the family fortune. But what he didn't understand was that he couldn't earn his way back into the family either. Becoming a hired hand and working for some level of favor just can't cut it. But many, like the younger son, still try.

"I'll do better this time, God. I'll do more good works. I won't do anything bad. I'll watch my language. I'll go to church every Sunday. I won't gossip. I'll pay all my taxes."

That's not God's way of salvation. My friends, there are no servants in God's family, only sons and daughters, fully adopted through God's gift of grace. Redemption is through faith alone, never by works.

Though the circumstances are oftentimes terrible, it is still a life-changing blessing when someone comes to the end of their resources and realizes his or her need for God. It is only then that they are ready to experience God's gift of eternal life—not as a servant but as a child of the King.

May we never forget that we are part of God's family as His children, not as servants trying to pay our way.

Thank you for your marvelous grace that makes me your child and you my Father.

FROM A LONG WAY OFF

*So he got up and came to his father. But while he was still a long way off, his father
saw him and felt compassion for him, and ran and embraced him and kissed him.*

LUKE 15:20, NASB

What a beautiful scene of reconciliation. The lost son was welcomed home with the full love and warmth of his gracious father. No grudges. No recriminations. No reminders of what he had done. No accusations. It is the devil that accuses humans; it is God who loves and redeems us. When you feel accusation in your heart, it is from satan, not God. Our conscience might call us to repentance, but when we hear "God is through with you," it is from the enemy.

The son started to tell his father of the plan he had come up with to earn his way back into the family: "Father, I have sinned against heaven and in your sight; I am no longer worthy to be called your son" (v. 21). But before he could volunteer as a servant, his father gave orders: "Quickly bring out the best robe and put it on him, and put a ring on his hand and sandals on his feet; and bring the fattened calf, kill it, and let us eat and celebrate; for this son of mine was dead and has come to life again; he was lost and has been found" (vv. 22–23). A celebration broke out! That's how God treats a prodigal who comes home. He throws a party!

What a wonderful picture of God's desire for the church. When a sinner comes to know God—and yes, when a believer who has fallen into sin is restored—it's celebration time. No accusations. No reminders. Just pure joy and celebration that the prodigal has come home.

*Father, give me your heart of joy when the lost come home to you.
Help me to never give up on the one who seems so far away from you!*

THE OLDER BROTHER

But [the older son] became angry and was not willing to go in;
and his father came out and began pleading with him.

LUKE 15:28, NASB

*A*pparently we don't have to wallow in a pigsty to have a piggy attitude. How could it be that we who have been saved by the grace and mercies of our loving heavenly Father could even think to resent another brother for the favor received from the Father.

Even though his father pleaded with him to join the party, the older brother said, "Look! For so many years I have been serving you and I have never neglected a command of yours; and yet you have never given me a young goat, so that I might celebrate with my friends; but when this son of yours came, who has devoured your wealth with prostitutes, you killed the fattened calf for him" (vv. 29–30).

We don't know if the older brother released his resentments. I hope so. For just as God is patient and loving toward the one who ran off, He is patient and loving with us when we let our attitudes turn sour and surly. But we must come in humility, knowing we have no power to handle this sin of pride.

Are you feeling resentment over the blessings and favor of another? Let's let that serve as a reminder that everything we have is from God: "Son, you have always been with me, and all that is mine is yours" (v. 31).

Thank you, Father, for all that you have given me.
You are so kind and loving toward me. I rejoice in you—and I rejoice
in all the ways you bless my brothers and sisters.

BEHOLD HIM

A Classic Devotion by Charles Spurgeon

But their eyes were holden that they should not know him.

LUKE 24:16, KJV

The disciples ought to have known Jesus, they had heard His voice so often, and gazed upon that marred face so frequently, that it is wonderful they did not discover Him. Yet is it not so with you also? You have not seen Jesus lately. You have been to His table, and you have not met Him there. You are in a dark trouble this evening, and though He plainly says, "It is I, be not afraid," yet you cannot discern Him. Alas! our eyes are holden. We know His voice; we have looked into His face; we have leaned our head upon His bosom, and yet, though Christ is very near us, we are saying "Oh that I knew where I might find Him!" We should know Jesus, for we have the Scriptures to reflect His image, and yet how possible it is for us to open that precious book and have no glimpse of the Well-beloved!

Dear child of God, are you in that state? Jesus feeds among the lilies of the Word, and you walk among those lilies, and yet you behold Him not . . . And why do we not see Him? It must be ascribed in our case, as in the disciples', to unbelief. They evidently did not expect to see Jesus, and therefore they did not know Him.

To a great extent in spiritual things we get what we expect of the Lord. Faith alone can bring us to see Jesus. Make it your prayer, "Lord, open my eyes, that I may see my Savior present with me." It is a blessed thing to want to see Him; but Oh! it is better far to gaze upon Him. To those who seek Him He is kind; but to those who find Him, beyond expression is He dear!

Father, keep my eyes open and my faith strong to always see Jesus.

SOLID ROCK

HE ONLY IS MY ROCK. . . .
I SHALL NOT BE SHAKEN.

FEBRUARY

My hope is built on nothing less
Than Jesus' blood & righteousness.
I dare not trust the sweetest frame,
But wholly lean on Jesus' name.

On Christ, the SOLID ROCK, I stand,
All other ground is sinking sand;
All other ground is sinking sand.

Praise be to my Solid Rock!

HE SPEAKS FIRST

There came a woman of Samaria to draw water. Jesus said to her, "Give Me a drink."
... The Samaritan woman said to Him, "How is it that You, being a Jew, ask me for a
drink since I am a Samaritan woman?" (For Jews have no dealings with Samaritans.)

JOHN 4:7, 9, NASB

I don't know what was on the mind of this woman the day she came to the
village well by herself. Was she on a journey—or was it just another day?

The glorious news is that it didn't matter what brought her to that place; what
mattered was that Jesus was there. As has so often been the case, He took her by
surprise. He wasn't aloof or unapproachable. In fact, going against the custom of the
day, he initiated the conversation. His request for a drink may have seemed straightforward and simple, but our kind and tender Savior was already reaching out with a
message of love to this lonely woman who had shut herself off from the world.

Isn't that just like Jesus? He makes the first move. He speaks the first words to
break down barriers of shame and alienation. He did it for this precious one we know
only as "the woman at the well," and He did it for me and for you. James 4:8 tells us
to draw near to God and He will draw near to us.

The true beauty of revealing Jesus is that He reveals himself to us. It can happen
anywhere—from a place of corporate worship with thousands of voices to a quiet
alone moment in the midst of a routine task. I encourage you to lean in, even just a
little. God is faithful to His Word. If you seek Him, you will find Him.

I don't know what is on your heart today, whether you are just surviving or
seeking your Savior. What I want you to hear is this: If you will look up and listen,
Jesus is speaking to you.

Father, you brought the world into existence with your words—
and you bring salvation to us through your words today. Help me to hear.

NEVER THIRST AGAIN

Jesus answered and said to her, "Everyone who drinks of this water will thirst again; but whoever drinks of the water that I will give him shall never thirst; but the water that I will give him will become in him a well of water springing up to eternal life."

JOHN 4:13–14, NASB

Her life was such a mess. We don't know why she had been married five times before—maybe a combination of divorce and widowhood. Whatever the reasons behind these devastating losses, she was now living with a man, perhaps giving up on the hope of true love and relationship represented in marriage.

She met Jesus at the well during the hottest part of the day. That has led many to speculate she was an outcast among the women of her village. Women traditionally did the heavy work of bringing water needed for cleaning and cooking into their homes during the coolest part of the day. It was also their time of fellowship. Had she been excluded?

What happens when Jesus enters the situation? He reaches out to her. He speaks to her. He asks her questions. He lets her know He knows all that is on her heart and mind. She pushes Him away by pointing out their differences, but Jesus gently persists and teaches her the meaning of true worship. And He offers the gift of a living water so she will never thirst again. Even when we feel we should be disqualified from all that Christ offers, grace beckons us back.

When was the last time you remembered and celebrated Jesus entering your life, meeting you at the place of your brokenness?

Father, I thank you for the moment you met me at the well
and gave me a love that could never be taken away.

IN SPIRIT AND IN TRUTH

But an hour is coming, and now is, when the true worshipers will worship the Father in spirit and truth; for such people the Father seeks to be His worshipers.

JOHN 4:23, NASB

The woman at the well could scarce believe that this stranger to her town spoke to her. Not with the words of condemnation and rejection she was used to, but with a magnificent mixture of authority, wisdom, and love. She knows in her heart that she has come face-to-face with someone who knows truth; she knows Jesus is a prophet.

But as someone well acquainted with heartbreak and loss, her first response was what so many of us have done when confronted with the love of God. She pushed away. She deflected. She made excuses. "Our fathers worshiped in this mountain, and you people say that in Jerusalem is the place where men ought to worship" (v. 20).

In His love and mercy for this outcast, Jesus reveals to the woman that true worship is not confined by place or race, but happens within the heart and is based on the Spirit and truth. She demurs one more time, saying that only the Messiah could make such a proclamation (v. 25). "Jesus said to her, 'I who speak to you am He'" (v. 26).

Her heart saw in a flash what scholars and leaders refused to see. Her life was changed. She was made new. A living water washed over her, cleansing her from all her sins, healing every hurt done to her and by her alike. The village outcast took off in a joyous run to tell everyone what had happened to her.

God of wisdom and love, thank you for sharing with me that worship begins in my heart, empowered by the Spirit, a proclaiming of truth!

WHY SPEAK WITH HER?

At this point His disciples came, and they were amazed that He had been speaking with
a woman, yet no one said, "What do You seek?" or, "Why do You speak with her?"

JOHN 4:27, NASB

They didn't say it out loud, but they sure thought it. Why is Jesus spending time with her? A Samaritan. Not a leader—just a lowly woman. Not a person of substance and character. Not someone worthy of His attention.

Have you ever thought like this ? If we are honest, every single one of us would have to fall on our faces and ask for God's mercy because we ourselves have failed to show mercy. When we met our wonderful Savior, our lives were changed. We became new. And there were some close associations we could not continue to experience in the same way, lest our hearts and minds be pulled away from our new life in Jesus Christ.

But bottom line, we were not worthy of the kindness, the patience, the mercy God showed us in Jesus Christ. How can we then exclude others? God's love is for everyone. His salvation is a gift offered to each and every person, regardless of background or current situation. A look at our own lives before salvation is a dramatic reminder that God comes to save the sinner.

Is there someone you have pushed away? I pray that we will see each person with the kindness and compassion and mercy with which Jesus looks at us.

***

I am grateful, heavenly Father, that when I was lost in my sins,
you had compassion and mercy on me.
Help me to share that same love and compassion with everyone I meet.

FEARLESSLY SHARE

So the woman left her waterpot, and went into the city and said to the men,
"Come, see a man who told me all the things that I have done."

JOHN 4:28, NASB

She was part of a despised community. She was an outcast within that community. She had lost at love, over and over, to the point that she had seemingly given up on the hope of a loving relationship.

How could this same woman run with all her might to the town square and not just whisper furtively to the women who were kept in the background, but go straight to the leaders of her village and shout, "Come, see!"?

The answer is simple. She met Jesus and recognized Him as the Savior of the world, the promised One who could forgive her sins, heal her brokenness, and put inside her heart the Spirit of truth. She had tasted a living water and experienced the joy of new life. She could not have kept this to herself no matter how hard she might have tried, no matter how fearful she might have been. She had received forgiveness and a joy that was overflowing from her life and spilling onto the lives of others.

Books and teachings on evangelism are a wonderful gift and something we should all pursue. But nothing can take the place of sharing our personal experiences of meeting the Savior, and telling the story of all He has done in our lives.

Have you run as hard as you can to share that joy lately? If not, take time to remember the place, that moment when you met Jesus and knew He truly was the Savior of the world, and the story of your life now. Go tell your story now.

Father, help me to share the incredible joy of salvation
through your Son, Jesus Christ.

HE KNOWS

*He said to her, "Go, call your husband and come here." The woman answered
and said, "I have no husband." Jesus said to her, "You have correctly said,
'I have no husband'; for you have had five husbands, and the one whom you now
have is not your husband; this you have said truly."*

JOHN 4:16–18, NASB

Throughout the Psalms, David teaches us that there is no lying to God. We truly come to Him "just as I am." This woman, broken, fallen, despised, knew what Israel's worship leader knew: Don't try to hide who you are, what you've done, but come to God in honest humility.

What did Adam and Eve do after they realized the horror of what they had done? "They heard the sound of the Lord God walking in the garden in the cool of the day, and the man and his wife hid themselves from the presence of the Lord God among the trees of the garden" (Genesis 3:8). Surely they knew and surely we know the futility of hiding our sin. God knows us. Jesus knew everything about this woman at the well.

So great is God's desire for an authentic relationship with us that He is moved by our honesty. He doesn't want us to come with a story or a façade, a perfect presentation of a masked life. He wants us. You. Me. Just as we are. Transformation—life change—begins not when we hide who we are and what we've done, but when we come in open, honest humility to our Savior, letting Him know our every need, loving Him with all that we are.

*Heavenly Father, may I never try to hide from your presence. Even in the moment when I
feel shame for an attitude or action, I come before you in honesty and all that I am.*

THEY BELIEVED

From that city many of the Samaritans believed in Him because of the word of the woman who testified, "He told me all the things that I have done."

JOHN 4:39, NASB

*W*hat will convince people to believe in Jesus? I am so thankful for those who can articulate a well-reasoned defense for Jesus' life and ministry; for His deity; for His existence today. But I also believe that what truly brings people to accept Jesus Christ as their Lord and Savior is the simple testimony of His followers. The story of what Jesus has done for us. It's His kindness that brings people to repentance and His kindness that draws us to himself today. I am so grateful to the Spirit of God beckoning my broken heart even in my teens, the living God drawing my heart. Through my saying yes to Him, He quenched my thirsty soul.

"He told me all the things that I have done." Jesus saw to the very heart of this woman and pierced the veil of her defenses. He offered her a living water so she would never thirst again. As a result, her whole town believed. Why? She simply told others what He had done for her. They already knew her life was a mess. But what blew their minds was when she ran up the hill to the village square and shouted, "I am different. I am new. I am not the woman you saw walk down to the well." That is the power of testimony.

Jesus is revealed in the changed lives of His beloved children. If He can do that for me, if He can do that for you, then someone He brings across our path can experience that magnificent moment of hope. Maybe, just maybe, He can do that for me.

God of love, thank you for making me a new person.
Bring people across my path whom I can share my simple story with.

THE FIELDS ARE READY

Do you not say, "There are yet four months, and then comes the harvest"?
Behold, I say to you, lift up your eyes and look on the fields,
that they are white for harvest.

JOHN 4:35, NASB

The woman at the well reveals so much about Jesus to us. Even when our lives are shut off from love, lost in sin, broken from the damage this world can inflict, He approaches us and speaks to us the words of love and acceptance our hearts are desperate to hear. His presence is a balm from the guilt and condemnation that brings sickness to our souls, no matter what face we show to the world.

In His own words, Jesus wraps up His short ministry to this forgotten little town in Samaria with the reminder that the fields are "white for harvest."

The time is now, lovely ones. The earth aches and groans under the strain of its choices. It trembles under the strain of greed and vanity, and yearns for the lover of our souls to bring ultimate hope.

Look around you. It's not four months away; it's not tomorrow. It's today. People need the Lord. All they are lacking is someone to tell the simple but life-changing story of what Jesus Christ has done. The story of the great love of God.

Loving Father, help me to see the opportunities to share your love
that are before me even as I pray these words.

THE SOLID ROCK

Therefore everyone who hears these words of mine and puts them into practice
is like a wise man who built his house on the rock.

MATTHEW 7:24, NIV

"Sing joyfully to the Lord, you righteous; it is fitting for the upright to praise him"
(Psalm 33:1).

My hope is built on nothing less
Than Jesus' blood and righteousness.
I dare not trust the sweetest frame,
But wholly lean on Jesus' name.

Refrain
On Christ, the solid Rock, I stand,
All other ground is sinking sand;
All other ground is sinking sand.

When darkness veils His lovely face,
I rest on His unchanging grace.
In every high and stormy gale,
My anchor holds within the veil.

When He shall come with trumpet sound,
O may I then in Him be found!
Dressed in His righteousness alone,
Faultless to stand before the throne.

My hope is built on you and you alone,
God my Father, Christ my Redeemer!

YOUR HEALING

They called him every name in the book and he said nothing back.
He suffered in silence, content to let God set things right. He used his servant body
to carry our sins to the Cross so we could be rid of sin, free to live the right way.
His wounds became your healing. You were lost sheep with no idea who you were or where
you were going. Now you're named and kept for good by the Shepherd of your souls.

1 PETER 2:24–25, THE MESSAGE

Is life tough right now? Are you being treated unfairly? Are you tempted to give up? Do you feel like God has forgotten you? First of all, remember the opening lines of God's message to you in 1 Peter. You are not forgotten. God knows you by name and knows exactly where you are and what you are going through. Take this opportunity to grow in your faith. Never, never, never ever forget that God is with you. That alone makes anything we go through bearable.

But then look to your Savior. Reflect on what He has done for you. Peter, once a coward but a follower of Christ who became mighty—not just in words but in valor—reminds us when we are in a season of adversity: "What counts is that you put up with it for God's sake when you're treated badly for no good reason. There's no particular virtue in accepting punishment that you well deserve. But if you're treated badly for good behavior and continue in spite of it to be a good servant, that is what counts with God" (vv. 19–20).

He is our model of perseverance—and He is our model of ultimate healing and victory. Don't give up. You can make it. Remember, when you are weak, He is strong.

You are my Deliverer, my Healer, my Friend, my Shepherd.
Victory is mine through you, O God!

INNER STRENGTH AND BEAUTY

*What matters is not your outer appearance—the styling of your hair,
the jewelry you wear, the cut of your clothes—but your inner disposition.*

1 PETER 3:4, THE MESSAGE

*P*eter's words were spoken to wives who were not being cared for and loved by their husbands like they should. But don't you think his holy counsel is good for all of us?

It's so easy to adopt an attitude of grievance and resentment. And certainly, all of us deserve to be treated right by those around us. But life doesn't always happen that way. The world is filled with people who can be unkind and rude. But the solution is not to become like those who don't treat others right. I can almost guarantee you won't get what you want—to be treated with love and affection—that way.

To his beloved friends who were scattered throughout the Roman Empire, Peter calls for a new kind of strength. A godly strength. An inner disposition of kindness and grace. He wants us to be like our Lord Jesus Christ. For the women he says: "Cultivate inner beauty, the gentle, gracious kind that God delights in. The holy women of old were beautiful before God that way, and were good, loyal wives to their husbands. Sarah, for instance, taking care of Abraham, would address him as 'my dear husband.' You'll be true daughters of Sarah if you do the same, unanxious and unintimidated" (vv. 5–6).

Wow. Isn't that a testimony of grace and strength under pressure? What a powerful message for wives—and husbands and children . . . all of us!

*You are holy, O God. And you call me to be holy. Let my inner disposition
reveal a strength and grace that brings glory to you.*

SHOW HONOR

The same goes for you husbands: Be good husbands to your wives.
Honor them, delight in them.

1 PETER 3:7, THE MESSAGE

God's word is both specific and universal. These words are written specifically to husbands—but it's such wonderful counsel for all of us. What a different world we would live in if people would fully let their hearts be changed by the love of Jesus Christ. What would happen in our workplaces, in our marriages, our families, our network of friends, our churches, if we would lead a revolution in honoring others, truly delighting in them? Is there any greater testimony of the grace you have received?

Have you fallen into patterns of grumbling about the people who are closest to you in life? Do you see the shortcomings and miss out on the blessings of lifting others up by the way you think and speak of them? Nothing is sadder than to see a married couple that began their life together with such love and enthusiasm to, after many years, no longer find joy in each other.

Friends, let's be obedient. Even if we don't feel like we are treated with the affection and dignity we deserve, let's be leaders. Let's be the ones who go the extra mile with kindness. It all begins when we look to Jesus and see how He treated us, even when we were far from Him and rejected Him.

Husbands, delight in your wife. Honor her. Children, honor your parents and delight in them. Wives, even if your husband has not yet taken the lead, help him become who he needs to be by the way you honor and delight in him.

You love me so much, O God. You delight in me, even when
I'm not such a delightful person. You honor me, even when I don't deserve honor.
May I treat others as you have treated me.

LOVING AND COMPASSIONATE

Summing up: Be agreeable, be sympathetic, be loving, be compassionate, be humble.
That goes for all of you, no exceptions. No retaliation. No sharp-tongued sarcasm.
Instead, bless—that's your job, to bless. You'll be a blessing and also get a blessing.

1 PETER 3:8–9, THE MESSAGE

God speaks to us so clearly and simply about holy living through the letter of Peter. It is a call to obedience, but it is not filled with a long list of rules. Really there is only one compelling rule: Love God and love others. When Jesus was asked what the greatest commandment was, He answered by saying there are two: "Love the Lord your God with all your heart and with all your soul and with all your mind. This is the first and greatest commandment. And the second is like it: Love your neighbor as yourself" (Matthew 22:37–39, NIV).

We make things too complicated. I like to keep life simple. Love God. Love others. We express our love to God in worship, and He loves to hear us lift our voices in praise. But we express our love to God when we love others like He does.

When you hear words of sarcasm come from your mouth, when you retaliate against someone who has spoken unwisely and unkindly, when your words and actions curse rather than bless, return to your love for God and ask Him to let that love overflow to those around you. All of them. No exceptions. You will bless them—and bless yourself.

You have been so compassionate and loving to me, O God.
Fill me with your grace and love so that others will say the same thing about me!

UNSTOPPABLE

If with heart and soul you're doing good, do you think you can be stopped?
Even if you suffer for it, you're still better off. Don't give the opposition a second thought.
Through thick and thin, keep your hearts at attention, in adoration before Christ,
your Master. Be ready to speak up and tell anyone who asks why you're living
the way you are, and always with the utmost courtesy.

1 PETER 3:13–15, THE MESSAGE

"I'm not making a difference." My friend, don't lose heart. Don't give that a second thought. When you express God's goodness in the world, you are indeed making a difference. You may not see the fruit of your labors instantly, but God himself notices and resides over every seed you are sowing. You are getting through. You are unstoppable.

Think of Jesus' earthly ministry. He worked with a ragtag band of followers that were sometimes slow to understand and live what Jesus was trying to teach them. At the time of His death and resurrection, there were still relatively few believers and followers. But the love of Christ changed the world. It conquered the power of sin and death. That same love—now flowing from your heart and life—will continue to build His kingdom.

Some reject us for our faith. But some reject us for our lack of faith. The greatest testimony of our life is when we are asked by others why we live the way we do. "How do I have what you have?" All God asks us to do is adore Christ, love others, and be ready to tell people what has happened in us. Are you ready to speak up?

My thoughts are on you, Lord. I adore you as I worship you with my life.
Let my life be seen by the world that they would come to me to find out
about this great love you have given me.

A CLEAR CONSCIENCE

Keep a clear conscience before God so that when people throw mud at you, none of it will stick. They'll end up realizing that they're the ones who need a bath.

1 PETER 3:16, THE MESSAGE

When we are criticized, it is so easy to respond defensively. It is natural to want to let people know how wrong they are about us. But Jesus is our model. When the religious leaders spoke against Him—even when He was being tried for blasphemy—He remained silent. He knew they had made up their minds to kill Him; He knew their hard hearts had blinded them to the obvious. He was content to go about His Father's business and let His life speak in His defense.

There may be a time when someone speaks words of judgment to you, and it is right to listen with a heart that is not defensive—to allow needed correction and insight into your life. But when someone is slinging mud at us from a hardened heart, we don't need to defend ourselves. Our life will do just that. Their very words will bring conviction to their heart. God will show them the difference between our heart and theirs. Our mature and grace-filled response may be the very thing that brings them to repentance.

I know this isn't easy; it really is a test of our faith to hear people speak nonsense against us. But what an opportunity to cling to our relationship with God, knowing that He is the only One we truly need to please. He is actually such a great Dad, He will cover and protect.

Are you under attack? Ask God to search your heart. When you know you are living for Him, your silence will speak volumes to your accusers!

You are my Defender, O God. In your presence my fear is silenced. I stand before you not because of my own goodness, but because of the blood of Jesus that has redeemed me.

THINKING LIKE JESUS

Since Jesus went through everything you're going through and more, learn to think like him. Think of your sufferings as a weaning from that old sinful habit of always expecting to get your own way. Then you'll be able to live out your days free to pursue what God wants instead of being tyrannized by what you want.

1 PETER 4:1–2, THE MESSAGE

The Christian life is one of joy and blessing, and even in the midst of heart-breaking times, we have a hope that we can confidently cling to. There are so many things He does for us and gives to us. But as we grow closer to God, we realize that a full life is not about what we get, but what we give. We find the true happiness of serving others out of love for God.

With Christ in our heart, with God at our side, we have everything we need in life. Sometimes it takes suffering to reveal to us just how rich we are. It is then we discover that our triumph is not just for this moment and this world, but also for all eternity. Suffering can remind us of what really matters and wean us "from that old sinful habit of always expecting to get your own way." We learn that wanting God's way is the key to freedom and true success.

Things not going your way? Are you facing hardships? What an opportunity to experience true freedom. Take this season to focus on desiring God's will in every area of your life. Then celebrate the freedom of living life as God intended you to.

Father, in good times and hard times, I worship you.
Your blessings flow into my heart and life no matter what is happening around me.
I want my will to be aligned with your will!

WIDE AWAKE IN PRAYER

Everything in the world is about to be wrapped up,
so take nothing for granted. Stay wide-awake in prayer.

1 PETER 4:7, THE MESSAGE

I don't know when Christ will return. I just know He will. A day is coming when every knee will bow and every tongue confess that Jesus is Lord. No exceptions: both the righteous and unrighteous. Perhaps this will happen in our life-time, but perhaps generations from now. I trust God's timing completely because I know that in His mercy He is drawing all who will listen and believe to receive the gift of salvation. I don't know when, but I know I need to be ready, whether I meet my Savior face-to-face in death or through His glorious coming.

God speaks through Peter to tell us to stay wide-awake in prayer. We get busy with so many distractions that we forget what matters and fall asleep in our spiritual lives. When we sleep spiritually, we forget how many people around us are lost in their sins; we put ourselves in the way of temptation; we stop asking God what His will is for our lives and demand our own way.

Time to wake up! We've slept long enough. Don't hit the Snooze button. Pray for God's will; pray for your loved ones; pray for those lost in their sins; pray that no sin will come between you and God. Prayer gives us the ability to take life on Planet Earth very seriously because we are able to see this is not all there is.

When was the last time you thought of eternity? Are you awake? Is your day and life filled with prayer?

You know the issues and people that are on my heart and mind before
I even bring them to you. Help me to be wide-awake to all that is around me
and all that you would have me to do, O God.

LOVE MATTERS MOST

Most of all, love each other as if your life depended on it.
Love makes up for practically anything.

1 PETER 4:8, THE MESSAGE

The New International Version translates this verse to say, "Above all, love each other deeply, because love covers over a multitude of sins." Does that mean our sins and disobedience don't matter to God? Of course not. It points back to the two great commandments Jesus gave us: Love God and love others. All sin arises when we don't do those two things. Conversely, when we love God and others and live surrendered to His Word and will, everything else we experience must bow to His promises.

When love is our purpose, when love is the goal, when love is our anchor, our lives and actions change to mirror the heart of our great God. When we love God with all our hearts, we trust Him so completely that we want His will in our lives because we know that is absolutely what is best for us. It's not even a question. We no longer let other gods rule our life. We don't demand our way and find ourselves on wrong paths. To serve others becomes the greatest joy, not the greatest burden.

As we come to the end of this word from God for all of us who are scattered throughout the world, we are reminded of the beauty and simplicity of pure religion. We learn to ask ourselves a simple question: Is my life an expression of love to God and others?

Let's keep it simple, dear friends. Love God. Love others.

Heavenly Father, I want my life to be a life of love. Nothing else matters.
I love you and ask that you help me love others more and more.

GIVE WHAT YOU GOT

Be quick to give a meal to the hungry, a bed to the homeless—cheerfully. Be generous with the different things God gave you, passing them around so all get in on it: if words, let it be God's words; if help, let it be God's hearty help. That way, God's bright presence will be evident in everything through Jesus, and he'll get all the credit as the One mighty in everything—encores to the end of time. Oh, yes!

1 PETER 4:9–11, THE MESSAGE

God loves a cheerful giver. A cheerful giver doesn't worry that there will be nothing left for him or her. Cheerful givers know that what they have in God is refreshed even as it is given away. Money is multiplied when invested as God teaches us. What God gives us is not a finite supply. Test Him. Give it away. You will find when you share love or wisdom or food to eat, your supply never runs out.

When we give from an awareness that everything we have is a gift from God, we are able to let others know that they are receiving not from us but directly from God—and so it is God who gets the praise and glory.

Peter points out the most obvious needs of food and shelter. But generosity goes beyond basic needs. Perhaps the greatest way we can be generous today is with our gift of time. Nothing will encourage someone who is struggling more than your willingness to stand beside them and help sort it out with the wisdom God has given you.

Don't forget that each of us has different gifts and different resources. All God asks is that we are generous with what He has given us! I was taught early, "Whatever you sow into God's kingdom, it may leave your hand, but it will never leave your life."

You have been so generous with me, O God. Thank you for the privilege of blessing others with all you have given me!

A SPECIAL WORD TO LEADERS

I have a special concern for you church leaders. I know what it's like to be a leader, in on
Christ's sufferings as well as the coming glory. Here's my concern: that you care for God's
flock with all the diligence of a shepherd. Not because you have to, but because you want
to please God. Not calculating what you can get out of it, but acting spontaneously.
Not bossily telling others what to do, but tenderly showing them the way.

1 PETER 5:1–3, THE MESSAGE

Peter knows the responsibility of leadership. He was one of the three in Jesus' inner circle. He was commanded to "feed my sheep." He also knew the anguish of failing his Lord when Jesus asked him to be close. He slept when Jesus needed his presence in prayer. He denied his Savior in the heat of battle.

So his words are particularly wise and powerful: Be diligent; do everything you do to please God, not out of obligation; don't lead for what you can get but because of what you can give; don't lord it over people but lead by example. All of us are leaders at times and need to take these words to heart.

I want to add something that is particularly on my heart. Would you commit to praying for your spiritual leaders? It seems that those God has called to lead often face much opposition and much temptation. Pray that their ministry will be powerful, and pray genuinely that they and their families would thrive under God's protection. Nothing bruises the reputation of the church and our faith more than when a leader falls into sin. Let's simply commit ourselves to praying for God's anointed.

Thank you for the spiritual leaders you have brought into my life, dear God.
Thank you for their gifts of preaching and teaching and encouragement.
Guide and protect their steps.

THE LAST WORD

Keep a cool head. Stay alert. The Devil is poised to pounce, and would like nothing better than to catch you napping. Keep your guard up. You're not the only ones plunged into these hard times. It's the same with Christians all over the world. So keep a firm grip on the faith. The suffering won't last forever. It won't be long before this generous God who has great plans for us in Christ—eternal and glorious plans they are!—will have you put together and on your feet for good. He gets the last word; yes, he does.

1 PETER 5:8–11, THE MESSAGE

Yes, He does. God always has the last word. Suffering lasts but a moment in view of eternity. Even when there is opposition, God's plans always prevail. And even though we have an enemy that would try to rob us of our faith, God has given us everything we need to stand strong and be victorious. All we need to do is stay alert and keep our eyes on Him. He will establish forever.

It is so easy to take our eyes off of God and look at the problems around us. That's when we get discouraged and fearful, giving the devil an opportunity to pounce. Don't forget, no matter how ferocious this lion from the pit of hell appears, he can do nothing to harm us. His roar is powerless against our faith. Do you believe that? If not, get your eyes immediately back on God. He is the One who is all powerful and who reigns forever and ever. Jesus is our Victor. We simply need to turn to Him when we feel under fire.

The adage "The only thing we have to fear is fear itself" is absolutely true in our spiritual life. God has eternal and glorious plans for you—trust Him at His word; for it is the final word!

*Even when I hear the roar of a lion, I turn to you and realize
I am safe in your presence, O God, my Protector.*

NEVER FORGOTTEN

The church in exile here with me—but not for a moment forgotten by God—
wants to be remembered to you. Mark, who is like a son to me, says hello.
Give holy embraces all around! Peace to you—to all who walk in Christ's ways.

1 PETER 5:13–14, THE MESSAGE

We end where we began in this beautiful letter from Peter. You are not forgotten. God knows you by name, knows where you live, knows every situation you are facing in life, and loves you so much.

Take joy in that. And share that joy with others. Peter tells these scattered Christians that Mark says hello and loves them very much. He wants them to receive their love and affection and give hugs all around. What a beautiful picture of Christian fellowship. God loves you. I love you. Let's show it to one another! Never miss an opportunity to tell your brothers and sisters in Christ how much you love them. Don't be cold and aloof. God has made us to walk in fellowship. He knows we thrive and grow when we are surrounded by people we love and trust. We are to be generous with all that God has given us, and that includes our affection for those who walk in Christ's ways with us.

Take a moment to thank God for those who have been a special encouragement to you. Take a moment to ask God who needs a word of encouragement and love from you right now.

Your love means so much to me, Father God.
I am so blessed with the love I receive from fellowship with other Christians.
Give me a generous spirit in showing them how much
I love and appreciate them. Help me to be an encourager.

WATCH OUT

*I could have confidence in my own effort if anyone could. Indeed, if others
have reason for confidence in their own efforts, I have even more!*

PHILIPPIANS 3:4, NLT

"Watch out for those dogs," Paul warns (v. 2). There is a conspiracy afoot. Some would rob the Philippians—and us—of the truth of our salvation. What makes the conspiracy so dangerous is it sounds rather innocent and even noble. Follow the law and be saved. Make a greater effort to be saved. Paul rejects this emphatically—salvation is through the death and resurrection of Jesus Christ alone—and says that if effort saved us, he would be the "most saved":

"I was circumcised when I was eight days old. I am a pure-blooded citizen of Israel and a member of the tribe of Benjamin—a real Hebrew if there ever was one! I was a member of the Pharisees, who demand the strictest obedience to the Jewish law. I was so zealous that I harshly persecuted the church. And as for righteousness, I obeyed the law without fault. I once thought these things were valuable, but now I consider them worthless because of what Christ has done. Yes, everything else is worthless when compared with the infinite value of knowing Christ Jesus my Lord. For his sake I have discarded everything else, counting it all as garbage, so that I could gain Christ" (vv. 3–8).

Let your light shine. Please God with your obedience and service. Show your salvation through your love for others. But never forget for a second that salvation is a gift from God. If you hear otherwise—watch out!

*Thank you for Jesus. I count nothing else in my life, nothing else I could do
as compared to knowing Jesus now and in eternity.*

PRESS ON

*I don't mean to say that I have already achieved these things or that
I have already reached perfection. But I press on to possess that perfection
for which Christ Jesus first possessed me.*

PHILIPPIANS 3:12, NLT

*H*e who began a good work in you will complete it. Don't give up. Press on. No matter how far you feel you've come—or how far you feel you have to go—don't stop now. Even if you miss the mark terribly, today is a new day. Live for "that perfection for which Christ Jesus first possessed" you.

It is natural to want to arrive at our destination. Having flown more miles than I'd like to count, I really understand wanting to "get there" now. I might ask, "Are we there yet?" more than my children do. We will get there soon enough. Life is so short and fleeting. Our task is to enjoy each step of the journey and press on toward the perfection Christ Jesus calls us to.

Can we ever truly achieve perfection? Paul is quick to point out he hasn't reached perfection, but he presses on. I actually draw great strength from knowing that God's mercies are new every morning, and so I press on. I also rest in the fact that God sees me as perfect in His sight, through the blood of Jesus and not my own works. What a relief. In the meantime, my goal and delight, with passion, humility, and sincerity, is to press on.

Not feeling very perfect just now? Press on!

*Dear God, I am so far away from perfection, but because of your love
for me and your high calling to me, I press on!*

REJOICE ALWAYS

Always be full of joy in the Lord. I say it again—rejoice!

PHILIPPIANS 4:4, NLT

As Paul nears the end of his letter of joy, what does he focus on? Joy, of course!

Have we caught the concern in Paul's heart? Do we realize how much he wants us to live a life of joy? God doesn't save us to be miserable and unhappy. He wants us to experience true happiness by knowing our Creator—and then showing the world how wonderful it would be for them to know God fully.

Not every circumstance feels good. But we can always determine to be joyful. Yes, oftentimes joy is a choice, an act of the will. That's why grumbling and complaining is so dangerous. Negative thoughts and words take us down a path to where everything feels impossible, too hard, unfair. But positive words and thoughts—as an act of the will and as an expression of our salvation—lead us to joy. Joy is also a fruit of the Spirit. I love this. Not by might or power but by the Spirit of God himself within us.

Rejoice in the Lord always and some will scoff. They will tell you it is not possible to be joyful at all times. But Paul himself, in his own life, shows us that it is indeed possible. God himself has made a way.

What is going on in your life right now? And how are you going to react to circumstances? Let's make Paul's joy complete—let's please God—and rejoice. You will discover that even if you didn't feel the joy when the words formed on your lips, the reality will soon follow.

---

*You are so kind and gracious, my Lord. Thank you for the gift of joy
that transcends and goes deeper than all circumstances in life.*

FIX YOUR THOUGHTS

And now, dear brothers and sisters, one final thing. Fix your thoughts
on what is true, and honorable, and right, and pure, and lovely, and admirable.
Think about things that are excellent and worthy of praise.

PHILIPPIANS 4:8, NLT

The old adage tells us "Garbage in, garbage out." I'm afraid too many of us who are believers in Christ don't take proper care of what we feed our minds. So much in the way of entertainment is not honorable. We are taught to be cynical and skeptical, even about truths of God. But God's Word doesn't warn us about the negative in these verses. Through Paul's letter to the Philippians, God tells us to fix our minds on the positive.

There is no better place to start than God's Word. How would our thoughts and actions be different if we started meditating on several verses throughout the day? There are many different ways to see that your world is steeped in God's truths. My heart and mind are very influenced by the music I listen to and sing. It is important that my home is filled with songs that declare God's Word. Whether it's through listening to the preaching of God's Word, Bible studies, time alone and with others in prayer, and great Christian books, today there is little excuse.

Is it any wonder why church is so important? Some think they can live the Christian life without a strong local fellowship, but I'm not one of them. I know how important it is for me to unite with others to fix my mind on what is right, pure, lovely, and admirable—to think about things that are excellent and worthy of praise.

What's on your mind? Is it excellent?

Like your servant David, I meditate on your Word, O Lord.
I fix my mind on what is excellent and praiseworthy. I fix my mind on you!

DON'T WORRY

Don't worry about anything; instead, pray about everything.
Tell God what you need, and thank him for all he has done. Then you
will experience God's peace, which exceeds anything we can understand.
His peace will guard your hearts and minds as you live in Christ Jesus.

PHILIPPIANS 4:6–7, NLT

What has you worried today? What is robbing you of peace and joy? Have you prayed about it? My prayer is that none of us will wallow in problems but turn heart and mind to the answer to our every problem and need.

I don't know how many times I have lost sleep worrying over different situations, when in the end, God turned the problem around in His way and in His time.

Jesus Christ is our Victor. He has provided us everything we need to be victors as well. But it's up to us to claim what is ours. Each and every encounter we have with Jesus—from salvation to every challenge we must face—presents us with the choice to believe or not believe, to walk in faith or doubt. It is the same with worries. We can focus on the problem or we can focus on our Redeemer.

Let this testimony from missionary and minister Elisabeth Elliot be our testimony when it comes to worry and uncertainty: "Because God is my sovereign Lord, I was not worried. He manages perfectly, day and night, year in and year out, the movements of the stars, the wheeling of the planets, the staggering coordination of events that goes on on the molecular level in order to hold things together. There is no doubt that he can manage the timing of my days and weeks."

I release my worries into your hands, O Lord.
Thank you for the gift of your peace, for guarding my heart.

DESPERATE SITUATIONS

A Classic Devotion by Mrs. Charles Cowman

The angel of the Lord came upon [Peter], and a light shined
in the prison: and he smote Peter on the side, and raised him up,
saying, Arise up quickly. And his chains fell off.

ACTS 12:7, KJV

This is God's way. In the darkest hours of the night, His tread draws near across the billows. As the day of execution is breaking, the angel comes to Peter's cell. When the scaffold for Mordecai is complete, the royal sleeplessness leads to a reaction in favor of the favored race. . . .

"There's a simplicity about God in working out His plans, yet a resourcefulness equal to any difficulty, and an unswerving faithfulness to His trusting child, and an unforgetting steadiness in holding to His purpose. Through a fellow-prisoner, then a dream, He lifts Joseph from a prison to a premiership. And the length of stay in the prison prevents dizziness in the premier. It's safe to trust God's methods and to go by His clock" (S. D. Gordon).

"Providence hath a thousand keys to open a thousand sundry doors for the deliverance of His own, when it is even come to a desperate case. Let us be faithful; and care for our own part which is to suffer for Him, and lay Christ's part on himself, and leave it there" (George MacDonald).

Difficulty is the very atmosphere of miracle—it is miracle in its first stage. If it is to be a great miracle, the condition is not difficulty but impossibility. The clinging hand of His child makes a desperate situation a delight to Him.

I cling to you, O Lord. Thank you for opening doors no man can open.
Thank you for delivering me at just the right time.

SHIELD

JESUS IS A SHIELD FOR US.
HE IS OUR GLORY.

MARCH

'Tis Grace that brought me safe thus far
and Grace will lead me home. ♡

The Lord has promised good to me.
His word my hope secures.
HE will my shield & portion be,
As long as life endures.

Glory be to King Jesus, my Shield!

A SPACIOUS LIFE

He brought me out into a spacious place; he rescued me because he delighted in me.

PSALM 18:19, NIV

Who can capture the well of emotions contained within the core of a grateful heart like David could? His ability to write the journey of his own heart is quite astonishing. Is it any wonder we love the Psalms so much?

In Psalm 18:19 we are told that God has brought us into a "spacious life." What a wonderful thought. Jesus didn't die to give us a great day today. No, He died to pull us out of our "self" lives and to present to us life in all its fullness: a life to be lived for others, a life to be lived for His glory.

When looking at what a spacious life actually means, I am reminded that the peace of God and His redeeming grace in our lives brings about the beauty of a spacious heart—one unencumbered by the troubles of this world or our own lives. A spacious heart has room for whatever God places in your world today, and all of it is possible only because He loves us so completely. So when you hear the voice of someone who wants to cut you down to size, who wants you to be "realistic" and not get carried away with grand ideas and plans to make a difference in this world, I hope you will always realize that is not God's voice. His plans are perfect and always involve increase one way or another.

Because the Father delights in us—He delights in you, He delights in me—He longs for us to come to Him, to live in Him, to accomplish all that He has designed for us to do. Now that is a large, spacious life, indeed. And this path of life is not just intended for a few lucky ones—no way—but for every man, woman, and child. Every nation, tribe, and tongue. For me. For you.

Gracious Father, when I get comfortable with a cluttered and complicated life, help me to experience the spacious life that your Word promises.

CLEAN HANDS

I have been blameless before him and have kept myself from sin.
The Lord has rewarded me according to my righteousness,
according to the cleanness of my hands in his sight.

PSALM 18:23–24, NIV

avid speaks of the reward that comes from "clean hands," but we should never understand this to be a works-based philosophy that declares, "If I am good, then God will do good things for me." In Ephesians 2:8–10, Paul clearly states: "For it is by grace you have been saved, through faith—and this is not from yourselves, it is the gift of God—not by works, so that no one can boast. For we are God's handiwork, created in Christ Jesus to do good works, which God prepared in advance for us to do."

It is not by works that we are saved, so what then is David talking about? This "man after God's own heart," having been slandered, takes a stand, voicing his integrity and vigorously defending his character. Charles Spurgeon writes, "There is no self-righteousness in an honest man who knows that he is honest, not even if he believes that God rewards him in providence because of his honesty; for this is often a most evident matter of fact. It would be self-righteousness indeed if we transferred such thoughts . . . into the spiritual kingdom. For there grace reigns not only supreme, but sole in the distribution of favors."

A life lived under the light of truth will bring rewards—just as God intended—but we must always remember where our help comes from and give the Lord all the glory due to His great name.

Father, you created me for works of service, and I praise you
for giving me the power to do just what you intended for me.

GOD'S SMILE

You, Lord, keep my lamp burning; my God turns my darkness into light.

PSALM 18:28, NIV

David lived in close communion with his God. Notice the ease with which David calls the Creator of heaven and earth "my God." How wonderful to show such awe and respect with such a comfortable—and comforting—familiarity, all in the same thought.

David had dedicated himself to the service of the Lord, heart and soul. For us today, the only way this is sustainable—the only way we keep our lamps burning—is through God's grace working in our lives, and the love of Christ literally transforming us from the inside out.

As I read the words of David, I find myself drawing such strength from his honest prayers. You can almost see God smile toward David as his heart is revealed.

Today, I pray you find the security that comes from knowing that every time your own heart stretches toward the Lord, there He is again, just waiting for your longing heart to trust Him.

God alone turns our darkness into light. It is the light of His love burning bright from within us. But lamps die out without fuel. What is the source of fuel? Trust in God is first and foremost. Worship Him through every season. Just as God honored David's willing heart, He renews the faithful heart today. If we are to live with the light of Christ burning brilliantly within us, we must always be ready to say yes to the will of God. Jesus himself said that His own food, His own sustenance, His own strength was found in doing the will of the Father (see John 4:34).

Father, keep my lamp burning through the fuel of a loving and obedient heart.

HE RESCUED ME

He reached down from on high and took hold of me; he drew me out of deep waters.
He rescued me from my powerful enemy, from my foes, who were too strong for me.

PSALM 18:16–17, NIV

David's anthem of love and gratitude found in Psalm 18 unfolds like the storyboard of a blockbuster epic movie. All seemed lost. Danger and death were all around. The situation was hopeless. But at just the right moment, the mighty warrior king appeared to save his people. David knew who that King was—and we know that same King today. What a magnificent God we serve.

The amazing words of Psalm 18 can first be found in 2 Samuel 22, so we know exactly what David was going through when he composed the song. He was surrounded by his enemies, but most significantly, he was hounded by the man he served faithfully, the king he fought for without regard for his own life, the one who had turned his face from God—King Saul. It is one thing to be attacked by known enemies. How much worse it is to be besieged by one we love and once trusted.

David was as mighty a warrior as ever lived, but he knew it was not his own strength that saved him. He acknowledged the true giver and preserver of life.

What are you in the midst of? Are you surrounded by danger, by betrayal at the hand of a loved one? Do you know you don't have the strength to withstand all you are facing? Do you feel like you are going under? In that moment, look up, don't lose heart, and hold fast to your faith. Your God will rescue you. Apply Psalm 18 to your life. It's one of my all-time favorites. God himself hears every cry and will always be there to walk you through any storm.

O God, you alone are my rescue. Thank you for reaching your
hand of grace and mercy to me when I thought all was lost.

WITH ALL MY HEART AND STRENGTH

I love you, Lord, my strength.

PSALM 18:1, NIV

*I*n Hosea 6:6, God speaks clearly to His people on what He wants from them: "I want you to show love, not offer sacrifices. I want you to know me more than I want burnt offerings" (NLT). God wanted His people to know and love Him. Is it any wonder that David was a "man after God's heart"? For what was David's first response to deliverance? He sang a song of love.

We use the word *love* quite often, and maybe this doesn't sound surprising to us. But consider that in David's time the people were not used to hearing the word *love* as part of their worship. Love was deemed as an attitude that was too familiar, not respectful enough. But David, a true leader, was never one to simply follow the crowd. No matter what others thought, he shouted out with all the fervor of his heart, "I love God!"

David never lost his deep sense of reverence and fear, but he got to the heart of the matter in expressing His love for God. In so doing, he taught the people of his day that true worship of God is rooted in a relationship of love.

Jesus tells us that redemption is not based on God's feeling sorry for us. He declares, "For God loved the world so much that he gave his one and only Son, so that everyone who believes in him will not perish but have eternal life" (John 3:16, NLT). God's act of love calls for our response of love. This is where the truth of our worship comes from.

What is the basis of your relationship with God today? Is it tradition? Fear? Or is it a passionate and fervent heart that loves the Lord with all your strength?

O God, all I can say today is that I love you with all my heart and strength.

HE HEARD MY CRY

But in my distress I cried out to the Lord; yes, I prayed to my God for help.
He heard me from his sanctuary; my cry to him reached his ears.

PSALM 18:6, NLT

"*He* heard me." What a truly amazing verse from Scripture. I know for many of you reading these words, as it is for me, that simple phrase is at the heart of your testimony. If you've forgotten even a tiny bit how God saved you, read through Psalm 18 again—and again. It brings tears to my eyes every time.

I can literally see the mighty power of God reaching down and plucking me out—His own, His beloved—from the grip of hell. Maybe this is why superheroes and superhero movies never seem to lose their appeal. Maybe this is a universal response of the heart, knowing deep down, no matter how hard some try to cover it up and block it out, that they—that each of us—truly need a Savior.

God heard David's cry for help. God heard my cry for help. God hears your cry. He hears even—and especially—your prayers that are uttered in desperation, without eloquence or formality; the prayers that see you at the end of yourself; prayers with only a glimmer of hope that there is a God in heaven who is listening. God knows your situation and hears you. And above all else, He is faithful.

There have been times in my life that I felt no one was listening or wanted to know the ache in my soul. But I know now that God himself was there all the time. He reached down and rescued me even as the cry for help formed on my lips. This is why I get so passionate about praising the King. He loves us, oh how He loves us.

God, I want to walk worthy of my Savior.
Pour out my life as a living sacrifice to you, my King.

POWER IN WEAKNESS

Each time he said, "My grace is all you need. My power works best in weakness."
So now I am glad to boast about my weaknesses, so that the power of Christ
can work through me.

2 CORINTHIANS 12:9, NLT

*I*n the world at large, people admire strength and look down on weakness. But in His Sermon on the Mount, Jesus tells us that blessed—happy to the core—are the poor in spirit, those who mourn, the merciful, the meek, even those who are persecuted (Matthew 5:3–10). In Christ's kingdom, there is a remarkable moment when worldly understanding is turned upside down—the weak are lifted up to the place of honor and the strong are found wanting.

Nowhere does that moment become more real to me than in worship. That's when I realize in every fiber of my being that the Maker of heaven and earth has reached down to me, His servant. That's when I realize how unworthy and powerless I am to experience the magnitude of His sovereignty, power, and might in my own strength. But His grace is abundant toward me, each and every moment.

Being poor in spirit is understanding what David, the great psalmist, knew deep in his heart when he said, "Know that the Lord is God. It is he who made us, and we are his; we are his people, the sheep of his pasture" (Psalm 100:3, NIV). It is the simple, humble, grateful expression of praise to the Holy One who is all-loving, all-knowing, and all-powerful.

Thank you, heavenly Father, for becoming my strength,
for lifting me up to a new way of life through your power.

A LOVING FATHER

O Lord, don't rebuke me in your anger or discipline me in your rage.
Have compassion on me, Lord, for I am weak. Heal me, Lord, for my bones
are in agony. I am sick at heart. How long, O Lord, until you restore me?
Return, O Lord, and rescue me. Save me because of your unfailing love.

PSALM 6:1–4, NLT

Can't you sense the angst of one who is struggling with his concept of a loving Father? What is your understanding of God?

Many who have not had great examples of loving earthly fathers have a hard time placing their trust in their heavenly Father. Maybe they can say the words, but deep down they don't feel it. Some believe God is in heaven, watching and hovering over us with a big stick, waiting to bring sickness, tragedy, and other "signs" of judgment to our lives if we do even one wrong thing—or worse, to teach us a lesson.

I was dismayed to hear a Christian couple say that a young boy's cancer was sent by God to test the family. It was so frustrating to see otherwise good-hearted and devout people thinking that our loving Father would treat them this way. Remember, we have an enemy who exists to kill, steal, and destroy, to rob us of all God intended for our good. Jesus wears the Victor's crown. Always will.

The Psalms are real. They speak the sweetest praise but also reveal our honest frustrations and impatience. If you are struggling to feel the love of God, that's the place to start: honesty. He will listen, which is in itself a sign of just how much He truly loves you.

God of love, help me to not let disappointments or hurts cloud my vision of you.
Help me to see you as you truly are.

ON OUR SIDE

So, what do you think? With God on our side like this, how can we lose?
If God didn't hesitate to put everything on the line for us, embracing our condition
and exposing himself to the worst by sending his own Son, is there anything
else he wouldn't gladly and freely do for us?

ROMANS 8:31–32, THE MESSAGE

Our view of God will affect everything from our self-perception and sense of worth to how we feel about those around us to how we trust the significant people in our lives.

Our view of God will affect the way we pray and worship. Do you pray joyfully and with a spirit of expectancy? Or do you expect not to be heard and for nothing to happen? Do you attend church with the tingling anticipation that God is waiting for you there with a word for your spirit—or do you go through the motions with a bland, bored attitude, seeing church attendance as another box to tick on your long list of to-dos?

Our view of God will eventually be heard through our speech and seen in our lives. For out of the abundance of our hearts, our mouths speak.

My dear friends, please don't miss the transforming truth that God is on your side. He loves you. He is your defender. He wants the very best for you.

Repeat Romans 8:31 over and over if this is your struggle. Say it with all your heart until you embrace and believe it in your heart. Then simply expect to experience His beauty and faithfulness painted across the fabric of your life. Be ready to live a life greater than you dreamed was possible. It won't be without trials for any of us, but we can rest in the assurance God is always beside us. He is on our side.

God, you are on my side. I thank you for that. I know that nothing—
not even attitudes I've struggled with—can prevail against you in my life.

A CHANGE OF TUNE

Return, O Lord, deliver me! Oh, save me for Your mercies' sake!

PSALM 6:4, NKJV

The psalmist tells the music director to present Psalm 6 with "stringed instruments" and an "eight-stringed harp." I would love to have heard what he came up with. This psalm is filled with the language of great sorrow, humiliation, and the hatred of sin, which are the most easily recognizable signs of a contrite and broken spirit. You don't have to be a musician to know the tune and instrumentation would be harsh and sad. I think it would have been played in a minor key.

But something happens in the midst of David's cry of lament. It begins in verse 4 when he calls out, "Return, O Lord, deliver me!" The absence of God is the problem here and is at the heart of David's woe. Did God really leave? I doubt it. I suspect David had turned his eyes elsewhere, and now he was discovering that living life in his own way created nothing but problems.

By the time we get to verse 9, David is able to proclaim, "The Lord has heard my supplication; the Lord will receive my prayer."

What a change of tune. From not believing God is near to the conviction that God will receive his prayer. I believe in my heart that the music director had a burst of musical genius that transformed this psalm into an anthem of inspirational praise in a major key!

Not feeling God's presence in your life? Make a change of tune in your heart, beginning with the rock solid belief that God will receive your prayer.

Thank you, Father, that even when I have let my attentions stray elsewhere, you receive me into your presence and hear my prayer.

STAND AGAIN

*Let all my enemies be ashamed and greatly troubled; let them turn back
and be ashamed suddenly.*

PSALM 6:10, NKJV

Throughout Psalm 6, David is remorseful, agitated, and broken. He is weary from groaning and crying. He sounds like a man depressed to the point of death: "For in death there is no remembrance of you; in the grave who will give you thanks?" (v. 5). This poet-warrior was in great fear of what lay ahead for him, terrified of the thought of living a life without God.

He was right. To think one can live life without God is the foolishness of much of our modern world. So many presume that they can live as a spiritual being without Christ holding it all together. A life lived in sin and unresolved internal issues will age the body at a far greater pace than life lived in the sun. Unforgiveness, bitterness, pride, even disappointment have the ability to rot the bones of man (see Proverbs 14:30).

As badly as weeping hurts, when it turns to a season of rejoicing, the joy is all the more intense and purifying. If you are going through a time of weeping, I pray it will end soon and that, with our friend David, you will rise from the ashes.

David, this man after God's own heart, refused to stay where he found himself. He confessed his sin and stopped blaming others for his woes. He rose in strength, rebuking his enemies and living again in the power of promise.

*Father, turn my sorrow to joy. I pray for a revelation of your
love and goodness so that I may sing again a song of rejoicing.*

A LOUD SHOUT

O Lord my God, I have taken refuge in you. Save me,
and rescue me from all who are pursuing me.

PSALM 7:1, GOD'S WORD

*P*salm 7 and Habakkuk 3 are the only two passages in the Bible referred to as a *Shiggaion*, which can be translated as a "loud shout." This is just another simple reminder that God wants our worship to be sincere and from the heart. Sometimes that will be quiet; sometimes it will be highly reflective; sometimes there will be tears; but sometimes our worship is to be loud—and in this psalm, very passionate. Throughout the Psalms, David models God's desire for us to come to Him "just as I am." He doesn't want us to pretend to be feeling one emotion when we are clearly feeling another. He doesn't want our performance; he wants us in truth.

In this case, David comes before God Almighty in anger. Loud anger. But isn't anger a sin? David's son, wise King Solomon, cautions: "Don't be quick to get angry, because anger is typical of fools" (Ecclesiastes 7:9). But Paul points out it is possible to be angry without sin when he says, "Be angry without sinning" (Ephesians 4:26).

The Psalms—Israel's songs of worship—covered the full spectrum of David's emotions, of our emotions. And Psalm 7 is a magnificent triumph of faith as David turns even the most disastrous event into a song.

Can you face what angers you and turn it into a song of praise? Maybe this is also part of our sacrifice of praise. What I do know is when I bring even my frustrations before the Lord, my heart is reminded of His faithfulness in it and through it all. Martin Luther said, "David made Psalms; we also will make Psalms, and sing them as well as we can to the honour of our Lord, and to spite and mock the devil."

Father, with David, I will shout aloud to you in both joys and sorrow; in victory
and defeat. With honesty I come, as you continue to turn tragedy to triumph.

RESCUE ME

Like a lion they will tear me to pieces and drag me off with no one to rescue me.

PSALM 7:2, GOD'S WORD

The context of Psalm 7 is that Cush the Benjamite has accused David of disloyalty to Saul, Israel's king and David's royal authority. For all of us, attacks from the outside are felt far less keenly than attacks from those closest to us. Cush and David knew each other. This was corrupt politics at their worst, where stabbing a friend in the back was an easy trade-off for personal gain. Because of the sad state of Saul's heart and mind, evidenced in large measure by an insane and intense jealousy of David, the king listened to the accusations, accepted them as truth, and then went after David with great ferocity.

The prayer of this shepherd comes through as he compares Saul's attack to a lion pouncing on a defenseless lamb, ripping it to pieces and devouring it, and then sauntering slowly to bask in the sun, with a proud smile of victory. A lion does what it does because of its nature. But the evildoer does so from a perversity of the heart. No wonder the phrase "evil smile" is something we all understand and instinctively dislike.

Of course, the only way a lamb can be left to attack by a lion is when there is no shepherd close-by to protect and rescue. And the marvelous news for David—and for us—is that our heavenly Father is not silent when His child is in danger. Do you feel powerless? Do you feel surrounded by danger on every side? Don't lose heart. Help is on the way. Call out to the Lord now, "Deliver me!" He is our strength and our shield.

You are the God who protects and rescues,
and I thank you and rest in that marvelous truth today.

FALSELY ACCUSED

Lord my God, if I have done this and there is guilt on my hands—
if I have repaid my ally with evil or without cause have robbed my foe—then let
my enemy pursue and overtake me, let him trample my life to the ground
and make me sleep in the dust.

PSALM 7:3–5, NIV

*J*ust like David, we become frustrated when others spread false accusations against us. Though they are not true, we are angry, confused, and hurt, in part because there is next to nothing we can do about it. Jesus both warned and comforted His disciples: "Blessed are you when people insult you, persecute you and falsely say all kinds of evil against you because of me" (Matthew 5:11).

What was David's defense? "My shield is with God, who saves the upright in heart" (Psalm 7:10, NASB). We catch an even clearer picture of David's integrity from the key verses of this study: "If I have done this and there is guilt on my hands . . . trample my life to the ground."

In life and leadership, you will make mistakes—and those around you will make mistakes as well. None of us are perfect. This is why we are all in need of God's great grace. We walk in this grace, and we are to offer this grace to others as they journey as well. This is part of our commitment to Christ and evidence of His miracle-working power in our lives. When you find yourself in a position where you could easily point an accusing finger—or have an accusing finger pointed at you—think, trust, and forgive. Remember always, in Christ, your hope is secure.

Father, my trust and commitment and love are found in you and in your Son.
Help me to know your words of approval are all that matter.

Hallelujah!
Jesus ♡ You have /
overcome the WORLD
Amen

FALSE ACCUSATIONS

"No weapon forged against you will prevail, and you will refute every tongue that accuses you. This is the heritage of the servants of the Lord, and this is their vindication from me," declares the Lord.

ISAIAH 54:17, NIV

There were seasons in David's life where his actions brought calamity. But much of the distress came to him in the moments when his life was filled with praise, thanksgiving, and obedience.

His tiny fledgling nation was surrounded by enemies on every side. And David faced his enemies—from the bear trying to steal his sheep to warring cities that wanted to destroy his people—with poise and courage. But the greatest woes in his life came from those closest to him. Later in life it would be a treacherous son. Early in his life it was marked by the rage of the man he tried to serve, King Saul.

"Kill him," his men urged David. His response? "He said to his men, 'The Lord forbid that I should do such a thing to my master, the Lord's anointed, or lay my hand on him; for he is the anointed of the Lord'" (1 Samuel 24:6).

What an incredible faith David had in his Lord. He understood that grace is not just a word from the Father to us, but is to be extended to each other.

Even as David honored Saul, it still did not protect him from lying tongues. There is a reason. Envy pursues goodness. It has been said, "The worst critiques come when we least deserve them." What is our response to be? We are to be bigger than the man who enjoys flying rumors and throwing stones, to flee from the market of rumor mongering. And we are to trust God with our character and reputation.

Thank you, Father, that you protect me not only from physical harm, but the damage caused by words. Help me to walk blameless in your sight each day.

I WANT TO FLY AWAY

My heart is in anguish within me; the terrors of death have fallen on me.
Fear and trembling have beset me; horror has overwhelmed me. I said,
"Oh, that I had the wings of a dove! I would fly away and be at rest."

PSALM 55:4–6, NIV

Have you ever wanted to just fly away from your problems? You aren't the first to feel that way. Even David hit such a low point in his life that all he wanted to do was escape and not face what was in front of him anymore. The solitude of a desert seemed more hospitable than what he was dealing with.

Psalm 55 also points to a parent's worst nightmare: total rejection from a child. This is the same way David prayed when his close friend and counselor, Ahithophel, deserted him to serve in the court of Absalom, who was attempting to dethrone his father (see 2 Samuel 15–17). When trust is broken, in whatever form it takes, it always brings about great disappointment, but how much more when it comes at the hand of a trusted friend and a family member.

Betrayal makes you feel very alone and very vulnerable. You can hear those emotions in David's heart when he says "I am distraught" (v. 2). It is the word that would describe the confusion of a demoralized army. David is demoralized.

But he doesn't run. The real problems of life can't be erased by a ride on the wings of a dove. He does what he calls us to do: "Cast your cares on the Lord and he will sustain you; he will never let the righteous be shaken" (v. 22).

Have you cast your cares on the Lord? I encourage you to truly place your cares on the greatest shoulders of all. Allow God's presence to bring rest to your concerned soul.

Father God, I bring to you the challenges of my life,
both big and small, knowing you will sustain me.

DRIVEN TO PRAYER

As for me, I call to God, and the Lord saves me.

PSALM 55:16, NIV

We have an enemy that would discourage and destroy us. He is a roaring lion (see 1 Peter 5:8); he sneaks up on us as an angel of light (see 2 Corinthians 11:14). Often his work is done through people who have resisted the grace and mercies of God. He besieges the small and the mighty and everyone in between. So all of us have experienced what David and other giants of the faith felt in the face of persecution and betrayal.

In Psalm 55, David describes his feelings of broken trust and the overwhelming grief that followed. His first response was to run away. We understand that. It is so easy to start to build walls of protection around our hearts so we don't get hurt again. But this is not the way forward for David or for us. I've had great revelation over the years that even if I am betrayed, I can still confidently climb the mountain of the Lord. No one can make that decision to live like this other than me. No betrayal can steal that from me. Only I can allow the joy of my Christian walk to be stolen from me through my reactions.

A good word to remember is that in the face of trials, when the enemy drives God's servant to prayer, the enemy has encouraged the spiritual renewal he sought to destroy.

David declares, "I call to God." That's the turning point for him and all of us. Are you under fire? You know exactly what to do next!

*God of heaven, I call upon you now. I don't have the strength
to handle my problems by myself. I turn to you!*

I TRUST YOU

But you, God, will bring down the wicked into the pit of decay; the bloodthirsty and deceitful will not live out half their days. But as for me, I trust in you.

PSALM 55:23, NIV

Sometimes the seas of life are smooth and a comforting breeze blows gently across our faces. Sometimes the seas are choppy—not terribly dangerous, but definitely uncomfortable. And sometimes storms rage across the waters of our lives, tossing us like a ship every which way. A tornado tears through a town. A hurricane devastates an island nation. Persecution rains down on devout and innocent villagers for no other crime than lifting up the name of Jesus.

The temptation is to assume God is with us in the good times but that we are alone when times are rough. If that wasn't true for the giants of our faith, including David, then why would that be true for us? I hope you will remember and embrace the truth that Jesus spoke when He said, "And lo, I am with you always, even to the end of the age" (Matthew 28:20, NKJV).

Is your life blissful at this moment? God is with you. Are there a number of problems and issues that gnaw at your sense of peace? God is still with you. Are you facing gale-force winds? All the more, God is near. He's not leaving you alone.

When David states, "I trust you," you can sense a new focus in his life. No longer is he preoccupied with his enemies—his problems—but his eyes are on the Lord. No matter what you are going through, only two parties ultimately matter in your spiritual life: God and you. Two is good company but three is a crowd.

When was the last time you said to God, "I trust you. I truly trust you"?

God, whether sunny skies or storm clouds, you are with me—and I trust you.

AMAZING GRACE

Out of his fullness we have all received grace.

JOHN 1:16, NIV

What turned John Newton, a man who was immersed in the slave trade, into a great reformer and a preacher of the gospel? An amazing grace, of course!

Amazing Grace, how sweet the sound,
That saved a wretch like me.
I once was lost but now am found,
Was blind, but now I see.

'Twas Grace that taught my heart to fear.
And Grace, my fears relieved.
How precious did that Grace appear
The hour I first believed.

Through many dangers, toils and snares
I have already come;
'Tis Grace that brought me safe thus far
and Grace will lead me home.

The Lord has promised good to me.
His word my hope secures.
He will my shield and portion be,
As long as life endures.

Thank you for your amazing grace that saved me, dear God.

NOT ONE FORGOTTEN

I, Peter, am an apostle on assignment by Jesus, the Messiah, writing to exiles scattered to the four winds. Not one is missing, not one forgotten. God the Father has his eye on each of you, and has determined by the work of the Spirit to keep you obedient through the sacrifice of Jesus. May everything good from God be yours!

1 PETER 1:1–2, THE MESSAGE

Have you ever felt left out? Ignored? Unimportant? Forgotten? Our Scriptures here are directed to the people of the day in which they were written, but it is also clear that they contain God's truth for every generation. When the apostle Peter wrote to Christians who had been scattered due to persecution, his assurance that "not one is missing, not one forgotten" still applies to us today.

My dear friends, one of the clear evidences that God loves us deeply is that He always seeks to talk to us. He does just that in Peter's first letter. Then we are immediately and explicitly told that God's divine interest is not vague, but specific. It is for each one of us. He knows us by name. He knows where we live. He knows our joys and sorrows. He knows our strengths and weaknesses. His eye is on us, you and me.

What does the God who knows us personally want for each of us? He is "determined by the work of the Spirit to keep you obedient through the sacrifice of Jesus." Obedience to God is no burden. It is a joy. It is when we truly begin to live life in full. And one of the marvelous results of obedience is that we actually get to receive and experience the "everything good" that is from God to us.

***

Hallelujah! I praise you for your goodness to me, O God. I thank you that you know me by name and love me enough to have died for my sins.

THE FUTURE STARTS NOW

*What a God we have! And how fortunate we are to have him, this Father
of our Master Jesus! Because Jesus was raised from the dead, we've been given
a brand-new life and have everything to live for, including a future in heaven—
and the future starts now! God is keeping careful watch over us and the future.
The Day is coming when you'll have it all—life healed and whole.*

1 PETER 1:3–5, THE MESSAGE

There is so much to see and say in these verses. I love how Eugene Peterson translates that we've been "given a brand-new life and have everything to live for." Do you believe that? Do you know just how fortunate we are? This is something for all of us to embrace, not just with head knowledge but deep in our heart.

Not only do we have the promise of a life filled with God here and now, but we also have the hope of heaven. We in the church have sometimes been criticized that we are so "heavenly minded that we are no earthly good." Perhaps that is true of some, but what is true is that Christians who keep their eyes on Jesus are of the utmost good here on earth. By His Spirit, we have been entrusted with this season in history.

For those who carry a pain or sorrow today, I affirm that God is keeping a careful and loving watch over you right now. And I encourage you to keep your eyes up, your expectation high, for our God has overcome the world. There is also great delight to know that day is coming when every tear is dried and we are healed and whole!

*Father God, we are so fortunate to have you, for without you, we can do nothing, our life
would have no meaning. Thank you for raising Jesus from the dead to give us new life.*

WALKING BY FAITH

You never saw him, yet you love him. You still don't see him,
yet you trust him—with laughter and singing. Because you kept on believing,
you'll get what you're looking forward to: total salvation.

1 PETER 1:8–9, THE MESSAGE

*P*eter was an eyewitness to Jesus. He heard His voice calling him from working his nets as a fisherman to becoming a fisher of men. He traveled with Jesus and saw the miracles, heard the teaching, and experienced the wonder of the resurrection. I find wonderful encouragement in the fact that Peter pays us a special compliment: We didn't see Jesus in the flesh, but we still trust in Him, we keep believing, we come before Him with laughter and singing—as if He were physically present in the same room with us before our very eyes.

To walk by faith, not by sight, has its own special reward. We are strengthened in our spirit and in our heart to fully experience the person of Jesus even if we can't touch Him in the flesh. What a joy and hope is ours, both now and in the future. In heaven we will experience Jesus as a physical presence.

We have the full riches of Jesus today in the here and now. Total salvation is ours because Jesus is the Victor over sin and death. But we still have a further hope that is ours in heaven. That is when the last remnants of sin and death are completely cast away in the perfection of our eternal home.

And so, with revelation overflowing from our hearts, we trust, we sing, we believe, we cling, we confess, we wait.

I come before your presence, my God, with a song in my heart and a smile on my lips,
knowing you are real and present in my life today and forever.

PROPHESIES FULFILLED

*The prophets who told us this was coming asked a lot of questions about this gift
of life God was preparing. The Messiah's Spirit let them in on some of it—that the
Messiah would experience suffering, followed by glory. They clamored to know
who and when. All they were told was that they were serving you, you who by orders
from heaven have now heard for yourselves—through the Holy Spirit—
the Message of those prophecies fulfilled. Do you realize how fortunate you are?
Angels would have given anything to be in on this!*

1 PETER 1:10–12, THE MESSAGE

*D*ear friends, it is so true. We are so blessed and so fortunate. What others longed for, we received. Even if we haven't yet seen Jesus in the flesh, through the gift of the Holy Spirit, we have still fully experienced the Messiah, God's Anointed One.

The prophets talked of His suffering and glory. They had ideas on what that might look like, but it is we, the church today, who have experienced the completed work of Jesus Christ, the Victor. Through His suffering He took the sin of the world on himself. Through His glory—the resurrection and ascension—He gave us a brand-new life, left us with the person of the Holy Spirit, and continues to intercede on our behalf before the Father.

There are things we will see and understand more clearly in heaven. But right now, we have everything we need to experience full salvation today. We are the recipients of what God's prophets and angels longed to see and experience. May we never forget how truly blessed we are!

*Thank you for sending Jesus Christ into the world to save us from our sins. Thank you for
being true to your Word and fulfilling your promise of victory over sin and death.*

DON'T BE LAZY

So roll up your sleeves, put your mind in gear, be totally ready to receive the gift
that's coming when Jesus arrives. Don't lazily slip back into those old grooves of evil,
doing just what you feel like doing. You didn't know any better then; you do now.

1 PETER 1:13–14, THE MESSAGE

eter warns against laziness and how detrimental it is to our spiritual vitality. He wants us to roll up our sleeves, not to earn our salvation, but as an expression of gratitude and worship. God is God. We are part of the creation. And yet we are to become more like God in our thoughts, attitudes, and actions. Peter calls it holiness. He says: "As obedient children, let yourselves be pulled into a way of life shaped by God's life, a life energetic and blazing with holiness. God said, 'I am holy; you be holy'" (vv. 15–16). A verse later, God's response to our laziness or diligence is described like this: "You call out to God for help and he helps—he's a good Father that way. But don't forget, he's also a responsible Father, and won't let you get by with sloppy living" (v. 17).

I hope you know by now that I am for you. I am an encourager. I believe in emphasizing the grace and mercy of our Father. But I still must speak out about spiritual laziness, something I think is a plague in today's church. I don't want to be harsh, but I want so much for you, for myself, for the body of Christ. The Christian life is to be enjoyed, but I want us to take it seriously; to be alert, attentive, awake, ready to say yes to all that He asks. I don't want any of us to "lazily slip back in those old grooves of evil, doing just what you feel like doing."

Let's pray for each other that we would walk worthy of our calling in Christ Jesus.

Thank you, heavenly Father, that you are God of love and mercy.
Thank you also that you expect my best—and that you provide the strength and grace
I need to please you with my life.

SACRED BLOOD

*Your life is a journey you must travel with a deep consciousness of God.
It cost God plenty to get you out of that dead-end, empty-headed life you grew up in.
He paid with Christ's sacred blood, you know. He died like an unblemished, sacrificial
lamb. And this was no afterthought. Even though it has only lately—at the end of
the ages—become public knowledge, God always knew he was going to do this for you.*

1 PETER 1:18–20, THE MESSAGE

Not one of us is perfect. Anyone who claims to be is delusional. The most faithful and godly Christians I have met are humble on that point. They don't brag about their goodness, but only wish they could please God more.

We still somehow get confused at times. We either tell ourselves that with more determination and hard work we can live exactly how God wants us to. Or, realizing we don't have the personal power to overcome temptation, we begin to take sin lightly and don't aspire to godliness.

We are not alone in our struggles. The only place we can turn to is God—and He points us to His Son and what Jesus Christ did for us on the cross. God forgives and empowers but at great cost: "He paid with Christ's sacred blood." This was His provision from the very beginning of days. He would do for us what we could not do ourselves, both in salvation and in godly living.

The reminder is so simple yet so powerful. Don't try harder; trust more. Rest in the finished, perfect work of the cross. Will you trust Him to help you live the life He has planned for you?

*Father, when I thought I was strong enough to live for you, I failed.
It was when I realized how much I needed you that I was able to begin the walk
of holiness. Please stay close to me and uphold me on my life journey.*

LOVE ONE ANOTHER

Now that you've cleaned up your lives by following the truth,
love one another as if your lives depended on it.

1 PETER 1:22, THE MESSAGE

*T*hroughout his letter to Christians scattered by persecution, Peter proclaims God's desire that we be holy. He tells us: "God said, 'I am holy; you be holy'" (v. 16). Never does he suggest we can earn our salvation, but he uses strong words and phrases to stress that we need to work well, not be lazy, think deeply, and basically avoid a casual and shallow Christian walk. In today's passage he affirms they have begun to walk in holiness—and then shares what the greatest evidence of godliness is: "Love one another as if your life depended on it."

Do you love your brothers in Christ that much? Do I? As if our lives depended on it? Do we love our children, our parents, our spouses as if our lives depended on it? Sometimes it is easier to show our love for God through big and dramatic ways. Oh, when God calls you to do something big in His name, by all means do it. Share His love with the world however He calls you to do so. But let's not forget that we express our holiness by the way we treat those closest to us—our families and our spiritual family in particular.

Will we be perfect at it? Of course not. Disputes arise. That's part of being human. But that's what offering and seeking forgiveness are for: restoring the love that God wants between our family and us.

Is there someone you need to seek forgiveness from or offer forgiveness to today?

Father, may I show love to you as I show love to the dear friends
and family you have placed in my life.

CLEAN HOUSE!

So clean house! Make a clean sweep of malice and pretense, envy and hurtful talk.
You've had a taste of God. Now, like infants at the breast, drink deep of God's
pure kindness. Then you'll grow up mature and whole in God.

1 PETER 2:1–3, THE MESSAGE

Bad intentions toward others. Pretending to be someone you're not. Coveting what others have. Gossip, slander, and harsh criticism. Who could Peter be talking to? He must be referring to those who have never experienced the love of God. Sadly, no. He is calling out his brothers and sisters in Christ. They know God and have tasted His goodness. Speaking to and through Peter, God is again reminding us: "I am holy; you be holy."

It's not just a matter of determining we won't have malice and pretense, envy and hurtful talk. We must return to the source of our salvation and the only hope we have of becoming grown up, mature, and whole in God. The place to start is God's pure kindness—His love and mercy expressed in Jesus Christ dying for our sins. As parents, we might not like it when a teenager acts immature, but we have patience because we know they are in the process of maturing. It is quite another thing to see an adult act immaturely. Someone might tell them, "Act your age!" Let's never stop growing more like God as we grow closer to God. I want to know Him better and love Him more this year than I did last year—and I want the same thing next year.

The question for each of us is one of housekeeping. Are there attitudes or actions we have allowed to take root in our life that are keeping us from the pursuit of holiness?

I have tasted your kindness, your goodness, your grace and mercy, O Lord.
May I never forget what I've experienced in you as I draw nearer to you in holiness.

CHOSEN ONES

But you are the ones chosen by God, chosen for the high calling of priestly work,
chosen to be a holy people, God's instruments to do his work and speak out for him,
to tell others of the night-and-day difference he made for you—from nothing
to something, from rejected to accepted.

1 PETER 2:9–10, THE MESSAGE

The talent shows on television are both exhilarating and heartbreaking to watch. Each week someone is chosen to continue in the competition, and we get to see his or her unbridled joy and excitement. But each week someone else is told that his or her talent wasn't good enough to move on. The cameras follow them backstage, where we witness their tears and sometimes anger at being rejected. We can feel their pain. They wanted to be somebody but feel like a nobody.

On the only stage that really matters in life, the stage where we stand before God Almighty, we hear, "You are the ones chosen by God." We are chosen for a calling and we are chosen to be His representatives. Let that sink in for a moment. Don't take it lightly or for granted. Our Lord does not treat us as the judges of a talent show would. We are always "enough" for Him. Come as you are.

You are chosen by the Creator of the universe—the One who knows you by name and never forgets you. He is the One who took us from "nothing to something, from rejected to accepted."

Dear friends, never doubt God's love for you. Never doubt how much He believes in you. He is confident that you can share with others what you received. What an honor and privilege. When you experience moments in life where you feel rejected and like nobody, never forget that you have been chosen.

Thank you for believing in me when I didn't believe in myself. Thank you for choosing me
when it seemed everyone else rejected me. I love you, my heavenly Father.

NOT OUR HOME

*Friends, this world is not your home, so don't make yourselves cozy in it.
Don't indulge your ego at the expense of your soul. Live an exemplary life among
the natives so that your actions will refute their prejudices. Then they'll be won
over to God's side and be there to join in the celebration when he arrives.*

1 PETER 2:11–12, THE MESSAGE

I like my home on Planet Earth. There is nothing bad about that, but it's still good for me to read God's Word on this very topic again. Throughout this wonderful letter to a scattered people—many of them not living where they had laid down roots due to persecution—Peter reminds them and us that we live both in the present and the future. As Christians, we have received the gift of salvation that is for today but which places in us the promise of heaven and eternal life.

That's why we aren't to get too comfortable here. This is not our final home. We are just passing through. We are to realize that our highest aspirations of life are fully realized in heaven. Our every action must be performed in view of eternity. We are not to become lazy and indulgent, but to live for the betterment and protection of our very souls. The good news is that when we build our lives around the future God has promised to us, the glorious hope we have in Christ Jesus, our present reality is all the sweeter. Life is not stifled but set free. We truly do taste the joy of heaven when we live for God today.

It's a good thing to enjoy and explore the life and present reality God has given us. But it's even better when we experience this life in view of eternity.

*Heavenly Father, thank you for all that is mine now and all
that is mine in eternity with you.*

GOOD CITIZENS

Make the Master proud of you by being good citizens. Respect the authorities,
whatever their level; they are God's emissaries for keeping order.

1 PETER 2:13, THE MESSAGE

When Jesus was asked whom we are to serve, He gave a brilliant but simple answer: "Give Caesar what is his, and give God what is his" (Matthew 22:21). There might be moments when civil disobedience is required for the Christian, but the principle that Peter sets forth is based on respect. And he extends that principle of showing proper respect beyond government: "Exercise your freedom by serving God, not by breaking the rules. Treat everyone you meet with dignity. Love your spiritual family. Revere God. Respect the government" (vv. 15–17).

Why does Peter get so specific in what he says about citizenship? And why would he tell Christians who had experienced intense government persecution to be respectful? Apparently some were claiming their spiritual freedom as a reason for not obeying laws that were established for a safe and ordered society. There is a spiritual freedom in Christ, but it does not exclude us from being good citizens. It also appears Peter was quite concerned that Christians maintain a positive testimony so that others might be saved.

We show respect to God in our praise and thanksgiving. But we also bring honor to His name by the respect we show to the rightful authorities in our world. He asks us not to judge, but to pray. We can all do that.

Father, I am grateful for living in a safe and ordered society. I honor you by honoring all
I come in contact with, including those within my government. And we pray for all those
living within conflict. Your kingdom come. . . .

THE NECESSITY OF PRAYER

A Classic Devotion by E. M. Bounds

Then shalt thou call, and the Lord shall answer; thou shalt cry,
and he shall say, Here I am. If thou take away from the midst of thee
the yoke, the putting forth of the finger, and speaking vanity.

ISAIAH 58:9, KJV

*I*t must never be forgotten that Almighty God rules this world. He is not an absentee God. His hand is ever on the throttle of human affairs. He is everywhere present in the concerns of time. His eyes behold, his eyelids try the children of men. He rules the world just as He rules the church by prayer.

This lesson needs to be emphasized, iterated and reiterated in the ears of men of modern times and brought to bear with cumulative force on the consciences of this generation whose eyes have no vision for the eternal things. . . .

Nothing is more important to God than prayer in dealing with mankind. But it is likewise all-important to man to pray. Failure to pray is failure along the whole line of life. It is failure of duty, service, and spiritual progress. God must help man by prayer. He who does not pray, therefore, robs himself of God's help and places God where He cannot help man. Man must pray to God if love for God is to exist. Faith and hope aid patience, and all the strong, beautiful, vital forces of piety are withered and dead in a prayerless life. The life of the individual believer, his personal salvation, and personal Christian graces have their being, bloom and fruitage in prayer.

All this and much more can be said as to the necessity of prayer to the being, and culture of piety in the individual.

Dear Lord, as I come to you in prayer, I ask for my heart to always be yearning
for you in prayer. Help me to always remember how important it is to you that I pray.

HOLY ONE

JESUS IS THE HOLY ONE OF GOD.
HE ALONE IS HOLY.

APRIL

Only Thou art holy,
there is _none_ beside thee,
Perfect in power, in ♡love♡ and purity.

HOLY, HOLY, HOLY! Lord God Almighty!
All thy works shall praise thy name,
in earth and sky and sea;
HOLY, HOLY, HOLY! Merciful and mighty,
God in three Persons, blessed Trinity!

HOLY ONE, be lifted high!

THE PLOT

*Then the chief priests, the scribes, and the elders of the people assembled
at the palace of the high priest, who was called Caiaphas, and plotted to
take Jesus by trickery and kill Him. But they said, "Not during the feast,
lest there be an uproar among the people."*

MATTHEW 26:3–5, NKJV

They met in back rooms and schemed. They would take Jesus by trickery. Take Jesus by trickery? Really?

Caiaphas and the religious leaders who plotted against Jesus were incredibly mistaken in their arrogance. Nothing caught or ever has caught Jesus by surprise. He was all human and all God—He already knew that His mission would hit the limits of human pain and suffering and would be preceded by rejection and betrayal. He knew exactly what awaited Him—what His Father sent Him to accomplish—and He gave himself to the task willingly with full obedience: "[Jesus] said to His disciples, 'You know that after two days is the Passover, and the Son of Man will be delivered up to be crucified'" (vv. 1–2).

No, Jesus wasn't tricked. But someone was: Caiaphas and his fellow conspirators. They were tricked through their own arrogance and the evil in their hearts. These religious leaders should have recognized Jesus first but became the blind leading the blind through hardheartedness.

We can still fall into the trap of self-deceit today. It always begins through pride and arrogance, somehow thinking that our ways are superior to God's ways. In this season when the church celebrates Jesus' mighty work of redemption, let's not miss the joy of complete obedience to God's will and plans for our life.

Thank you, God, for giving us Jesus to deliver us from our sins.

BURIAL PREPARATION

Now when Jesus was in Bethany, at the home of Simon the leper, a woman came to Him with an alabaster vial of very costly perfume, and she poured it on His head as He reclined at the table.

MATTHEW 26:6–7, NASB

What a beautiful expression of love and devotion—this woman gave her most valuable possession to Jesus out of the fullness of her heart.

Not everyone was impressed with her extravagance: "But the disciples were indignant when they saw this, and said, 'Why this waste? For this perfume might have been sold for a high price and the money given to the poor'" (vv. 8–9). When we express the deepness of our heart in doing good for the Savior—with no thought or worry of cost—some might think we are crazy. But that's okay. They just don't understand—yet. Jesus has the final word in the matter, and He tells the disciples to leave her alone because she has done something good to Him.

This woman's act of worship revealed her absolute love for Jesus. But Jesus said it went beyond a good deed in the moment: "For when she poured this perfume on My body, she did it to prepare Me for burial. Truly I say to you, wherever this gospel is preached in the whole world, what this woman has done will also be spoken of in memory of her" (vv. 12–13).

How amazing. Even if we aren't aware of it, when we pour out our heart to Jesus in extravagant love, our deed echoes through eternity. Today is a day for extravagant love. No one else's opinion matters. Let your love spill over into life.

Your gift of Jesus was such an extravagant love, God.
May our love be an expression of the love you have put in our heart.

THE BETRAYAL

Then one of the twelve, called Judas Iscariot, went to the chief priests and said,
"What are you willing to give me if I deliver Him to you?" And they counted out to him
thirty pieces of silver. So from that time he sought opportunity to betray Him.

MATTHEW 26:14–16, NKJV

An enemy can seek to harm us, but an enemy can't betray us. Betrayal can only come at the hands of someone we love and trust. That's why betrayal is so utterly painful. What is done to the heart is devastating.

Perhaps you still bear the scars of a betrayal from someone close and dear to you: a sibling, a spouse, a child, a parent, a dear friend, or even a close business associate who robbed you of the trust you held for them. Jesus understands the hurt you feel. He experienced denial and betrayal at the deepest level.

So much has been written about Judas Iscariot. Some have pointed out that he must have held a special place of trust among the disciples as the keeper of the purse. Others speculate that his motivation for conspiring against Jesus was to force Him to show His greatness. Judas' betrayal certainly revealed Jesus' greatness, but whatever his reasons, they pierced Jesus to the core. His follower, His constant friend of three years, was rejecting everything he had learned and experienced.

We know how the story of Judas ends and are saddened at such a waste of human life. Think of Jesus' pain, knowing that Judas would fulfill prophecy through his suicide. If only Judas had comprehended in his heart how good, how merciful, how ready to forgive our Savior is—even toward those who have betrayed Him.

Heavenly Father, you loved me even though I was lost in my sin.
You did not count my betrayal against me, but welcomed me into your family
through the blood of my Savior.

IN REMEMBRANCE

*And as they were eating, Jesus took bread, blessed and broke it, and gave
it to the disciples and said, "Take, eat; this is My body." Then He took the cup,
and gave thanks, and gave it to them, saying, "Drink from it, all of you. For this is
My blood of the new covenant, which is shed for many for the remission of sins."*

MATTHEW 26:26–28, NKJV

We are forgetful. We need help to remember what is important. That's why countries erect monuments and statues to commemorate key figures and events in their history. Most weddings include a fabulous picture album that can be enjoyed through the years as a reminder of vows made on a blessed day. At the everyday level of life we keep a calendar or write notes on Post-its and leave them in spots we are sure to see so we can remember tasks and appointments.

Throughout the Old and New Testaments, almost five hundred times, God's Word instructs us to "remember"—and most often the call is to "forget not" the mighty acts of God in creation and salvation. Over and over Moses said to the children of Israel: "Remember that you were slaves in Egypt and the Lord your God redeemed you. That is why I give you this command today" (Deuteronomy 15:15, NIV). The psalmist declared, "I will remember the deeds of the Lord; yes, I will remember your miracles of long ago" (Psalm 77:11, NIV).

In a simple meal with His disciples, Jesus offers the wine and bread as symbols of His body and blood so that they—so that we—will never forget His magnificent sacrifice that broke the power of sin in our lives. In the Lord's Supper, in worship, in thanksgiving, let's remember God's goodness to us.

*Your mighty deeds are too numerous to count.
We remember you in our praise and worship today, O God.*

THE DENIAL

*Peter answered and said to Him, "Even if all are made to
stumble because of You, I will never be made to stumble."*

MATTHEW 26:33, NKJV

*P*eter was quite adamant that he would never betray his Master. Even after Jesus quoted from the prophets—"Strike the Shepherd, and the sheep will be scattered" (Zechariah 13:7)—to let him know he would, Peter persisted: "Even if I have to die with you, I will not deny you!" (Matthew 26:35). After speaking these words with such passion, Peter did deny his Lord. And as Jesus hung on the cross, Peter was not beside Him to make good on his promise to die with Him.

When Judas betrayed his Lord, he cut himself off from friends and killed himself. Peter—ashamed, embarrassed, and shaken to his core—returned. The coward became bold for his Lord. He defied those who threatened to take his life if he continued to preach the gospel. And at the end of his life, he fulfilled his vow that he would die before denying his Lord. Legend tells us that he didn't feel worthy to hang on a cross like Jesus, and asked to be hung upside down instead.

Peter is our model of triumphantly overcoming failure. He experienced the completed work of salvation delivered by Jesus and lived with a power that was not previously evident in his life. Our words are so important and powerful to shape our lives, but we can't stop there. Let's live in the power that Jesus offers us through faith.

*I walk in your grace and power today, my God.
May I never deny you—not because of my own strength,
but because of the strength you alone provide me.*

YOUR WILL BE DONE

Again, a second time, He went away and prayed, saying, "O My Father,
if this cup cannot pass away from Me unless I drink it, Your will be done."

MATTHEW 26:42, NKJV

*I*n speaking of eternity and judgment, C. S. Lewis said, "There are only two kinds of people in the end: those who say to God, 'Thy will be done,' and those to whom God says, in the end, 'Thy will be done.'"

The consequences of demanding our will over God's will are eternal. In His love and kindness toward us, God does not force His will on us. He offers unconditional love, but it is our choice to accept or reject it. He does allow us to demand that our will be done, but eternity without Him is the result.

Jesus knew His mission, and He knew the torturous suffering that accompanied obedience to God. In his humanness, He asked if the cup that contained all the sins, all the evil, all the pain of humankind could be avoided. He didn't even wait to hear His Father's response. He simply and powerfully restated, "Your will be done." That's how great His love of the Father was. In that simple phrase He shows us what it means to completely trust in the goodness of God. We can entrust our life into His hands. Jesus also teaches us the most important prayer any of us can utter: Your will, O God.

Do you completely trust in the goodness of God today? Are you willing to believe His will for your life is perfect for you, even if the cost seems high? I want that so much for you. I want that so much for my life.

Not my will, but your will be done, O God.

WAKE UP

And He came and found them asleep again, for their eyes were heavy. So He left them, went away again, and prayed the third time, saying the same words. Then He came to His disciples and said to them, "Are you still sleeping and resting?"

MATTHEW 26:44–46, NKJV

*W*e've all slept in before. I think all of us can relate to the feeling when we're so tired we can barely keep our eyes open and all the energy we seem to have is just enough to fall in bed and sleep. I'm sure the disciples were exhausted from the Holy Week activities on the Jewish calendar and more so from the stress of being under the constant demands of friends and foes alike.

But Jesus, their Teacher, needed them at His side. He specifically asked Peter and the two sons of Zebedee—James and John—to stay close: "My soul is exceedingly sorrowful, even to death. Stay here and watch with Me" (v. 38). It was the brothers who initiated the conversation on who was greatest among the disciples when their mother asked Jesus if the two could have seats of honor on His right and left hands when His kingdom was revealed. They didn't yet understand the nature of His kingdom, and by falling asleep they showed once again they weren't ready to wear the mantle of service. They couldn't stay awake in their Friend's darkest hour.

We live in a world that is lost and in a moment of intense darkness. Have we fallen asleep when our Lord and Savior has asked us to stay awake with Him? Are we sleeping in spiritually and letting momentous events and opportunities pass us by? My dear friends, let's wake up and draw close to Jesus. The world needs us.

Father, forgive us when we have sought comfort and rest in moments you have called us to battle.

THE ARREST

But Jesus said to him, "Put your sword in its place, for all who take
the sword will perish by the sword. Or do you think that I cannot now pray
to My Father, and He will provide Me with more than twelve legions of angels?
How then could the Scriptures be fulfilled, that it must happen thus?"

MATTHEW 26:52–54, NKJV

Caiaphas did not trick Jesus. Jesus was not taken by the brute strength of soldiers. Jesus willingly gave himself up for arrest in order to obey His heavenly Father. He wasn't hiding. He didn't resist. He was certainly no weakling. He was powerful enough to walk boldly into the torture that awaited Him. He had an army of angels that could have slaughtered the best that Rome had to throw at Him. The guards fell in fear at the sight of one angel on the day of Jesus' resurrection. They might have died of fright at what Jesus could have called to His defense. Jesus, with calm resolution, told Peter to put his knife back in its sheath and gave himself to the authorities.

In His arrest, we again see a powerful picture of the Jesus we know and love, sacrificing himself on our behalf. *The Message* translates the wonderful passage in Philippians 2 like this: "When the time came, he set aside the privileges of deity and took on the status of a slave, became human! Having become human, he stayed human. It was an incredibly humbling process. He didn't claim special privileges. Instead, he lived a selfless, obedient life and then died a selfless, obedient death—and the worst kind of death at that—a crucifixion" (vv. 6–8).

Selfless and obedient. But always and ever a conqueror. This Jesus, our Savior, defeated death and sin. Now, that's true strength!

❧

Mighty God, mighty Savior—thank you for giving yourself
on our behalf to conquer sin and death.

THE FIRST TRIAL

Then the high priest tore his clothes, saying, "He has spoken blasphemy!
What further need do we have of witnesses? Look, now you have heard His blasphemy!

MATTHEW 26:65, NKJV

What a show Caiaphas put on for his co-conspirators when he tore his clothes. Isn't it ironic that this supposed defender of the faith broke the law in his fervor? In Leviticus 21:10, the high priest is specifically prohibited from uncovering his head or rending his clothes. But Caiaphas wasn't really concerned with truth. He had hatched a scheme to rid himself of this prophet who spoke with authority he did not have.

He called for witnesses. Finally, two men were willing to say that they had heard Jesus say, "I am able to destroy the temple of God and to build it in three days" (Matthew 26:61). But that wasn't enough to convict Jesus. Silent throughout most of this sham, it was Jesus who finished what Caiaphas couldn't accomplish when he acknowledged, "It is as you said," in response to the demand, "I put you under oath by the living God: Tell us if you are the Christ, the Son of God!" (vv. 63–64).

Once again we discover that everything happened according to God's will, not the scheme of men. Oh, Caiaphas played his part. Unable to rouse the crowd through his words, he did all he could to fan the flames of the worst in human emotion: fear, anger, and cruelty.

But in each step of the Passion, we don't see a Jesus who is led, but a Jesus who leads. He is the Lord of life. My friends, in our own lives, let's continue to discover the peace and power that comes through following the lead of Jesus in willing obedience.

You are worthy of all praise and thanksgiving, my Lord.
Thank you for showing us the joy of obedience, even obedience unto death.

THE ROOSTER CROWS

Then he began to curse and swear, saying, "I do not know the Man!"
Immediately a rooster crowed. And Peter remembered the word of Jesus who
had said to him, "Before the rooster crows, you will deny Me three times."
So he went out and wept bitterly.

MATTHEW 26:74–75, NKJV

*P*eter denied Jesus three times. The first time, Peter's response was evasive: "I do not know what you are saying" (v .70). In his second denial he gave an oath and said, "I do not know the Man!" (v. 72). In his third denial, Peter cursed and swore he didn't know Jesus.

Do you notice the progression? He goes from evasive to certain and then to angry, curse-filled declaration. Isn't that like sin in our lives? It begins with a small indiscretion and proceeds to defiant, angry rebellion.

We are so blessed to have a merciful and forgiving heavenly Father. No matter what we've done, no matter how many times we've done it, He hears our bitter cry of sorrow and call for forgiveness. That is God's nature. Never forget that, no matter where you find yourself spiritually.

But better still, let's open our hearts to the correction of the Holy Spirit immediately. Let's not let sin progress and take hold in our lives. An instant turning to God for help and strength is always the best path. It's not that God will ever give up on us, but there is always the danger that we will give up on ourselves. You are too valuable for that. Listen, yield, follow.

Father, I will listen for your voice and turn from any denial of you,
any action or attitude that separates me from fellowship with you.

THE SUICIDE

Then [Judas] threw down the pieces of silver in the temple
and departed, and went and hanged himself.

MATTHEW 27:5, NKJV

*S*uch a tragedy. Such a sad story. I am reminded of Saul from the Old Testament. Anointed as king of Israel, he allowed his mind and life to be twisted by fear and jealousy to his eternal ruin. Judas too was singled out by God. He was chosen to walk in the footsteps of Jesus for three years as one of the Twelve. He heard the teachings and witnessed the miracles. He shared meals and laughter and tears with a band of brothers under the unwavering guidance of Jesus Christ.

"Then Judas, His betrayer, seeing that He had been condemned, was remorseful and brought back the thirty pieces of silver to the chief priests and elders, saying, 'I have sinned by betraying innocent blood.' And they said, 'What is that to us? You see to it!'" (vv. 3–4).

How could such a close follower of Christ come to such a place? Did it start with a small sin? Did he never settle the issue that Jesus must be our Savior and Lord? Did he let fear and doubts choke out his faith? Over time, most of us will see someone who was once close to God pull away and break fellowship. It is heart-breaking, to say the least.

We can't lose heart, even if we fail. For anyone who feels they are losing the battle for their soul, return to the words of John: "But if we confess our sins, he will forgive our sins, because we can trust God to do what is right. He will cleanse us from all the wrongs we have done" (1 John 1:9, NCV).

Forgive me for any sin in my life, O Lord. Cleanse me from all unrighteousness.

PILATE

When Pilate saw that he could not prevail at all, but rather that a tumult
was rising, he took water and washed his hands before the multitude, saying,
"I am innocent of the blood of this just Person. You see to it."

MATTHEW 27:24, NKJV

Shouldn't this story be a little different? Shouldn't God's chosen people be wise and compassionate? Shouldn't a Roman governor be cruel and merciless? Pilate did not have clean hands in this public hearing, no matter how many times he washed his hands in front of them to take that claim. He knew Jesus was innocent and should be released. Yet he was afraid of the mob and tried to bargain with them. When that didn't work as he planned—and despite prophetic warnings from his wife—he passed the judgment of death but blamed the people. It does not matter that he said this blood would be on the people's heads; he is the one who spoke the words.

How could the people have chosen Barabbas—a criminal and murderer—over Jesus? One was a destroyer. The other brought hope and healing everywhere He went. We can make excuses that the religious leaders preyed on their emotions and took advantage of them. But like Pilate, they too spoke the words and accepted the responsibility for Jesus' death with their own tongues.

As we approach Golgotha, the place where Jesus was crucified, we are given a vivid reminder of our personal responsibility when presented with how we will respond to God's claim on our lives. There is no one else who can do it for us. We can blame no one else if we don't accept the love of Jesus Christ with faith. I encourage you today: Choose Jesus. It is never too late.

Heavenly Father, I choose your Son—Jesus—your gift to us and the giver of life.

THE MOCKING

When they had twisted a crown of thorns, they put it on His head,
and a reed in His right hand. And they bowed the knee before Him and
mocked Him, saying, "Hail, King of the Jews!"

MATTHEW 27:29, NKJV

What makes people cruel to one another? As people who know God's Word, we know the answer. The sin of Adam introduced Original Sin into the world. We are born with a sin nature that naturally rebels against God. We live in a fallen world where all manner of evil is possible. Yet cruelty still takes us by surprise, though it is well chronicled throughout history and into our day. I've traveled to countries torn by war and strife that permeates every corner of life. Life under such conditions is heartrending.

These Roman soldiers went far beyond following orders. Perhaps some can understand their gambling over the possessions of a condemned prisoner—their thinking would be that He wouldn't be needing them anymore—but to mock and brutalize Him as they did is simply repulsive.

As we walk with Jesus on His path to the cross, we are reminded that the depths of depravity, the capacity for evil, the cruelty of the unsaved human heart are evidence of what a glorious Savior we need. To some, much of sin seems rather harmless and a matter of preference rather than the same seed as Original Sin.

God is so good. He blesses us in so many ways. But let's not be naïve to the fact that this is a fallen world we live in, capable of unimaginable depravity and cruelty. Never take sin lightly. That Jesus was willing to die for all of us is of eternal consequence.

Forgive me my sins as I forgive those who sin against me.
Lead me not into temptation but deliver me from evil.

THE BLASPHEMY

And those who passed by blasphemed Him, wagging their heads and saying,
"You who destroy the temple and build it in three days, save Yourself!
If You are the Son of God, come down from the cross."

MATTHEW 27:39–40, NKJV

God has granted us the freedom to receive or reject Him. But not without consequences, good and bad. Paul reminds us that "the wages of sin is death, but the gift of God is eternal life in Christ Jesus our Lord" (Romans 6:23).

He also reminds us: "God also has highly exalted Him and given Him the name which is above every name, that at the name of Jesus every knee should bow, of those in heaven, and of those on earth, and of those under the earth, and that every tongue should confess that Jesus Christ is Lord, to the glory of God the Father" (Philippians 2:9-11).

Blasphemy—speaking ill of God—will not be allowed to continue forever. One very important reminder for all of us in our casual and very profane day is that the fourth of the Ten Commandments is "You shall not take the name of the Lord your God in vain, for the Lord will not hold him guiltless who takes His name in vain" (Deuteronomy 5:11). Does speaking God's name carelessly rise to the level of blasphemy? Let it be enough to know that we must treasure the name of the One who saved us. How can we worship the same name we use as an expression of anger?

The mob blasphemed Jesus. Blasphemy abounds everywhere you look or listen today. Let us never disrespect the One who died that we might live.

Your name is above all others, my God and Deliverer.
I honor you and your name with all my words, my praise, and my life.

FORSAKEN

*Now from the sixth hour until the ninth hour there was darkness
over all the land. And about the ninth hour Jesus cried out
with a loud voice, saying, "Eli, Eli, lama sabachthani?" that is,
"My God, My God, why have You forsaken Me?"*

MATTHEW 27:45–46, NKJV

*H*e hung on the cross alone. Jesus carried all the sins of the world, of every person past, present, and future. But He bore them alone. For He alone could bear them. Not you, not I, not the kindest person who ever lived. Only Jesus. In His pain—physical, spiritual, and psychological—He called out to His Father. Isn't it amazing that in His moment of absolute abandonment, Jesus still clung to the Father?

The nobility of Jesus could not be ignored. The crowd that showed up for a spectacle grew ever quieter. The sky darkened. I don't know this as fact, but I truly doubt there was any singing in heaven that day.

The prophet Isaiah foretold this moment when he declared, "But He was wounded for our transgressions, He was bruised for our iniquities; the chastisement for our peace was upon Him, and by His stripes we are healed" (Isaiah 53:5).

My friends, because Jesus endured the cross, He has given us the power to endure whatever we must face in life. Even when the sky grows dark and we feel abandoned by all we love, God is there with comfort and healing. Never alone; never forsaken; always loved. That is the promise of the cross. Don't ever lose heart. Look to the cross and victorious King, who conquered sin and death on it. He has overcome the world.

*Thank you that you are with me to the very ends
of the earth, my Savior and Friend.*

HE IS RISEN

Now after the Sabbath, as the first day of the week began to dawn,
Mary Magdalene and the other Mary came to see the tomb.
And behold, there was a great earthquake; for an angel of the Lord descended
from heaven, and came and rolled back the stone from the door and sat on it.
His countenance was like lightning, and his clothing as white as snow.
And the guards shook for fear of him, and became like dead men.

MATTHEW 28:1–4, NKJV

Hallelujah! This is the defining moment that changes everything. Christ's work is completely fulfilled. Sin and death are defeated. The Father has raised His Son from the dead—and we get to experience that miracle with Him. We too will be raised from the dead. The grave is not our final resting place. There is a celebration that awaits us in heaven. Any injury and disappointment experienced in the here and now no longer has the power to diminish our lives. We have the power to be victors in life, no matter what the circumstance or battle before us.

In John's divine revelation of heaven he writes: "Then I heard what sounded like a great multitude, like the roar of rushing waters and like loud peals of thunder, shouting: 'Hallelujah! For our Lord God Almighty reigns'" (Revelation 19:6, NIV). How can we read about the resurrection and not say hallelujah? David exhorts us: "Exalt the Lord our God and worship at his footstool; he is holy" (Psalm 99:5, NIV).

As we've walked in Jesus' footsteps through His death and resurrection, this is the moment to stop and savor the simple phrase, "He has risen, just as He said" (Matthew 28:6, NIV). Now is the time to say "Hallelujah!" and express our praise to God.

You are risen, O Lord, just as you declared. Hallelujah!

WORSHIP AT HIS FEET

And as they went to tell His disciples, behold, Jesus met them, saying, "Rejoice!" So they came and held Him by the feet and worshiped Him. Then Jesus said to them, "Do not be afraid." Go and tell My brethren to go to Galilee, and there they will see Me."

MATTHEW 28:9–10, NKJV

Mary and Mary Magdalene went to the tomb to pay their respects to their fallen Teacher and Friend. Instead they were met by an angel—"His appearance was like lightning, and his clothing was white as snow" (v. 3)—and then they saw Jesus himself: "Suddenly Jesus met them. 'Greetings,' he said. They came to him, clasped his feet and worshiped him. Then Jesus said to them, 'Do not be afraid. Go and tell my brothers to go to Galilee; there they will see me'" (NIV).

What a glorious moment. Think of what they had been through and witnessed with their own eyes: Jesus dying on the cross and now alive. What else could they do but fall at His feet and worship? Both the angel and Jesus sent the women to let others know what they had seen with their own eyes. He sends us to do the same thing—tell people what we have seen and experienced when we meet the risen Christ.

One thing I don't want us to miss: Why did Jesus appear first to two women? The answer is so simple. They were the ones who showed up first. Do you go to find Jesus? Do you seek Him out in worship? James 4:8 says, "Draw near to God and He will draw near to you." Friends, we can worship our Lord in any place at any time, with others or alone. And I still believe in the great power of gathering together as His body, on purpose, our hearts desperate for His presence. Our resolve is strengthened as we do not forsake the gathering together as the great day approaches. Don't miss seeing Him in a special way because you didn't show up!

Thank you, Lord, for revealing yourself to me. Thank you for meeting me when I turned my face and heart toward you. I love and worship you. Thank you for your church.

THE BRIBE

Now while they were going, behold, some of the guard came into the city
and reported to the chief priests all the things that had happened.
When they had assembled with the elders and consulted together,
they gave a large sum of money to the soldiers, saying, "Tell them,
'His disciples came at night and stole Him away while we slept.'"

MATTHEW 28:11–13, NKJV

At least you can say this for Caiaphas: He was persistent. He schemed to trick Jesus. The problem is he was only tricking himself into believing he could thwart God's will. He was not the first nor will he be the last to think he can stand against God. It is just not possible. God's Word will be taken to the ends of the earth. On the day of judgment every knee will bow to the Lord God Almighty.

This man was anointed to be God's representative to the people and to petition God for mercy on their behalf. He had so lost his way through arrogance that he was in direct opposition to his call. He forgot the counsel of Solomon, who wrote, "Pride goes before destruction, a haughty spirit before a fall" (Proverbs 16:18, NIV). Friends, there is a wonderful and liberating confidence that God gives us. But the warning that pride precedes spiritual ruin still holds. Celebrate and enjoy your successes, but give God all the thanks and glory.

Christ has risen, just as He said. Hold firm to that truth. It will be revealed in eternity. Some will speak against God—every generation has its blasphemers and wolves in sheep's clothing. Don't let anyone deceive you. The resurrection is our hope of glory!

I put my hope and trust in you alone, my Lord and Savior.

THE COMMISSION

*"Go therefore and make disciples of all the nations, baptizing them
in the name of the Father and of the Son and of the Holy Spirit,
teaching them to observe all things that I have commanded you;
and lo, I am with you always, even to the end of the age." Amen.*

MATTHEW 28:19–20, NKJV

Whatever God gives us is to be shared. When blessed financially, we share with those in need. When we are given a special insight from God's Word, we share with a group or friend. When God lifts our spirits, we encourage the discouraged. When we have a roof over our heads and food on the table, we offer hospitality. Most importantly, when we receive the gift of salvation, when we are made His disciples, we make it our purpose in life to help others become disciples.

Every one of us needs a teacher. But every one of us also needs to be a teacher. It doesn't mean we will stand before a large audience or have a classroom we are responsible for. It may be a son and daughter we read Bible stories to in our home. It may be a friend we meet with over coffee to read a passage of Scripture and pray together. Being a disciple maker is as simple as helping someone else experience the risen Jesus and draw closer to Him—just as happened in our own lives.

Who helps you become a disciple of Jesus Christ? Who do you help become a disciple? Let's go into all the nations and into our own neighborhoods to share Christ and strengthen others as we go about our lives.

*Father, your gift of salvation is so precious to me.
Your teachings and your will are the path of peace and joy.
Help me to share that with my world.*

HOLY, HOLY, HOLY!

Day and night they never stop saying: "'Holy, holy, holy is the Lord God Almighty,' who was, and is, and is to come."

REVELATION 4:8, NIV

*L*et's join our voices with heaven and never stop praising our Lord!

Holy, holy, holy! Lord God Almighty!
Early in the morning our song shall rise to thee;
Holy, holy, holy! Merciful and mighty,
God in three Persons, blessed Trinity!

Holy, holy, holy! All the saints adore thee,
Casting down their golden crowns around the glassy sea;
Cherubim and seraphim falling down before thee,
Which wert, and art, and evermore shalt be.

Holy, holy, holy! Though the darkness hide thee,
Though the eye of sinful man thy glory may not see,
Only Thou art holy; there is none beside thee,
Perfect in power, in love, and purity.

Holy, holy, holy! Lord God Almighty!
All thy works shall praise thy name, in earth and sky and sea;
Holy, holy, holy! Merciful and mighty,
God in three Persons, blessed Trinity!

*God, you are perfect in power, love, and purity and worthy of all my praise.
I sing my praise to you today.*

THE GOD WHO LISTENS

Arise, Lord! Lift up your hand, O God. Do not forget the helpless.

PSALM 10:12, NIV

I love the way the psalmist has such a great relationship with his God that he cries in anguish on behalf of a hurting humanity, fully expecting to awaken the answer of heaven. Things are tough for those he loves, but he hasn't given up and he hasn't lost his faith. He knows that God will hear him. "Lift up your hand, O God. Do not forsake these children who are being persecuted and crushed." We can't help but feel brokenhearted for the trials so many have to endure. But we can rest assured God will save His beloved—and He will call the wicked to account.

I think there is a very subtle and important lesson in the prayer of the psalmist. It is easy to put much focus on pointing out and discussing wicked deeds, when actually we can use that same energy for doing something about it. It is God's job to judge; it is our job to share His love. We don't know what He knows and can't see what He sees. So we must keep our focus on loving others, offering what assistance is possible, praying for them with the passion of the psalmist, and lifting the name of Jesus to both the persecuted and the persecutor.

Even to the persecutor? Absolutely. The love of our Father is so grand and amazing that no one is beyond His saving grace. If the man who was the persecutor of the church could become its first missionary, then no one is beyond the reach of God's love.

Father, save the persecuted and helpless. Call the wicked to account.
Help me to bring your light and love to the world.

THE HARDHEARTED

Why does the wicked man revile God? Why does he say to himself,
"He won't call me to account"?

PSALM 10:13, NIV

ardheartedness is one of the most costly tragedies in life. The man described here is a real example of the ultimate pride. "God won't call me into account. He can't do anything about my sins. I don't answer to God."

Godless pride brings such a loss of perspective. "I can sin without any repercussions." This is a lie from the pit of hell itself. God declares that He hates sin. The Word says, "For the wages of sin is death." Thankfully, mercy and compassion actually help describe who our Jesus is, and He will forgive any—even the most hardhearted—who turn to Him. Again, our focus must return to His love. His compassion upon the lowly and downtrodden is too wonderful to find words to express.

Many blame God for the inhumane treatment that millions suffer daily at the hand of the wicked. We must always remember, because of the gracious nature of our Lord, everyone has a will. When this gift is abused, when hearts are unyielded to the power of the Holy Spirit, the results are tragic.

Disappointments, a jaded outlook on life—right through to willful sin and pride—are all devastating to our spiritual life. Let's let the warning of the hardhearted remind us to stay open to anything and everything God has to say to us. We do this by staying in His Word, by welcoming His presence as we worship Him, by serving others, and by simply taking the time to listen as He speaks.

Father, keep my heart tender toward you and the needs all around me.
If there are areas where my heart is not open to your will and ways, speak to me
and give me the grace to allow your work in me right now.

FATHER TO THE FATHERLESS

But you, God, see the trouble of the afflicted; you consider
their grief and take it in hand. The victims commit themselves to you;
you are the helper of the fatherless.

PSALM 10:14, NIV

*D*on't miss what I'm about to write. It's too important for our day and age to skip over. If you grew up in a home with no father or with a father who was unkind or not really there for you, God is and always will be the defender of the fatherless. Thank God for the example of wonderful earthly fathers. If you have a great dad, make sure you take the time to appreciate him today. But many today can testify to not having a loving earthly father. The fatherless generation is looking for examples as they raise their own children. But praise be to God, He is the ultimate example of true fatherhood, full of grace, wisdom, guidance, and most of all, unconditional love. He hears and responds to the prayer of the afflicted. He pays special note to the fatherless. He is there to encourage, strengthen, rescue, and heal all the helpless. Be assured, no matter how grim circumstance may be for you or those you love, God adopts, defends, and gives dignity to all of humanity, even those who are betrayed and damaged. God is, after all, our loving heavenly Father.

Please remember, you are not alone and you are not unloved. You are completely valued by the One who created you and knew you even before you came to be. You have the most wonderful Father you could ever imagine.

You are my Father and my God. Thank you that I am your child.
Thank you that you heal and rescue me when I am hurt. Thank you for never
abandoning me—you are always there for me and all your children.

NO MORE FEAR

Break the arm of the wicked man; call the evildoer to account for his wickedness
that would not be found out. The Lord is King for ever and ever; the nations
will perish from his land. You, Lord, hear the desire of the afflicted;
you encourage them, and you listen to their cry, defending the fatherless and
the oppressed, so that mere earthly mortals will never again strike terror.

PSALM 10:15–18, NIV

We no longer need to live in terror. Think of that. No more fear.

But what about those who are oppressed? What if there is another war? What if something bad happens to my child or another loved one? I wish I could declare that no bad things will ever happen again in this world. But this psalm tells us there are still wicked in the world. They will not get away with their sins and will be called into account, but yes, they will still do evil things.

The reason we need not live in fear is that we must trust God. With God beside us every moment of the day, we are safe—even when bad things happen, even when God's timing is not our timing. He is our refuge. Remember that as life unfolds before you and circumstances change, you are God's child.

"But I still feel afraid." In Psalm 125 we are told God is an immovable mountain. Even if the earth seems to shift under our feet, He is solid; He is steadfast and never changing. He is always by our side, whatever our day holds.

I taught my girls from when they were young, "God has not given us a spirit of fear, but of power and of love and of a sound mind" (2 Timothy 1:7, NKJV).

Speak this over your life every day.

───❦───

Father, with you beside me, my life is secure now and throughout all eternity.
Thank you for revealing yourself to me as all powerful so that my faith is sure
even when there are tremors under my feet.

DON'T WORRY

Don't worry about anything; instead, pray about everything. Tell God what
you need, and thank him for all he has done. Then you will experience God's peace, which
exceeds anything we can understand. His peace will guard your
hearts and minds as you live in Christ Jesus.

PHILIPPIANS 4:5–7, NLT

What has you worried today? What is robbing you of peace and joy?
Jesus doesn't want us to live with worry. He asks, "Can any one of
you by worrying add a single hour to your life?" (Matthew 6:27, NIV).

Corrie ten Boom, the great Christian teacher and writer who suffered so much
during World War II because her family protected Jews from the Nazis, said, "Worry
does not empty tomorrow of its sorrows; it empties today of its strength." This is not
spoken from someone naïve and simpleminded but from one who was tested by fire.

George MacDonald, the nineteenth-century British preacher and author, said,
"It is not the cares of today, but the cares of tomorrow, that weigh a man down. For
the needs of today we have corresponding strength given. For the morrow we are told
to trust. It is not ours yet. It is when tomorrow's burden is added to the burden of
today that the weight is more than a man can bear."

Philippians is Paul's letter of joy. Is it any wonder he addresses the topic of worry?
He doesn't want his friends' joy stolen from within. His antidote? Pray about everything. My friends, I'll ask again, what is worrying you today? Let it go. Turn to God
in prayer.

I bring my worries before you, Lord, as an act of obedience. I pray that you
would help me to guard the joy and peace you have gifted to me through
constant communication with you.

ALWAYS CONTENT

*Not that I was ever in need, for I have learned how to be content
with whatever I have. I know how to live on almost nothing or with everything.
I have learned the secret of living in every situation, whether it is with
a full stomach or empty, with plenty or little.*

PHILIPPIANS 4:11–12, NLT

The early hymn reminds us to "Praise God from whom all blessings flow." It's true; God meets our every need. But that doesn't mean there won't be struggles and some tough days in this world. They come to all of us, and it is no sign of our gracious Lord's disfavor—never think that for even a second. You can walk in total faith and still face hardship. But you will never be poor. Eternal life is both something in the future and a spiritual richness in the present. Are you facing tough times? Never forget God is the God of deliverance.

Paul has such a profound message as he concludes this letter: Be content with whatever. Tough circumstances don't shake his faith and don't make him feel sorry for himself. Whatever—bring it on. He shows us the power of poise—a positive attitude and demeanor even when the bullets are flying all around us.

Poise can seem like a superficial posture, almost like one is acting as if everything is okay when things really aren't. I believe true poise goes much deeper and is a reflection of what we really believe inside of us. Paul's confidence in the goodness of God was so strong and sure that not even an empty belly threw him off his game. He was content whatever. I know my God is good, and I want to show that to the world, whatever.

*I declare my confidence in you, O God, at this moment. I walk in contentment,
no matter what is happening around me, because of your favor toward me. Thank you.*

I CAN DO ANYTHING

For I can do everything through Christ, who gives me strength.

PHILIPPIANS 4:13, NLT

o you believe that? Do you believe you can do all things through Christ Jesus? Now that's what I call a bold and confident faith! Paul's not bragging; he's stating something that is as sure as the sun rising in his heart and mind.

If there is a trial in your life, you are up to the task. How do I know it? Because you can do all things through Christ.

Is there a task that God has laid before you? Even if it seems bigger than your vision and abilities, you can get it done. Why? Because you can do all things through Christ Jesus.

If you have a question about what road you should take in life, you can make the right first step at the fork in the road. How can you know? Because you can do all things through Christ Jesus.

Let's not focus on the trials, the tasks, or the questions in life. Let's unite our hearts with Paul and focus on Jesus Christ. He is the source of our strength and confidence. Then we can declare with Paul, "I can do everything through Christ, who gives me strength."

Even if I feel a lack of confidence and boldness,
your strength turns me into a victor.
I turn to you with all my trials, tasks, and questions today, O Lord.

A REWARD FOR YOUR KINDNESS

As you know, you Philippians were the only ones who gave me financial help when I first brought you the Good News and then traveled on from Macedonia. No other church did this. Even when I was in Thessalonica you sent help more than once. I don't say this because I want a gift from you. Rather, I want you to receive a reward for your kindness.

PHILIPPIANS 4:15–16, NLT

*P*aul has told his friends in the city of Philippi he is content whether he is at a feast or going without food. Even with an empty stomach and purse, he can do anything through Christ Jesus. He even gives them assurance that the God who has met his needs will meet theirs.

So when Paul "hints" that another gift from them would be to his benefit, it is for their own good: "I want you to receive a reward for your kindness."

Paul is echoing the words of Jesus: "Give, and you will receive. Your gift will return to you in full—pressed down, shaken together to make room for more, running over, and poured into your lap. The amount you give will determine the amount you get back" (Luke 6:38). When meeting with the elders in Ephesus, Paul put it this way: "And I have been a constant example of how you can help those in need by working hard. You should remember the words of the Lord Jesus: 'It is more blessed to give than to receive'" (Acts 20:35).

My friends, for followers of Christ, it is impossible to give without receiving something back. It may not come back from the person or group we gave to. It may not come in the exact form we expected. But be assured, giving is rewarded! What gift do you have to give today?

Father God, make me a joyful giver, not because of what I get back, but because my gift is given to you. Thank you for the many ways you reward my kindness.

ALL YOUR NEEDS

And this same God who takes care of me will supply all your needs from
his glorious riches, which have been given to us in Christ Jesus.

PHILIPPIANS 4:19, NLT

Why could Paul be so joyful in the face of imprisonment, hunger, and even the opposition of his friends? He had experienced the glorious riches of knowing Jesus Christ, and he knew that nothing else in life could compare.

The first thing we can ask ourselves is whether we recognize just how rich we are for knowing Jesus Christ. This is a gift from God himself. It is not temporary, but eternal. It doesn't have to be guarded because it can't be stolen. It doesn't have to be hoarded, because its supply is endless. When my own father was wasting away due to cancer, he said to me, "I already have my miracle, for I know Jesus. I know His saving grace." My dad taught me that nothing, simply nothing, not in death or in life, can compare to the glorious riches of knowing Christ.

Jesus commands us: "Do not store up for yourselves treasures on earth, where moths and vermin destroy, and where thieves break in and steal. But store up for yourselves treasures in heaven, where moths and vermin do not destroy, and where thieves do not break in and steal" (Matthew 6:19–20, NIV).

The amazing thing is that our eternal reward is with us here and now. God, who prepares a glorious home in eternity for us, also meets our every need on earth. He loves us and is kind. Is it any wonder His will is done on earth as it is in heaven when it comes to His beloved children? That's you. That's me.

Let's take time today to reflect on the glorious riches we have been given in Christ Jesus our Lord.

Thank you, kind and gracious God, for all you have given me here in this world
and throughout eternity in heaven through your Son, Jesus Christ.

THE POWER OF PRAYER

A Classic Devotion by Andrew Murray

*Now thanks be unto God, which always causeth us to triumph in Christ,
and maketh manifest the savour of his knowledge by us in every place.*

2 CORINTHIANS 2:14, KJV

When a general chooses the place from which he intends to strike the enemy, he pays most attention to those points which he thinks most important in the fight. Thus there was on the battlefield of Waterloo a farmhouse which Wellington immediately saw was the key to the situation. He did not spare his troops in his endeavours to hold that point: the victory depended on it. So it actually happened. It is the same in the conflict between the believer and the powers of darkness. The inner chamber is the place where the decisive victory is obtained.

The enemy uses all his power to lead the Christian and above all the minister, to neglect prayer. He knows that however admirable the sermon may be, however attractive the service, however faithful the pastoral visitation, none of these things can damage him or his kingdom if prayer is neglected. When the church shuts herself up to the power of the inner chamber, and the soldiers of the Lord have received on their knees "power from on high," then the powers of darkness will be shaken and souls will be delivered. In the church, on the mission field, with the minister and his congregation, everything depends on the faithful exercise of the power of prayer.

In the conflict between Satan and the believer, God's child can conquer everything by prayer. Is it any wonder that Satan does his utmost to snatch that weapon from the Christian, or to hinder him in the use of it?

Heavenly Father, I lay hold of the victory you have granted to me through prayer.

THE GATE

JESUS IS THE GATE
BY WHICH WE ARE SAVED.

MAY

To God be the glory,
   GREAT things he hath done!
So loved he the world
   that he gave us his Son,
Who yielded his life
   an atonement for sin,
And opened the LIFE GATE
   that all may go in.

O come to the Father, through Jesus the Son,
And give him the glory, great things
HE has done.

      Praise Jesus, the Lord!

ABIDE IN ME

*Abide in Me, and I in you. As the branch cannot bear fruit of itself unless
it abides in the vine, so neither can you unless you abide in Me.*

JOHN 15:4, NASB

*J*esus was a masterful storyteller, holding crowds spellbound with powerful
and lovely word pictures from a variety of familiar scenes of everyday life.
Though most of us are not farmers, we still understand easily his lessons from the
world of agriculture. In John 15 He tells skillfully of a vineyard.

I've been told that grapes are a difficult fruit to grow. It takes the right soil, the
right weather—and the diligent hand of a master gardener. A wonderful vineyard
doesn't happen because some seeds are thrown on the side of a hill and then left alone.
What a beautiful reminder that we have a Master Gardener who cares for us deeply
and who is present in all moments of our growth, never casting us aside to fend for
ourselves.

There is one very profound difference between our spiritual life and the life of a
branch in the vineyard. God, in His infinite love, does not force us to associate ourselves with Him. He calls for us to freely choose Him through our will and our love.
But He reminds us that we will never bear the lush, delicious fruit He has intended
for our lives without our decision to be connected to Him, to abide in Him, to live in
Him.

Where do you abide? Where do you plant the roots of your heart and mind? Is
it in the magnificent life-giving Vine who is Jesus Christ? No matter how hard we
strive, without that divine connection, our lives will always be less than what God
intended for us.

⁓⊱⊰⁓

*I give you my love and my will, O Father. I put my life in your hands.
I abide in you through Jesus Christ my Lord.*

ASK WHATEVER YOU WANT

If you abide in Me, and My words abide in you,
ask whatever you wish, and it will be done for you.

JOHN 15:7, NASB

That can't be right, can it? Whatever we wish? We can come to our heavenly Father through Jesus Christ our Lord and ask whatever we want—and it will be done? Isn't that presumption? Isn't that just a little too bold?

Not according to our wonderful Savior!

I am sure that God has been asked for things of little value to the one asking and for the building of His kingdom. But we are still invited by God himself to ask what we desire. And the miracle is that when we are connected to Jesus Christ as part of God's beautiful vineyard, as we keep His commandments, as we abide in His love, our prayers and desires change. As we live in fellowship with our Savior, more and more, we want what He wants. Our prayers are less careful and timid but become bolder as we pray from the overflow of our heart: "Your kingdom come, Your will be done, on earth as it is in heaven" (Matthew 6:10).

That's the prayer life I want. That's the relationship with God I desire with all my heart. I want to know Him through Christ Jesus so well that my words of praise and my words of request are echoes of heaven. I want wherever I take my stand to literally be a place of heaven on earth.

It all begins when we abide in Him who came to give us life. Are you abiding in Jesus today?

Heavenly Father, more than anything else, I want your will to be done here,
in my life, on earth, as it is done in heaven.

HIS JOY IN ME

*These things I have spoken to you so that My joy may be in you,
and that your joy may be made full.*

JOHN 15:11, NASB

*W*hen we abide in Christ, when we obey His commands, when we want His will done in our world and in our lives, a joy unspeakable wells up from His Spirit within us, a joy that we could never experience through a life lived apart from Jesus. That famous song from another generation, "I Did It My Way," promises so much but delivers so little. No fullness of joy will be found apart from abiding in the Vine. The joy that Christ brings is not circumstance-dependent.

What a promise. What a hope. We can experience a joy that transcends any challenges or setbacks the world throws at us. Deeper than a superficial and temporary happiness to be chased, it is something that our kind and gracious heavenly Father gives to us through His Son.

In my own life there are still moments of discouragement and disappointment. But I live with a deep and abiding joy that nothing in this world can take away. It is joy unspeakable and full of glory, promised to us as a fruit of the Spirit.

If your life is lacking in joy today, don't chase after momentary pleasure. Don't even worry about joy. Just draw closer to Jesus. Abide in Him, obey Him, desire His will in your life more than anything. Just as you can't bear fruit apart from Him, so it is impossible to manufacture true joy. But never forget that He is faithful and will do exactly what He said. He will give you His joy.

*I am forever grateful, O God. I gave you my life and you gave me your joy.
Thank you for the fullness of joy that you give as a gift of love.*

GLORIFYING MY FATHER

My Father is glorified by this, that you bear much fruit,
and so prove to be My disciples.

JOHN 15:8, NASB

*O*ne of the great confessions of God's church began with this simple declaration: "Man's chief end is to glorify God, and to enjoy him forever" (the first statement of The Westminster Confession).

I confess today that I want to glorify God. I want to enjoy Him forever. And how does Jesus tell us we can do just that? It is by bearing much fruit. *The Message* translation of the Bible describes the fruit of the Spirit this way: "But what happens when we live God's way? He brings gifts into our lives, much the same way that fruit appears in an orchard—things like affection for others, exuberance about life, serenity. We develop a willingness to stick with things, a sense of compassion in the heart, and a conviction that a basic holiness permeates things and people" (Galatians 5:22).

I want to live that way. I know I don't have the strength in my own power to do it, but fruit is something He brings into our lives. No longer is a fruitful life a matter of trying harder but a matter of trusting more. Abiding in Christ is trusting Him with everything we have and are. It is walking in His ways because we believe with all our hearts His ways are best.

Are you tired of trying harder and failing? Are you ready to trust Him more, to abide in Him, to put every fiber of your being into His care? The results will blow your mind. You will bear much fruit and prove for all the world to see that you are His disciple. Stunning!

I give you all glory, God my Father—in my worship and in the fruit of my life.
I love and trust you with all my heart.

OBEY MY COMMANDS

Just as the Father has loved Me, I have also loved you; abide in My love.
If you keep My commandments, you will abide in My love; just as I have kept
My Father's commandments and abide in His love.

JOHN 15:9–10, NASB

*O*bedience is not the most popular of words in modern culture. For many people, obedience feels like a mean and unreasonable burden or request. Even many who know Jesus worry that an emphasis on obedience will turn our living faith into a religion of works, where people will think they can earn salvation and favor with God.

When I read the words of my Savior, "Keep my commands," I see no such conflicts. For obedience is the lifestyle based on our response to love: The Father loves Jesus; Jesus loves us; Jesus abides in His Father's love through His obedience; we abide in Jesus' love through obedience. There is no burden in that. There is no claim that we have earned our salvation. Our obedience is the love between us and God spilling over into our lives.

My own life is full of imperfections, and full of God's saving grace. Because of God's magnificent love for me, I want to obey God. I want to do His will. I want to glorify Him. I don't want to do anything that turns my face from Him or His from me. I want nothing between God and me.

My heart and life are committed to worshiping God. As long as I have breath I will shout of His goodness. I will declare that He is with us. I will praise His name. I will proclaim His faithfulness to all I can. I will write and sing songs of worship to the best of my ability. And I will love and worship Him through obeying His commands.

I love you, God. I love you with my life. I love you with my songs.
I love you with my words. I love you with my obedience.

MY REFUGE

Be merciful to me, O God, be merciful to me!
For my soul trusts in You; and in the shadow of Your wings I will
make my refuge, until these calamities have passed me by.

PSALM 57:1, NKJV

David is under attack—not from enemy nations but by one whom he loves and whom he has faithfully served. King Saul has descended into spiritual darkness and psychological madness. One of the biggest ways this is manifested is a jealous rage toward David. Perhaps the contrast of David's heart toward God and his own state of raging insecurity has painted an even bigger target on David's back. David's flight of escape is a roller-coaster ride of hiding in the depths of caves and the heights of mountain crags.

David's faith declares: "I will cry out to God Most High, to God who performs all things for me. He shall send from heaven and save me; He reproaches the one who would swallow me up. Selah. God shall send forth His mercy and His truth" (vv. 2–3).

My friends, if only we would follow David's heart and ways when we feel under siege by the world around us. He doesn't curse his life or his God. He cries out to Him. That alone indicates his faith has not wavered. Then David acknowledges that God "performs all things for me." He stands strong knowing that God's mercy and truth will be sent in response to his cry for help.

When life seems against you, don't look down, but rather look up and cry out to God Almighty!

Thank you, Father, for your mercy and truth that comfort
and deliver me no matter what is happening around me.

IN ALL THINGS, WORSHIP

My soul is among lions; I lie among the sons of men who are set on fire,
whose teeth are spears and arrows, and their tongue a sharp sword. Be exalted,
O God, above the heavens; let Your glory be above all the earth.

PSALM 57:4–5, NKJV

There are tough circumstances and really tough circumstances. David is obviously experiencing the latter. His word pictures are terrifying. On the run from Saul, he is walking in the midst of lions, fiery warriors with teeth like spears and arrows. That would be enough to make even the bravest man melt into a puddle of fear. Aren't there times when all of us have had enough? We just can't bear any more.

What does David do? Forsake his faith? Surrender to his enemies? Never! He does the unthinkable, the unimaginable. David leads a worship service. Surrounded by enemies, his life hanging in the balance, he cries out, "Be exalted, O God, above the heavens; let Your glory be above all the earth."

Nothing fills my heart and soul with joy like the experience of worship. Is it any wonder we can experience God so deeply and fully in the Psalms? Jesus, my Savior, the Victor, quotes from them throughout His earthly ministry. The Psalms capture and express the heart of Jesus so beautifully.

What is going on in your life today, in this season of your life? My friend, even if you're hiding in a cave on the mountaintop, worship God today. Praise Him; exalt Him; stand in awe of His glory.

Be exalted, O God, above the heavens; let your glory be above all the earth!

SHOUTS OF JOY

My heart is steadfast, O God, my heart is steadfast;
I will sing and give praise. Awake, my glory! Awake, lute and harp!
I will awaken the dawn. I will praise You, O Lord,
among the peoples; I will sing to You among the nations.

PSALM 57:7–9, NKJV

When we worship, we acknowledge that God is our Creator, the giver of all good things, worthy of all our honor and praise, the One who knows us best and loves us most, and we announce and declare that God is among us! We also realize that we are the created. We didn't make ourselves. Our life is not our own; it is to be lived for the One who gifted us with it. Worship acknowledges who God is—and through Him we know who we are.

That's why worship changes us from the inside out, and even if our circumstances don't change, we magnify God's great name above it all. In His presence we find joy and strength for every situation.

Chased like a rabbit with a mountain lion right behind it, surrounded by hardship, David continues his worship service. His cry of desperation becomes a triumphant shout of joy. My friends, what more is there? Lift your voice and then add some instruments—loud enough to wake up the dawn!—and praise your God with a song of praise. Nothing will renew a steadfast heart as worshiping the mighty God who created us!

I will sing praises to you all day, O God! My heart is steadfast when
all around me swirls. I praise you before all the peoples of the world!

ALWAYS WORKING

Paul, a prisoner of Christ Jesus, and Timothy our brother, to Philemon
our beloved brother and fellow worker, and to Apphia our sister, and to Archippus
our fellow soldier, and to the church in your house: Grace to you and peace
from God our Father and the Lord Jesus Christ.

PHILEMON 1–3, NASB

When Paul wrote to the Philippians from a Roman prison, we can't help but notice that no matter what his situation, he never stopped expressing his joy of knowing Christ. His life was filled with praise and worship in any and all circumstances. In this short one-chapter letter to a fellow believer, we see that Paul never stops working either. In this letter he makes an appeal on behalf of a runaway slave. Isn't it interesting that even though he is enslaved as a prisoner, Paul is thinking of others? He can't help himself.

I believe there's a lesson in watching Paul's tireless work on behalf of others. I think we get worried that if we give ourselves away we will run out of energy and personal resources. Rest is a necessary gift God gave to us to recharge our batteries. And Sabbath is God's idea in protection of our souls. Yes, rest is vital. But Paul's life shows us that when we give ourselves away to the right things at the right time, God keeps filling us up with more of His grace and strength.

As Isaiah put so beautifully and powerfully: "Yet those who wait for the Lord will gain new strength; they will mount up with wings like eagles, they will run and not get tired, they will walk and not become weary" (40:31).

Father God, I give myself in service to you, knowing that you supply all my needs.
Thank you for giving me the strength I need for each day to do your work.

YOUR LOVE AND FAITH

I thank my God always, making mention of you in my prayers,
because I hear of your love and of the faith which you have toward
the Lord Jesus and toward all the saints.

PHILEMON 1:4–5, NASB

Paul is ever caring, ever believing, and ever praying for and on behalf of his friends scattered about the world. He traveled by foot or by ship, so it was incredibly difficult to maintain relationships. Yet Paul, under the inspiration of the Holy Spirit—and with great effort and cost—wrote letters of encouragement and instruction to lift those in his circle of influence. This small letter is filled with both.

In a few short verses Paul is going to ask Philemon to go against the customs of the day and his rights as a citizen of the Roman Empire not only to forgive a runaway slave but to free him. This sounds so simple and straightforward in our day, but his request was revolutionary for those times.

I am inspired by Paul's approach to this brother in Christ. He didn't agree with him and his actions, but he saw the grace within Philemon. How many times have we sat back and focused on the negative and what we see wrong in others? Paul models a grace-filled approach to confronting the tough issues in life. It's not like he was a man without backbone who only sought to flatter others. We know he could be a ferocious lion when required. But in his letters we can see how he really saw and approached others—and it is a beautiful reminder of how we should approach difficult situations.

Thank you, God, that you did not look at me and see only my faults
and weaknesses. You saw in me potential to make a difference in your kingdom.
Help me to see and approach others the same way.

MY APPEAL

*Therefore, though I have enough confidence in Christ to order you
to do what is proper, yet for love's sake I rather appeal to you—since I am
such a person as Paul, the aged, and now also a prisoner of Christ Jesus.*

PHILEMON 1:8–9, NASB

Boldness is a good thing. But so is gentleness. King Solomon contrasts the righteous and the wicked and tells us, "A gentle answer turns away wrath, but a harsh word stirs up anger" (Proverbs 15:1).

I get the strong feeling that in his human nature—before meeting Christ on the road to Damascus—Paul would have been a bulldozer in conversation and argument. He was, after all, a trained scholar and lawyer. I can feel the hand of the Holy Spirit on his heart and mind as he writes this letter to Philemon. "I can order you to do the right thing"—but no, Paul curbs the words that might have stirred up resistance and brings what he wants to happen as a request. Perhaps he gave more honor in the circumstance than the circumstance deserved, but he is still modeling how God approaches us through Jesus Christ.

Let the words of Paul penetrate your heart. Yes, we have rights we can demand. But as recipients of grace, my rights lay by the wayside as my heart responds to this incomprehensible amazing grace.

*Father, let my words, even in tough situations,
show your grace and love through my life in this world.*

SETTING CAPTIVES FREE

*I appeal to you for my child Onesimus, whom I have begotten
in my imprisonment, who formerly was useless to you,
but now is useful both to you and to me.*

PHILEMON 1:10–11, NASB

When Jesus returned to His hometown and announced His purpose, He said: "The Spirit of the Lord is upon Me, because He anointed Me to preach the gospel to the poor. He has sent Me to proclaim release to the captives, and recovery of sight to the blind, to set free those who are oppressed" (Luke 4:18).

We need to be reminded that slavery is not a horror that is only found in history books. The horror of slavery still holds much power in this world, sometimes just out of our sight. We need to pray for the oppressed of our day. We need to help wherever and whenever we can.

Is it any surprise that Paul put so much focus on a slave? While a prisoner himself, Paul met a runaway slave who became a convert and a dear brother to him. Onesimus was a man who ran away from work while a slave but worked joyfully and with all his heart when he was set free. What a marvelous picture of grace.

Paul knew the heart of Jesus, so it is little wonder he wanted to see this oppressed brother set free. What is our work in this world to be? The same as Christ's, the same as Paul's: setting the oppressed free!

---

*Father God, help me to bring the message that we can be free from
all chains that bind us. I pray that my life reflects yours,
living to see people set free from spiritual chains—and chains
of oppression in this world. In Jesus' name.*

FREED TO LOVE

But without your consent I did not want to do anything,
so that your goodness would not be, in effect,
by compulsion but of your own free will.

PHILEMON 1:14, NASB

God is God. He is all powerful. He can do anything He wants. He doesn't have to ask us to bow before Him. He can force us to. But God is a God of love and relationship, and He desires us to love Him freely. We know this from human relationships. What kind of marriage would it be if one spouse forced another to show love? How would you know when any appearance of love was real?

In the same way, Paul presents Philemon with a choice. You can do the right thing because you are ordered to—or because you desire to. Which is better for Philemon—what will please God? We know the answer.

Is there anything in your life today that does not honor God or others? Or maybe you are engaged in some sort of service but for all the wrong reasons. Could it be that God has spoken to you and is speaking to you about it right now? If there are issues in your life you are dealing with, I pray you will learn not to focus on the issue, but to focus on Jesus and embrace the Holy Spirit bringing about the desired change. It all comes out of love and respect for Him. The important thing today is to listen for God's voice and do whatever He would ask of you freely and joyfully, because you love Him and live to please Him.

Search my life, O God. Let the words of my mouth, the meditations
of my heart, and all my deeds bring glory and honor to you.

A NEW BROTHER

For perhaps he was for this reason separated from you for a while, that you would
have him back forever, no longer as a slave, but more than a slave, a beloved brother,
especially to me, but how much more to you, both in the flesh and in the Lord.

PHILEMON 1:15–16, NASB

Part of the wonder of being a Christian is that we serve a living God, the One who performs the miraculous continually. Some miracles are visible, while others happen within the heart and are outworked in change within our lives. I have seen married couples who could barely stand the sight of each other have a relationship of love and joy restored. That's a miracle. I have seen proud, angry, and profane people become joyful, loving saints who speak gentle words of humility and wisdom. That's a miracle. I've seen my own life restored from one that was broken and defeated to one that I pray is being poured out as my thank-you offering to God every day.

Philemon has the opportunity to experience a miracle. Onesimus, once his slave, can become his brother. He will no longer be someone Philemon can't trust and who has to be vigilantly watched after. He will become someone Philemon can trust with his life. All Philemon has to do is see him with the eyes of Christ and release him.

We carry grievances and judgments in life that don't make us safer or wiser; they simply wear us down. Are you holding a grudge? Is there someone you need to set free with the power of forgiveness flowing straight from God's heart through yours? You can not only witness a miracle today but experience one.

Dear God, I am tired of carrying the weight of prejudice
and unforgiveness and judgmentalism in my heart. I give all that to you
and ask for you to do a miracle in my life and relationships today.

MY ACCOUNT

~·e·⁓·e·~

If then you regard me a partner, accept him as you would me.
But if he has wronged you in any way
or owes you anything, charge that to my account.

PHILEMON 1:17–18, NASB

*P*aul is willing to pay whatever is required to secure Onesimus's freedom. He won't hesitate to reach deep into his pockets and give whatever he has. But he does remind Philemon that he has probably prepaid anything that Onesimus might owe him: "I, Paul, am writing this with my own hand, I will repay it (not to mention to you that you owe to me even your own self as well)" (v. 19).

Paul strikes a hard bargain to get what he wants. He simply reminds Philemon—and us—that anything we think we might be giving up or losing as children of God cannot compare to all that God has done for us. It always comes back to grace. We have been given so much more than we deserve. God has lavished on us His love and blessings. And at the cross, where the fullness of grace is revealed on earth to us through Jesus, the accounts are settled once and for all. Our lives are changed forever. We can never look at our account and claim we have given more than we have received. What a crazy thought!

Whenever we are tempted to feel sorry for ourselves, to claim that life isn't fair, let's always return to the love of our Savior, Jesus Christ. Let's give up and surrender anything God asks of us with instant obedience and all joy. Just remember, God is faithful to His Word. Hold on unswervingly to the promise of God over your life.

I am forever grateful to you for your love for me, O God. Even when I was
lost in my sins with no hope or resources to find salvation, you reached down to me.
Thank you for the opportunity to share your love in my world.

Victors Crown

You are salvation, You are hope, Heaven's angels all surround All delight is found in ...
That YOU wash ... the bride

You're my help, my Defender,
My Savior ~ my friend ... by your
grace I live ~ breathe to worship
You

Hallelujah!
Jesus ♡ You have !
overcome the WORLD
Amen

TO GOD BE THE GLORY

For God so loved the world that he gave his one and only Son,
that whoever believes in him shall not perish but have eternal life.

JOHN 3:16, NIV

What a lovely day to reflect on the great things God has done for you and me.

To God be the glory, great things he hath done!
So loved he the world that he gave us his Son,
Who yielded his life an atonement for sin,
And opened the life gate that all may go in.

Refrain
Praise the Lord, praise the Lord,
Let the earth hear his voice!
Praise the Lord, praise the Lord,
Let the people rejoice!
O come to the Father, through Jesus the Son,
And give him the glory, great things he has done.

O perfect redemption, the purchase of blood,
To every believer the promise of God;
The vilest offender who truly believes,
That moment from Jesus a pardon receives.

As I lift up my voice to you, O God my Redeemer,
I pray that the world will truly hear my voice and be saved.

A BLESSED WALK

Blessed are those whose ways are blameless, who walk according to the law of the Lord.
Blessed are those who keep his statutes and seek him with all their heart.

PSALM 119:1–2, NIV

Henry Blackaby wrote, "God's commands are designed to guide you to life's very best. You will not obey Him, however, if you do not believe Him and trust Him. You cannot believe Him if you do not love Him. You cannot love Him unless you know Him."

Think about David in that light. This man after God's heart truly knew Him, loved Him, trusted Him, believed Him, and found such blessing and joy in obeying Him. In that order.

"Blessed are those who walk according to the law of the Lord." My friends, have you discovered the absolute joy and delight of obedience? Are you experiencing His very best for you right now?

If that's a question in your mind, the place to start isn't beating yourself up or living in regret. Return to the basics. Do you believe and trust Him? Do you love and know Him?

Throughout this marvelous psalm, David will remind us of the beauty of God's Word. That's where we get to know Him and His ways as the Spirit not only teaches us about Him—as important as that is—but also allows us to experience God directly.

What an opportunity to seek Him with all our heart. Seek Him and He will find you!

Thank you, Lord, for revealing yourself to us. Thank you for giving us
a sure foundation of belief and trust. Thank you for the gift of your Word,
which guides us into life's very best!

THE PATH OF PURITY

I have hidden your word in my heart that I might not sin against you.

PSALM 119:11, NIV

Psalm 119 is the longest book in the Bible. David, God's specially anointed poet and king, wrote a stanza beginning with each letter of the Hebrew alphabet. He begins the letter B with a question: How can a young person stay on the path of purity? Maybe he was thinking of his own temptations as a youth. Maybe he had in mind one or all of his sons as he wrote this special psalm.

One thing I want to say to all parents reading this is that the greatest gift we can give our children is a knowledge and love of God's Word. Taking them to church is wonderful, but there is also the greatest value in embracing the pattern of God's Word transforming us in all environments in life. Very few material gifts we give our children will go with them into adulthood. Maybe they will keep a favorite toy in a box as a sentimental reminder of childhood. But give them God's Word, and it is an ever-present companion to them all the days of their life.

David tells us the greatest defense against sin is "hiding" God's Word in our heart. That can mean memorizing—almost a lost and forgotten discipline in our day—but what's most important is described in verses 10–16: recounting out loud, meditating on, rejoicing in, delighting in, never neglecting His Word. Seek God in His Word. He will find you and keep your paths pure.

Thank you for the gifts of wisdom, guidance, joy, strength,
and knowing you more that you give us through your Word.

OPEN MY EYES

Open my eyes that I may see wonderful things in your law.

PSALM 119:18, NIV

Two people walk down the same road. One sees the beauty and majesty of God's creation in a sunrise or sunset, in the color of the sky, in trees and plants. The other sees nothing to find joy in and grumbles. What's the difference? One had his eyes truly open.

How many times do we miss blessings simply because we weren't looking for them? We get busy and distracted. We get stuck in bad moods. We think too much about ourselves—what I need and want. When our minds are stuck on all that is wrong, we miss all the wonderful things God puts in our path.

There is an old Chinese proverb that says, "When the student is ready the teacher will arrive." Could this be true of God's Word? Could it be that until our eyes and hearts are open, we are going to miss the wonderful things that God has for us to learn and live?

David's prayer was so simple: "Open my eyes." But it was profound. He was surrounded on every side by his enemies. What was he asking God to do? He wanted his focus to be on God's provision as found in His Word—not on his problems. Where are your eyes focused now? God's promises and provisions or your problems?

Open my eyes to the wonders awaiting me in your Word, O Lord.
Thank you for revealing Jesus to me in the pages of my Bible.

STRENGTHEN ME

My soul is weary with sorrow;
strengthen me according to your word.

PSALM 119:28, NIV

*I*t's ironic that when we need God and His Word the most, we are tempted to turn inside ourselves and wallow in self-pity. Tough times and sorrows are the very times we need God the most. David understood this and not only survived incredible forces arrayed against him but thrived in the process. By turning his heart toward God in life's most excruciating moments, he was inspired in his heart to give us the Psalms, those wonderful and heartfelt expressions of worship and dependence.

By all means, turn to wise and trusted friends in your moments of need. And don't be afraid to express your full gamut of emotions—David shows us that God wants us to come before Him with full honesty, even when we have doubts or feel anger. But my brothers and sisters, most of all turn to God in worship, in prayer, and in eagerly seeking Him and His counsel in the Word of God. Pray for open eyes to receive the wisdom, the correction, and the encouragement you need to not only survive but thrive in the battles of life.

If you've ever doubted even for a moment the power of God's Word, read through all of Psalm 119 again. And again. Meditate on these beautiful words and promises. Let them sink deep into your being. Let them become God's strength in your hour of need.

You are the all-knowing God. All wisdom is yours.
You know me best and love me most.
I thank you for the wisdom you share directly with me
through your Word.

NO MORE WORTHLESS THINGS

Turn my eyes away from worthless things;
preserve my life according to your word.

PSALM 119:37, NIV

Never have there been so many words and images coming at us 24/7. They come through our senses and enter our minds. But so many of them are worthless and lead to worthless thoughts. Never has there been a greater need to watch what we watch, to monitor what we see and hear, to protect our children from the enemy's assault through worthless things and images.

Paul's counsel in Philippians 4:8 is expressed so well in *The Message* translation: "Summing it all up, friends, I'd say you'll do best by filling your minds and meditating on things true, noble, reputable, authentic, compelling, gracious—the best, not the worst; the beautiful, not the ugly; things to praise, not things to curse."

David hit a point in his life when he knew that he had to get his mind back on the things of God. Revenge, discouragement, lust, greed—none of the ugly emotions of life were going to get him through his trials. Only God could do that. So that's where he needed to refocus his mind and life.

Where is your focus today? The beautiful or the ugly? Things to praise or things that are to be cursed? Things of eternal value or things that are worthless? Turn from the worthless and ponder the true, the noble, the authentic, the reputable, and the gracious. It took David deep into the heart of God and will do so for us!

Father, I fix my mind on you today. I won't allow the petty
distractions of the world to rob me of the power of your Word
that sustains and keeps me in all situations.

ACCORDING TO YOUR PROMISE

May your unfailing love come to me, Lord, your salvation, according to your promise;
then I can answer anyone who taunts me, for I trust in your word.

PSALM 119:41–42, NIV

*R*eally, should we worry about what others think when we know we are pleasing God? In our spiritual life, we know the answer is no—others' opinions of us can't compare to what God thinks of us when we are walking in His will. But in light of our humanity, in the flesh, we are tempted to set others right in their faulty judgments.

David was under assault. He had lost his kingdom. It wasn't his enemies from godless countries he had gone to war against, but his son Absalom, who had deposed him. He was humiliated. Those who were once his friends had become his enemies, serving Absalom instead. They taunted David. Some were undoubtedly jealous and delighted in seeing a true warrior brought low. This made them feel bigger somehow.

David understands that not only are they taunting him but they are taunting God. They have lost sight of the One who anointed David and delivered him and the entire nation from their enemies. He wants them to see with their own eyes his deliverance so they can see again the Deliverer. In this sense, David is not about justifying himself but proving God and His faithfulness to all doubters.

When you feel the need to justify and defend yourself, follow David's lead and do all you can to honor God and His faithfulness. When you honor Him, you are trusting God with all the tender places of your heart and obeying His Word above all other temptations. This is how we delight the Father's heart.

I am so humbled, Lord, that when I lift you up, you lift me up. Your love for me
is unfailing. Your promises and salvation are sure. I know my trust in you and your
Word will always be proven in this life and the life to come.

PRESERVE MY LIFE

Remember your word to your servant, for you have given me hope.
My comfort in my suffering is this: Your promise preserves my life.
The arrogant mock me unmercifully, but I do not turn from your law.

PSALM 119:49–51, NIV

No matter how low you feel, no matter how under siege your life seems to be, know for certain your life will be preserved. God is the God of comfort and hope. He is El Shaddai, the God who supplies all your needs.

I love how Joni Eareckson Tada talks of this comfort: "You don't have to be alone in your hurt! Comfort is yours. Joy is an option. And it's all been made possible by your Savior. He went without comfort so you might have it. He postponed joy so you might share in it. He willingly chose isolation so you might never be alone in your hurt and sorrow."

When David turns to God in prayer and praise, he already sees and experiences the Savior who will come to the world seven hundred years later. He reveals God as He will be seen and experienced in Jesus Christ. Not everyone had faith to recognize what David was pointing out to them. Not everyone today has the faith to accept the loving God who is fully expressed in Jesus through His Word.

But you have opened this book and have chosen to spend time with God each day in His Word and in worship because your faith has made you alive. That means that whatever hope, comfort, and strength you need today is already yours in Christ Jesus.

I praise you, God. You give me hope and comfort sufficient for all my needs.
I will never turn from you and your ways.

FILLED WITH YOUR LOVE

The earth is filled with your love, Lord; teach me your decrees.

PSALM 119:64, NIV

*Y*es, my friends, it is good to be aware of what is happening in our world. We need to be informed and concerned. But perhaps there is a time when we need to turn off the television and tune out the other things in life that seem to focus on the negative. There is heartache in our world to be sure. But the earth is filled with God's love. He is greater than all else.

I have heard testimony from those who have taken a "fast" from news and entertainment in order to get their thoughts and focus back on the Lord and to grow spiritually. I think that's an excellent idea. We have fasted from food to get our mind on spiritual things. But there are other things that fill us up to the point that we are not attuned to what God wants to say to us.

You know David wasn't oblivious to the trials and tribulations around him. He experienced too many personal hardships to ever be naïve to the suffering of others. Yet this man who was well acquainted with grief looks up to God, and his soul takes flight as he sees God surrounding him. Others would have given up. David is just getting started. He worships and studies every word from the lips of God.

We all have sorrows and hardships come our way. But look to your Creator, look to your Savior, seek Him with all your heart in the pages of the Word. Be prepared to be blown away by the discovery that the world is filled with His love.

*Teach me your decrees, O God. Help me to understand
what you want from me. I praise you for your love that surrounds me,
even when I am in the midst of troubles.*

MORE PRECIOUS THAN GOLD

The law from your mouth is more precious to me
than thousands of pieces of silver and gold.

PSALM 119:72, NIV

*J*esus asked these questions of His disciples after a rich young ruler had refused the gift of eternal life: "What good will it be for someone to gain the whole world, yet forfeit their soul? Or what can anyone give in exchange for their soul?" (Matthew 16:26). Paul warns his young protégé Timothy: "For the love of money is a root of all kinds of evil. Some people, eager for money, have wandered from the faith and pierced themselves with many griefs" (1 Timothy 6:10).

Our God is so good and gracious and kind. Following Him sets up the conditions for peace and prosperity—even though in our fallen world this is so often marred. All of us have been blessed by God in countless ways, and some have been blessed financially as well.

David sets the very same contrast that Jesus and His followers did. Notice he doesn't say money is bad and of no worth. If God loves a cheerful giver, then He certainly doesn't mind someone with something to give! But the contrast is that our spiritual lives are so valuable, not even a treasure chest filled with gold, silver, and precious jewels can compare.

David has lived in the palace and he has hidden in a cave. He knows both wealth and severe need. He is in a unique position to tell us that no earthly fortune can compare to the greatness of knowing God and living for Him. Make sure today that your heart is set on treasure that cannot be eroded.

Your love, your will, your guidance—those are the treasures
I crave most in my life, God. Thank you for the riches that are mine through
knowing you through Jesus Christ my Lord.

YOUR HANDS

Your hands made me and formed me; give me understanding to learn your commands.

PSALM 119:73, NIV

*A*ll throughout Psalm 119 we learn of the many blessings of knowing God's Word. And because of those blessings David continues to emphasize, we know God and His will for our lives through getting our heart and minds into His Word. Open your eyes so you can see what He wants to show you. Seek Him in the Word so that He can find you there. Ask Him to be your Teacher. Meditate. Obey. Believe. Trust. Each section of this marvelous psalm is a call to action. The Bible is not to be a casual acquaintance in your life, but a constant companion.

As David talks to God in the Word, he comes back to the basis of God's claim on our lives. "Your hands made me and formed me." God is our Creator. He is not someone we ought to get to know and maybe serve. He is the One we must get to know and serve as we worship Him and experience life as He created it for us. Trust me, the response of a heart transformed through God's Word is a life that is consecrated to His will and purpose, fueled for service.

As you have read David's words—words that were given to him from God himself—have you resolved to spend more time in the Word? As we just read yesterday, silver and gold are valuable, but they can't compare to the treasure you receive from God's Word.

You have been invited by God Almighty to get to know Him, to sit at His feet and be taught, to receive countless promises and provisions—all through filling your heart, mind, and soul with His Word. I pray your answer will be a mighty yes!

Thank you for inviting me to know you through time together in your Word.
Thank you for the promise to be my Teacher and Guide through each verse of the Bible.

EVERYONE WHO CALLS

Everyone who calls on the name of the Lord will be saved.

ROMANS 10:13, NLT

*D*o you have a loved one who doesn't know Jesus as Lord and Savior? Are you discouraged by the depravity of modern culture? Does it feel to you as though the kingdom of God is losing ground?

Don't lose heart. Paul declares that there is good news for absolutely every person on the face of the earth. No matter how they have previously lived—wicked, indifferent, whatever—their lives can change in an instant when they call on the name of Jesus.

If the greatest joy in life is serving God and sharing His Son with others, then this verse can only make us happy. Of course we are heartbroken that so many are lost, but we also know that if we truly make Jesus known with our lives and actions, then there are opportunities each day to "pull someone from the fire."

One poignant reminder is that it is God's work to convict and judge. The Holy Spirit draws people to the Father, and our job is to represent Christ well in all that we are. When we find ourselves judging and condemning—writing people off as too hopeless—this verse is a gentle correction to believe in the power of the gospel to change lives. If God declares that everyone who calls on the name of the Lord will be saved, then it is absolutely true.

Give me a heart filled with hope and love, dear God. Help me to not look at others with an attitude of indifference, but to realize just how much you love them and want fellowship with them, how much your heart desires every one of us home.

FOR HIS GLORY

*For everything comes from him and exists by his power and
is intended for his glory. All glory to him forever! Amen.*

ROMANS 11:36, NLT

This sounds very much like a call to worship. Paul is very logical in presenting God's Word to us, but he is also emotional and passionate when he thinks of the Savior that knocked him off his feet and transformed his life forever.

He explains that everything that exists comes from God and is intended for His glory. But then Paul can't help himself. He has to shout. It bubbles up in his spirit and overflows with a loud, passionate cry: "All glory to him forever!"

It's a wonderful thing to grow in our understanding of God's Word. Study and discipline are wonderful. But also remember that God calls us to worship Him with expression from our voices, our songs, our hands raised in honor, our instruments. Sometimes we have to stop all the doing and just allow the "being in Him" to flow out of us in praise. Simply lift your heart and voice in praise. God wants all of us. That includes our minds and hearts, our thoughts and emotions, our songs. . . .

I hope and pray we never become too sophisticated and "proper" to ever allow our praise to be hindered and lessened due to a what-will-people-think attitude. Shout to the Lord, lift Him up. Our lives are to be an expression of praise to His glorious name. All that we are and have been given is intended for His glory. So go ahead and shout it: All glory to Him forever!

*All glory to you, my Father. With everything I am,
with everything you have given me, I bring it before you in worship,
giving you all the glory.*

HIS PERFECT WILL

I plead with you to give your bodies to God because of all he has done for you.
Let them be a living and holy sacrifice—the kind he will find acceptable. This is truly
the way to worship him. Don't copy the behavior and customs of this world, but let God
transform you into a new person by changing the way you think. Then you will learn to
know God's will for you, which is good and pleasing and perfect.

ROMANS 12:1–2, NLT

How can we know God's good, pleasing, and perfect will for our lives? It starts when we acknowledge that anything we do is "because of all he has done" for us. And from there we give our bodies to God. Paul isn't talking about just our physical bodies. He is talking about everything we are. He calls us to give ourselves completely to God, not a part or corner of our lives withheld. It is the same as when we pray, "Not my will but your will be done."

What is God's will for us? He wants us to say "Your will be done" through a complete commitment. Everything else in life is just the small stuff. If we will declare that we are willing to do anything God wants us to do and live that out, we will have discovered His will for our lives. That's when we are no longer conformed to the evil patterns of this world but are transformed. A life given in worship to the Lord announces clearly which kingdom we belong to. My personal prayer is that my life would be marked by His presence, that whose I am would never be a mystery.

When God makes us different, it is not for the sake of being different. He wants His people to be different in order to make a difference, to be the hands and feet of Jesus. That's us! Think about that. Pray about that. Ask yourself, "Have I given myself completely to God?"

In view of your mercy, because of all you have done for me, O Lord, I offer myself
completely to you. Not my will, but yours be done in and through me!

YOUR GIFT WELL DONE

In his grace, God has given us different gifts for doing certain things well. So if God has given you the ability to prophesy, speak out with as much faith as God has given you. If your gift is serving others, serve them well. If you are a teacher, teach well. If your gift is to encourage others, be encouraging. If it is giving, give generously. If God has given you leadership ability, take the responsibility seriously. And if you have a gift for showing kindness to others, do it gladly.

ROMANS 12:6–8, NLT

Never look with envy at the gifts others have or how God uses them in ministry. You can admire them, learn from them, and be inspired by them, but don't let even the smallest dab of comparison establish root in your heart. Others are who they are in Christ. You are not called to be them. You are called to be you! The best *you* can only be achieved through you being you. And God has gifted you. He doesn't ask you to use others' gifts. He wants you to fully employ your gifts.

Paul has already called us to offer our bodies as living sacrifices, and that includes our gifts. It is always possible that our gifts will give us a great reputation and usher many blessings into our lives. But don't let that be the reason you exercise your gifts. Your gifts are to glorify God and make His name known to others. When our gifts become an exercise in pride and personal gain, there is always danger close ahead. Be careful. Repent. Ask God to renew your spirit of serving as an expression of love and worship to Him. Serving God is part of our holy calling. Thank God today for the gifts He has given you, the things that bring you to life on the inside.

When we give all we have to God, oh what a difference we make in our world, and how fulfilling it is as we go about what we were born to do!

I give myself to you, God, completely and without reservation. Take the gifts you have given me and use them to glorify you and make your wonderful name known!

IF GOD IS FOR YOU

A Classic Devotion by Richard Baxter

❧

If God be for us, who can be against us?

ROMANS 8:31, KJV

o not be discouraged at the difficulties and oppositions that will rise up before you when you begin resolvedly to walk with God. Discouragements turn multitudes from religion, and provide a great temptation for many young beginners to turn back. Israel in the wilderness was ready to retreat to Egypt. God himself will have his servants and his graces tried and exercised by difficulties, and Satan will quickly raise up storms before us, as soon as we are set out to sea.

But God is on your side and has all your enemies in his hand, and can rebuke them, or destroy them in a moment. O what is the breath or fury of dust or devils, against the Lord Almighty! In the day you entered into a covenant with God, and he with you, you entered into the most impregnable rock and fortress, and covered yourself in a castle of defence, where you may (modestly) defy all adverse powers of earth or hell. If God cannot save you, he is not God.

O think on the saints' triumphant boastings in their God: "God is our refuge and strength, a very present help in trouble" (Psa. 46:1). If all of the world were on your side, you might yet have cause to fear. But to have God on your side is infinitely more!

Christ the Captain of your salvation has gone this way before you, and now he is engaged to make you a conqueror! Do not be afraid where Christ is leading the way.

Thank you for making me a conqueror through Jesus Christ. Thank you for Jesus.
It's His love that allows me to overcome all discouragement and opposition.

SAVIOR

JESUS IS INDEED
THE SAVIOR OF THE WORLD.

JUNE

Blessed assurance,
    Jesus is mine!
O what a foretaste of glory divine!
Heir of salvation, purchase of God,
Born of his Spirit,
    washed in his blood.

This is my story, this is my song,
Praising my SAVIOR
    all the day long.

SAVIOR, you are worthy
    of PRAISE!

Jesus

EVERY TIME I THINK OF YOU

Every time I think of you, I give thanks to my God.

PHILIPPIANS 1:3, NLT

He was in prison, facing the very real possibility of martyrdom. Some of his disciples and fellow ministers weren't being much help to him, but rather were causing further problems for him because of petty jealousies. Yet Paul, not one of the original disciples of Jesus but still called to be an apostle of Christ, writes a letter filled with joy and hope. I wish that all my emails and phone calls and times together with my beloved friends were always filled with such grace, no matter what the circumstances.

Wouldn't you love to hear someone say to you, "Every time I think of you, I give thanks to my God"? What a fabulous word of encouragement. What a beautiful expression of love. And we know with Paul it was not just a casual and polite remark; he meant it. He did it. His life was not focused on himself, but on his Lord Jesus Christ and those whom he reached with the gospel.

There are two powerful questions for us to ponder in this short little verse, aren't there? Who are we thinking about? And whom are we giving thanks to God for? We all need a reminder that we truly become who God created us to be when we stop thinking about me, me, me—and focus on others with the good news of Jesus. Even as I write these words, I want you to know that I am praying for you today, and I genuinely give thanks to God for you.

***

Thank you, heavenly Father, for all those who have encouraged me with their encouragement and prayers. I bring dear friends before you today, thanking you for giving me an opportunity to be a part of their lives.

WHENEVER I PRAY

Whenever I pray, I make my requests for all of you with joy.

PHILIPPIANS 1:4, NLT

*I*n this letter of joy, Paul lets his friends in Philippi know just how much he loves them. He thinks of them often. He thanks God for them. And he brings their needs before his heavenly Father, not out of some duty or determined act of discipline—though discipline is a good thing—but out of joy. Praying on their behalf is no chore, but a delightful part of his day.

He was under lock and key, so perhaps he had more time to think and pray, but I have the strong feeling that if Paul's days were just as active and busy as normal for this man who worked tirelessly to take the gospel to the world, he would still have prayed for the needs of those he loved so much in the same way.

Who are you thinking about? Who are you thanking God for? Who has needs that you can bring before the Father with joy? There is such an important lesson in this verse and in those questions. It is no sin to want to be happy and experience joy. But so often we try to find it by focusing on self: my needs, my ambitions, my interests. My dear friends, we already know what an ineffective way to find happiness that is. Our God created us to find fulfillment and joy in doing His work, in serving others, in living with the compassion of Jesus in this world.

*As I bring the needs of my friends before you today,
my Father and my Friend, I do so with joy and thanksgiving!*

MY PARTNERS

For you have been my partners in spreading the Good News about
Christ from the time you first heard it until now.

PHILIPPIANS 1:5, NLT

*P*aul was a hateful and much feared man before meeting his Savior on the road to Damascus. But all that energy, all that intellect, all that passion that was so misused as a persecutor of the church was completely given for God's glory and work on earth once he truly met Jesus. Isn't that the way God does things? He has such a lovely way of transforming what is ugly into something that is beautiful, something that was meant for harm into something that brings healing, a person who brings words of death into a person who brings words of life.

How many of us have the same testimony as Paul? God turned our worst into His best. I can't think of a more powerful reason that all of us need to guard our hearts against judgmentalism. That one we think has no redeeming value and who could never be saved could become the next Paul.

Beatings, shipwrecks, and the shadow of death were no match for Paul's zeal to share the good news about Christ. This man who stood alone at the stoning of Stephen can't help but celebrate his close relationships—his partners—based on the good news of Jesus Christ. He will later allude to some who caused him trouble because of jealousy and too much ego, but Paul is even thankful for them. Have you celebrated and thanked those who are your partners in all areas of your life?

Father, you have blessed me beyond anything I deserve through the people
you have brought into my life. I thank you for my life partners.

THE GOOD WORK

And I am certain that God, who began the good work within you,
will continue his work until it is finally finished
on the day when Christ Jesus returns.

PHILIPPIANS 1:6, NLT

God has done so much in and through you—in and through me—but He is not done with us yet! We aren't finished, so He isn't finished. What a marvelous truth and promise. There is always opportunity for us to grow more and more into Christlikeness because Christ himself lives inside us.

We have all had to live through moments of failure. None of us are perfect. But never forget that we have many reasons to thank God for how far He has brought us. And we have even more reason to thank Him that He will continue that work that is already started in us.

I would also add that we need to extend the grace of this verse to others. When you look around at church and feel judgmental toward others for what you perceive as their lack of spiritual progress, remember quickly, God isn't finished with them yet. A good work has begun, and God will continue to bring it to completion for the day that Christ returns. Our job isn't to heap condemnation but to provide encouragement and spur our brothers and sisters in Christ to live more fully in faith and love.

God, I thank you for the presence of Jesus Christ in my heart and life.
I thank you for the good work you have begun in me.
And I thank you for your patience and kindness for my shortcomings
at this present moment—and your faithfulness to transform me
into the person you have created me to be.

A SPECIAL PLACE IN MY HEART

So it is right that I should feel as I do about all of you, for you have a special place in my heart. You share with me the special favor of God, both in my imprisonment and in defending and confirming the truth of the Good News.

PHILIPPIANS 1:7, NLT

We know what Paul is talking about in this verse. We have experienced this kind of relationship ourselves. There are some people we have met in life who hold a special place in our heart. They have been there for us in the tough times—for Paul it was his several imprisonments—and we have a spiritual connection with them where our hearts and minds are so united that we see life the same way. Paul goes on to say to these dear friends of his: "God knows how much I love you and long for you with the tender compassion of Christ Jesus" (v. 8). Have we let these incredibly special people in our lives know how much we love them?

My prayer for you today is that you would have brothers and sisters in Christ who occupy this kind of place in your heart. You know they are there for you whether you are on the mountaintop or in prison. And I pray that you and I would also be this kind of person for someone else, that because of love and loyalty, we would have a special place in someone else's heart. Just look around and you will see the person who needs your help in a time of imprisonment, the one who feels forgotten. Look around and discover again how we really do need each other.

The favor of God is too wonderful to describe. But it becomes even greater when shared with others.

Dear God, help me to show my brothers and sisters in Christ how much I love them. Help our bonds of faith and love to grow and deepen as we model the love you have for us.

OVERFLOW MORE AND MORE

I pray that your love will overflow more and more, and that you
will keep on growing in knowledge and understanding.

PHILIPPIANS 1:9, NLT

Don't stop now. You have grown so much in knowledge and understanding since the day you met Jesus Christ as your Lord and Savior. But go further, dear friend. Don't get bogged down by distractions and self-focus. Turn your heart toward God and gain greater levels of His wisdom. Don't be satisfied with a lukewarm religion, but seek knowing God with all your heart, soul, and strength.

Rest in the love of Jesus and you will experience more of His love. It's not that God starts loving you more, but that your heart is more open to receiving it. What happens next is nothing short of miraculous. His love will overflow and spill into all areas of your life. Your spouse, your children, your co-workers, your neighbors, complete strangers—no one can help but be impacted by the love of Jesus overflowing from your heart. Even those who are resisting the grace of God will be touched, even if they don't experience God's salvation—yet. Your love will not go unnoticed and will not be ineffective.

God wants to fill you up with His Spirit—the Spirit that gives us God's wisdom. We can't do this through our own efforts, but we do have a part, which is to say, "Yes, Lord, I am yours." Are you ready to overflow?

Fill me with your love, O God. I thank you that you
dwell in my heart so that I can share you with all sincerity and power.
I say yes to your will today. I say yes to you.

PURE AND BLAMELESS LIVES

*For I want you to understand what really matters, so that you may live
pure and blameless lives until the day of Christ's return.*

PHILIPPIANS 1:10, NLT

The people Paul wrote to lived in a day and age much like the day and age we live in, filled with self-centeredness and upside-down values and pursuits. Paul wants his beloved children to "understand what really matters" and not be caught up in the emptiness of the culture around them. Knowing what matters—seeing the world the way God does—leads to pure and blameless lives.

Charles Spurgeon put it so well: "I would sooner be holy than happy if the two things could be divorced. Were it possible for a man always to sorrow and yet to be pure, I would choose the sorrow if I might win the purity, for to be free from the power of sin, to be made to love holiness, is true happiness."

I'll say again for emphasis: The weakness of our humanity is that we think we can experience true happiness by focusing on ourselves. We've all done it and know better, but the pull to live for self rather than God is part of what we were born with. My friends, let's choose the Jesus-centered life—the most important step in understanding "what really matters"—and discover the joy and fulfillment that comes through living a pure and blameless life.

*Lord, I want my life to matter, and I know that begins with
understanding what matters to you. I put my hope and trust in you today.
Lead me in your wisdom and ways.*

THE FRUIT OF YOUR SALVATION

May you always be filled with the fruit of your salvation—the righteous
character produced in your life by Jesus Christ—for this will bring
much glory and praise to God.

PHILIPPIANS 1:11, NLT

I love to glorify my God in worship, lifting my voice and heart in praise and thanksgiving. My soul is filled afresh every time I gather with a congregation of brothers and sisters who unite voices and hearts to honor our God. He is worthy of our worship.

Paul reminds us that "righteous character" brings much glory and praise to God. So I want my life—my decisions and relationships and everyday walk—to be just as much of a worship celebration to my Father God.

Paul puts it so beautifully when he writes that our righteous character is "produced in your life by Jesus." Just as we had no means by which to earn our salvation, we have no means to walk the walk—it is only through putting our complete faith in Jesus Christ.

Let's commit ourselves together to a life of truthful worship, lifting our voices together in songs of praise. But this is only the start of the story, or maybe I should say, the overflow of our thanksgiving to God. I pray we also commit ourselves to a daily walk of "righteous character," believing the One who is within us will do for us what we can't do for ourselves and give us the strength to serve like Jesus teaches us to serve.

Thank you, God, for the gift of Jesus. Thank you that He is in my heart and life,
producing righteous character and every good fruit.

BOLDLY SPEAK GOD'S MESSAGE

And I want you to know, my dear brothers and sisters,
that everything that has happened to me here has helped
to spread the Good News.

PHILIPPIANS 1:12, NLT

*W*hat good can happen when your ministry is cut short and you are thrown into captivity? For the apostle John, banished to the island of Patmos, he was visited by Jesus himself and given a divine revelation that is just as powerful and relevant today as when it was given to John. For Paul, getting tossed in jail meant there would be new Christians and even greater boldness in sharing the good news by his friends: "For everyone here, including the whole palace guard, knows that I am in chains because of Christ. And because of my imprisonment, most of the believers here have gained confidence and boldly speak God's message without fear" (vv. 13–14).

Whatever hardship you are facing today, trust in God that He is using the circumstance to bring His good and perfect will to pass. You just never know what the Lord will do through your trial. Queen Esther was put in a royal palace—and risked her life—to save her people. Joseph was thrown in a pit, sold into slavery, and then falsely accused and imprisoned—but he too saved his people.

Don't lose heart over the burdens you are carrying or any hardship you must bear. God is near. He loves you. You are not alone. He will save you. Not only that, you are in a position to reveal Jesus with power and clarity through His strength.

O God, help me to reveal Jesus to my world, no matter what
my circumstance and situation. Thank you for a power that comes
from His presence inside my life.

PURE MOTIVES

It's true that some are preaching out of jealousy and rivalry.
But others preach about Christ with pure motives.

PHILIPPIANS 1:15, NLT

*H*ow would you feel about people who saw you in prison and did things to make your time there even harder? It would be hard to feel and show grace toward them. But Paul, the persecutor turned missionary, shows us that he practices what he preaches. He urges us to draw near to Christ so we can "understand what really matters"—and in the moment of his testing he lives it.

He recognizes those who preach with a pure heart: "They preach because they love me, for they know I have been appointed to defend the Good News" (v. 16). But he is charitable even toward those who have let their ego get out of line: "Those others do not have pure motives as they preach about Christ. They preach with selfish ambition, not sincerely, intending to make my chains more painful to me" (v. 17). Does he write them off and condemn them? Not at all. His conclusion is this: "But that doesn't matter. Whether their motives are false or genuine, the message about Christ is being preached either way, so I rejoice. And I will continue to rejoice" (v. 18).

That is a man whose life was forever changed by meeting Jesus. The persecutor became a forgiver. And he knew what matters most—Christ being preached. I want that perspective and joy for you—and for me.

Even when there is conflict around me, even when there are
those who don't support me or wish me well, I will rejoice that
my reactions and life will reveal Jesus to my world.

NEVER BE ASHAMED

*For I fully expect and hope that I will never be ashamed, but that
I will continue to be bold for Christ, as I have been in the past.
And I trust that my life will bring honor to Christ, whether I live or die.*

PHILIPPIANS 1:20, NLT

Because of the fall of Adam and Eve and the natural sinfulness of the human heart that was passed onto all of us, there are those who will oppose God with all their strength. Paul was one of them. It was on his way to persecute believers in Jesus Christ that Jesus knocked him off his horse, blinded him, and spoke directly to him: "Saul! Saul! Why are you persecuting me?" (Acts 9:4). Never, never, never give up on the person in your life who seems most opposed to the gospel.

Now Paul is approaching the end of his journey and ministry on behalf of the One he persecuted. His hope is that "I will never be ashamed, but that I will continue to be bold for Christ." We may never be persecuted for our faith—though we don't know that for sure. But certainly, if we live for our Lord, we will face opposition. Some will make jokes at our expense in an attempt to embarrass us. We might be excluded and left out from some fellowship and activities to "put us in our place."

Let's not be discouraged. Rather, let's consider it a badge of honor. If Jesus, Paul, and so many heroes of the faith faced opposition from sinful men, then we are in good company. The best company. Don't be discouraged or ashamed. Be bold in sharing the good news and in honoring Christ, whether in life or death.

*O God, give me a boldness of spirit that I may reveal you
to the world no matter what opposition I face.
My hope is in you. My identity is found in you.*

LIVING FOR CHRIST

For to me, living means living for Christ,
and dying is even better.

PHILIPPIANS 1:21, NLT

I confess that I like being alive. I like my life. I want to live a long and fruitful life here on earth. I want to be here for my loved ones and friends. I want to see my grandchildren grow up and serve God. I want to continue to share in the sweet fellowship of my brothers and sisters at church. I don't know if Paul's words have totally sunk in—"for to me, living means living for Christ, and dying is even better"—but I understand along with him that our greatest joy now and in eternity is found in Jesus Christ.

That doesn't make it easy to look at life fully as Paul did. We love our family and friends so much and can't imagine being without them. And Paul did recognize just how special life in the here and now is: "But if I live, I can do more fruitful work for Christ. So I really don't know which is better" (v. 22).

Ultimately, the message of these verses is the same message Paul proclaimed throughout his ministry: Christ comes first. Put your total faith and love in Him. Everything else is secondary—but everything else becomes better and more lovely when we love Christ first. We love our family and friends—and even those who would be our enemies—so much better when we have fallen totally in love with Jesus.

Father God, my first love is Jesus Christ.
May I never lose that love and passion.
Thank you that Jesus is with me now and forever.

CITIZENS OF HEAVEN

Above all, you must live as citizens of heaven, conducting yourselves in a manner worthy of the Good News about Christ. Then, whether I come and see you again or only hear about you, I will know that you are standing together with one spirit and one purpose, fighting together for the faith, which is the Good News.

PHILIPPIANS 1:27, NLT

It is hard to understand that the world we live in—the only world we know—is only a temporary home. It's easy to understand when visiting other countries that I'm not in my country, my town, my home. I'm a visitor. But when I return to my house, it definitely feels like home.

Paul teaches us that heaven is our destination, the place where we will live infinitely longer than our days on earth. We may not be able to completely comprehend that in our hearts, but we do understand that our perspective must be expanded into the spiritual realm. Then we will understand "what matters most." Paul reminds us that our conduct matters. Our character brings much glory to God. And when our walk is "worthy of the Good News about Christ," we demonstrate that we have already assumed our heavenly citizenship. We live in the here and now, but we stand with other Christians with "one spirit and one purpose, fighting together for the faith."

When God created our world, He declared it to be "very good." We are to enjoy and savor the joys of this world. But we are to never forget that this is not all there is to life. Eternity, residing in our hearts on earth, will eventually be our heavenly reality. Let's unite with one spirit and one purpose and show the world we are citizens of heaven.

Our Father, may your will be done on earth as it is in heaven. Empower us to bring your will to earth through how we live today.

NOT INTIMIDATED

Don't be intimidated in any way by your enemies. This will be a sign to them that they are going to be destroyed, but that you are going to be saved, even by God himself.

PHILIPPIANS 1:28, NLT

*A*re you fearful and intimidated when people oppose you? I am pretty certain most of us have stood in Peter's shoes. Except maybe Paul. I can't think of a time when he backed down. He was truly a man of boldness.

Has anyone understood the mind of Christ like Paul? Oh, he seemed to grow discouraged at times, but he understood so clearly what ultimately matters in life—knowing Jesus. That is why he refused to back down or lose heart no matter what his circumstances. In fact, he still experienced sheer joy even when facing death. He saw suffering as a means to ministry and a privilege: "For you have been given not only the privilege of trusting in Christ but also the privilege of suffering for him" (v. 29).

For anyone experiencing fear and distress over current circumstances, Paul's anthem of joy, his letter to the Philippians, is required reading. This is the book of the Bible to read over and over until we understand that God's gifts of confidence, hope, and joy are ours to claim—not at some future date when life seems more under control—but even in the midst of fierce battle.

What does this boldness say to our enemies? It tells them that nothing they do can defeat us, for God himself will save us. It also tells them that their current course of action will lead to their own destruction—and beautifully, due to the great story of grace, some will be saved along the way. Nothing brings more joy than to see one who fought God fall in love with God through Jesus.

I stand not in my own strength, but through you, the God of my strength and salvation.

MAKE ME TRULY HAPPY

Is there any encouragement from belonging to Christ? Any comfort from his love?
Any fellowship together in the Spirit? Are your hearts tender and compassionate?
Then make me truly happy by agreeing wholeheartedly with each other, loving one
another, and working together with one mind and purpose.

PHILIPPIANS 2:1–2, NLT

We love to make the people we love happy. I love my husband, children, and grandchildren so much, and I want them to be truly happy. Young or old, single or married, I am sure you feel the same way too.

Paul's whole life is dedicated to pleasing Christ and making Him known to the entire world. He doesn't care about his own comfort and wealth. He has found the secret of contentment whether he has much or little. But in these verses he does ask his friends for a favor. And to let them know how big of a deal this is to him, he appeals to their love for him. What does he want from them? Unity. Stop fighting; love one another; work together with one mind and purpose.

If his beloved children in the faith will do those three things, his joy will soar beyond the clouds. Like David, Paul was one of those men who knew the heart of God. If agreement, love, and working together among believers bring Paul this much happiness, you can be sure it pleases the heart of God.

Are you in conflict with someone? Maybe you feel you've done everything you can to make things right. But is there anything else you can do? It would please God so much.

Heavenly Father, my heart's desire is to please you. Help me in all my relationships.
Help me to foster peace, love, and unity of purpose even when I feel my way is the best
way. Thank you for granting me humility and strength in equal measure.

BE HUMBLE

Don't be selfish; don't try to impress others.
Be humble, thinking of others as better than yourselves.
Don't look out only for your own interests,
but take an interest in others, too.

PHILIPPIANS 2:3–4, NLT

We worry too much about impressing a fickle audience of those around us when the only One we truly need to please is God.

When Samuel was led by God to the house of Jesse to anoint the next king of Israel, he couldn't help but be impressed by one of David's older brothers for his height and good looks. But God spoke an incredible truth into his heart: "But the Lord said to Samuel, 'Do not consider his appearance or his height, for I have rejected him. The Lord does not look at the things people look at. People look at the outward appearance, but the Lord looks at the heart'" (1 Samuel 16:7, NIV).

Once again we are reminded to take our focus off self and focus on being a blessing to others. We worry about outward appearance when God is most concerned with what is inside us. Despite our fears, humility doesn't make our lives less but puts us on the path to true greatness. When the disciples wanted to know who was greatest in the kingdom, what did Jesus do? He modeled servanthood by washing their feet. Genuine humility is seen in our actions, not just our words.

Are you unhappy? Do you feel lost and lacking in purpose? Focus on the needs of others and serve as Jesus did.

Lord, I want to see the world as you do, focusing on how I can be
a blessing and bring your truth to everyone around me.

THE ATTITUDE OF CHRIST

You must have the same attitude that Christ Jesus had.

PHILIPPIANS 2:5, NLT

*S*o what was the attitude of Christ Jesus?

Though he was God, he did not think of equality with God as something to cling to.

Instead, he gave up his divine privileges; he took the humble position of a slave and was born as a human being.

When he appeared in human form, he humbled himself in obedience to God and died a criminal's death on a cross.

Therefore, God elevated him to the place of highest honor and gave him the name above all other names, that at the name of Jesus every knee should bow, in heaven and on earth and under the earth, and every tongue confess that Jesus Christ is Lord, to the glory of God the Father.

Philippians 2:6–11

Bible scholars believe that in this passage, Paul quoted the oldest hymn of the Christian church, that this would be sung or recited in the earliest church meetings. Wow! Not only are we privileged to worship with fellow believers around the world—but through God's Word we can worship with fellow believers across centuries.

Meditate on these powerful words and understand that you are sharing the same words with those who walked and talked with Jesus in human form.

❧

I stand in amazement, O God, that I can worship with the same heart and words of praise as the saints who have come before me. Thank you!

REVERENCE AND FEAR

*Dear friends, you always followed my instructions when I was with you.
And now that I am away, it is even more important. Work hard to show the results
of your salvation, obeying God with deep reverence and fear. For God is working
in you, giving you the desire and the power to do what pleases him.*

PHILIPPIANS 2:12–13, NLT

I so believe in grace. There is simply no way to earn our salvation. That comes from God's kindness. He loved us when we didn't love Him. He forgave our rebelliousness. He reached out to us through Jesus Christ and did something for us we could not do ourselves. Our works will not save us.

But grace is not an excuse for sloppy living, and it doesn't mean we don't take works seriously. Paul encourages us to "work hard to show the results of your salvation, obeying God with deep reverence and fear." What Paul says next is truly remarkable: "God is working in you, giving you the desire and the power to do what pleases him." That means the same grace that brought our salvation is the same grace that enables us to live out our salvation in obedience.

For anyone who feels defeated in their spiritual life—and most of us have felt that way—all you need to do is turn to Jesus. If you feel as though you are lacking the necessary desire and power to live victoriously, never forget that the fullness of God is at work inside you. The same grace that saved you will be there with overcoming power. Confess your need to God and anticipate His grace-filled answer.

*Father God, when I don't have the desire or power to live the life
you have planned for me, help me to always remember to turn to you and acknowledge
your presence in my life. Thank you for your grace.*

SHINE LIKE STARS

*Do everything without complaining and arguing,
so that no one can criticize you. Live clean, innocent lives
as children of God, shining like bright lights in a world
full of crooked and perverse people.*

PHILIPPIANS 2:14–15, NLT

Based on popular television fare, it would seem that everyone wants to be a star. Some are motivated to do something special. Others simply want to be rich and famous. To be famous for being famous. Interesting times.

God is our Creator and created us for fellowship with Him. No one knows us like God. He knows our heart and what gives our lives purpose and meaning. Here's the good news: He actually wants us to "shine like stars." And not just by the world's standards or values, but to truly shine from the inside out, bursting with the life that Christ has given us. I guarantee that when we live for God, our lives will be defined by His presence and power. Paul tells us to cut out the negativity and "live clean, innocent lives as children of God." The result is we shine like stars—not just stars, but bright stars—in a dark and crooked world.

Have you been caught up in our culture of arguing and complaining? Take God's Word to heart. Don't feel the need to be so grown-up that you have to find the negative—live with the innocence of a child! I long for and love such simplicity in my own life. You will too!

*I want to shine like a star so that people see you and give you glory,
dear God. Give me the innocence and purity to stand out as a powerful
testimony in this generation that is aching for you.*

SHARE MY JOY

Yes, you should rejoice, and I will share your joy.

PHILIPPIANS 2:18, NLT

What an amazing man of God. Paul had no concern for death—as long as the truth of Jesus was proclaimed. Many of his friends were undoubtedly hoping and praying for his deliverance from imprisonment at the hands of Rome. Paul was even more concerned that they hold firmly to the faith: "Hold firmly to the word of life. And then I will be able to boast on the day of Christ that I did not run or labor in vain. But even if I am being poured out like a drink offering on the sacrifice and service coming from your faith, I am glad and rejoice with all of you" (vv. 16–17, NIV).

Paul's letter to the Philippians is a gospel of joy. Imprisonment is not enough to rob us of God's joy. Neither is being on the receiving end of jealousy and resentment from others. Not even the threat of death can rob us of joy. It would seem that we alone can push true joy from our lives when we let our focus stray from the wonder of Christ and a concern for others.

I am so thankful for Philippians and Paul's lovely invitation that we share in the same joy. I want to pass that joy on and say to you, Rejoice, share in this joy. The Word says this is the day that the Lord has made. We will rejoice and be glad in it! Joy unspeakable, full of glory!

Thank you for a joy that goes so deep into my being that no external circumstance can take it away from me. You are so kind to me, Lord.

BLESSED ASSURANCE

*Let us draw near to God with a sincere heart and with
the full assurance that faith brings, having our hearts sprinkled to cleanse us
from a guilty conscience and having our bodies washed with pure water.*

HEBREWS 10:22, NIV

I have many memories of standing next to my Nan in church as she sung this song with every fiber of her being. If you have given your heart to Jesus, then be assured He is yours—and that's something to sing about!

> Blessed assurance, Jesus is mine!
> O what a foretaste of glory divine!
> Heir of salvation, purchase of God,
> Born of his Spirit, washed in his blood.
>
> *Refrain*
> This is my story, this is my song,
> Praising my Savior, all the day long;
> This is my story, this is my song,
> Praising my Savior, all the day long.
>
> Perfect submission, all is at rest
> I in my Savior am happy and blest,
> Watching and waiting, looking above,
> Filled with his goodness, lost in his love.

*Savior God, I am happy and blessed.
Thank you for filling me with your goodness and love.*

HOPE IN YOUR WORD

My soul faints with longing for your salvation,
but I have put my hope in your word.

PSALM 119:81, NIV

*M*aybe we can't quite relate to David the giant killer, but we can relate to David in the way he expresses his raw emotions. "My soul faints with longing." All of us have had moments of such intense longing in life that we thought we might fall over in a faint. David calls out to God from the depths of his discouragement in the very next verse when he says, "My eyes fail, looking for your promise; I say, 'When will you comfort me?'" (v. 82).

Does this indicate David has lost faith in God's promise to him? Not at all. He has already declared, "I have put my hope in your word." He may get knocked down, but his faith is resilient enough that he never stays down. I don't believe his sense of desperation indicates less faith, but rather emphasizes just how much faith he really has. If his hope is sure in the midst of such sorrow, then that is indeed a true faith.

Have you made your declaration of hope in God and His Word? You might not be feeling an urgent need to declare your hope. Thank God for His goodness and for the peace you are experiencing. But don't be lulled to sleep. Life will always be filled with sweetness as well as challenges. When the challenges come, we need a sure anchor for our soul. Our anchor is Christ. In Him I have put my trust.

My hope is in you, O Lord. I don't put my hope in the false securities
the world promises. I believe in you and your love
and your faithfulness to carry me through every condition of this life.

THE ETERNAL WORD

Your word, Lord, is eternal; it stands firm in the heavens.
Your faithfulness continues through all generations; you established the earth,
and it endures. Your laws endure to this day, for all things serve you.

PSALM 119:89–91, NIV

Nations and civilizations and cultures rise and fall. Leaders are here today and gone tomorrow. Big ideas and discoveries promise to define the world as it really is, only to be proven inadequate by another round of ideas and discoveries. But not everything passes away. God himself is eternal; He has no beginning and no end. From the heart of the eternal God comes His eternal Word. It is based on His love and faithfulness for those He created, for you and me.

Is it any wonder David could endure trials and tribulations of every kind? He was a man of the world, well acquainted with military arts and diplomacy. He had keen insights into the human heart. But his might with the sword and in negotiations were never the source of his steadfastness. For David, it always came back to God's faithfulness. God created him, chose him, anointed him, protected him, strengthened him, used him. God never failed him. He knew without a shadow of a doubt God's Word would never let him down.

It is so for you and for me. God will never let us down. Situations will change. Ideas will come and go. But His faithfulness, His Word is eternal and will be with us forever.

Thank you that in a world of change I can count on you
and your promises, God. I will serve you all my days.
I delight in your will and your teachings.

I LOVE YOUR WORD!

Oh, how I love your law! I meditate on it all day long.
Your commands are always with me and make me wiser than my enemies.
I have more insight than all my teachers, for I meditate on your statutes.

PSALM 119:97–99, NIV

I certainly believe in showing great respect to the learned. I delight in hearing the words of a wise Bible teacher. My heart is fed as God's Word is explained with deeper insight and great revelation. But our friend David points out that God's Word is accessible to all of us.

When we hold fast to and meditate on the words from the Bible, we are given insights and understanding; we are taught how to walk wisely in order to avoid evil; we are taught obedience; and life in Christ is modeled for us continually. All this comes from the Holy Spirit, the One Jesus said would live in us and teach us all of God's words.

I think the elders and teachers that David was referring to were those who knew about God but didn't actually know God. They understood the meaning of every word in the Law and Prophets but didn't believe in them enough to live them.

In James we read, "Do not merely listen to the word, and so deceive yourselves. Do what it says. Anyone who listens to the word but does not do what it says is like someone who looks at his face in a mirror and, after looking at himself, goes away and immediately forgets what he looks like" (1:22–24).

My friends, let's be hearers and doers of God's Word. Your obedience will open the floodgates of the wisdom and insights God desires to impart to you!

Thank you for teaching me how you want me to live my life in simple but radical faith and love, dear Lord. Thank you for increasing my wisdom and understanding as I walk in your ways.

SWEETER THAN HONEY

How sweet are your words to my taste, sweeter than honey to my mouth!

PSALM 119:103, NIV

When young Hebrew children were sent to school—perhaps the simple home of the village teacher—to learn God's Word, the first passage they learned was Deuteronomy 6:4–5: "Hear, O Israel: The Lord our God, the Lord is one. Love the Lord your God with all your heart and with all your soul and with all your strength." The tradition was that after they memorized these words that were to be the heart and soul of everything else they learned, each child was given a treat covered in honey. From the earliest age they were taught that God's Word is sweet to the taste!

As we continue through Psalm 119, the longest chapter in the Bible, and David's revelation on the beauty, guidance, protection, wisdom, wonder, faithfulness, and joy found in God's Word, I challenge you to stay hungry for His Word, not allowing the reading of it to become a chore to you, just another thing you have to do. No, my friends, digging into God's Word, seeking Him there with all our heart, is sweeter than honey. When we draw near to God through His Word with expectation and enthusiasm, we discover a world of delight that lifts burdens and gives the answers we so desperately need.

Have your recent experiences in Bible reading been less than fulfilling? Ask God to meet you there. Ask God to reveal himself to you. Tell God how much you love Him and how you long to see Him there. Then open your Bible and prepare yourself for a treat that is sweeter than even honey.

Thank you, Savior God, for the joy you have given me in life.
Thank you for the joy I receive in your Word.

A LAMP AND A LIGHT

Your word is a lamp for my feet, a light on my path.

PSALM 119:105, NIV

God's Word is given to us as a light and a lamp. As a light it illuminates the world as it really is and allows us to see what we could not see in darkness. Because of the fall there are things we just don't "get" in the natural. We need God's Word to understand Him and our true spiritual nature.

There is something very important to understand here. The light we receive is not just about what goes into our mind. It is to guide our steps on the path we must walk. God's Word is given for every aspect of our life. If we stay in a safe place and never step out in faith, the lamp we have been given stays right there with us. But God's Word is not just for our delight; it is to be lived and shared in a dark world.

Throughout Scripture oil is a symbol of the Holy Spirit—the One inside us, our Teacher. He is the oil that fuels our light, Christ in us, the hope of glory. We read His Word and we worship Jesus as a response to His love for us, and through being near to Him we are fueled. Maybe your morning devotion times have become too much of a routine: read a devotional thought, read a Bible passage, say a prayer. All of this is beautiful, but if your heart is not engaged, you are simply going through the motions. Go for a walk, pray and look up, speak out Scripture, play worship music, and invite God to be near. What matters is that God's words become more than words to you. They will bring life and light, revelation and truth.

Your Word has guided and protected me so many times in life, O Lord.
I'm certain that there have been times when I didn't even know you were keeping
my feet from a dangerous path. Thank you for being my Light and lamp.

STREAMS OF TEARS

Streams of tears flow from my eyes, for your law is not obeyed.

PSALM 119:136, NIV

*D*avid has such a passion for God's Word in his own life and in the lives of others. He celebrates the deliverance he has received from obeying God's Word. But his heart is broken at the plight of the lost and the wicked who are living without God and His wisdom in their lives.

Just look around, and you can't miss the needless and senseless self-inflicted hurts and sorrows so many experience from refusing to acknowledge God and living outside the guidance and protection of His Word.

But this is a call and reminder that we have the great privilege of being able to share the love and light of Christ that has been shared with us. After all, each one of us was lost and bumping around in the dark before some brought the good news of Jesus Christ to us. I am so thankful.

David encourages us to allow our hearts to be moved with compassion for those who need Jesus, to let tears flow down our cheeks for those living without God. Who is God drawing you toward with the love and light He has put in your heart? You'll be surprised by how receptive people are.

Thank you for the one you sent into my life to show me how much you love and care for me, my Lord. I am forever grateful to them for being the messenger of your good news in Jesus Christ. Thank you that I can share your love with someone who is desperate for your saving grace today.

THE PEACE OF GOD'S WORD

Great peace have those who love your law, and nothing can make them stumble.
I wait for your salvation, Lord, and I follow your commands.

PSALM 119:165, NIV

There is a peace that is ours that the world can neither give nor take away. The prophet Isaiah says, "The fruit of that righteousness will be peace; its effect will be quietness and confidence forever" (32:17).

David is contrasting the love of the world with the love of God's law that John describes in the gospel and letters he wrote in the New Testament. When our love is for doing our will and getting our own way, when our love is in chasing after all the temptations the world offers, a noisy strife and a loss of peace with self and others always follows. The things we thought were going to make us happy become the very things that bring us such turmoil. C. S. Lewis said, "God cannot give us a happiness and peace apart from himself, because it is not there. There is no such thing."

True happiness, true peace is only found in seeking God with all our heart. When we love God and His Word, we are able to walk with integrity and a quiet calm that defies everything happening all around us. There may be evil and heartache surrounding us that can bring persecution and turmoil into our lives, but we can still experience a peace that is beyond understanding in Christ Jesus.

Psalm 119 has been about focus; focus on God's Word. Turn your eyes and attention to the things of God, for He is our peace.

You are the God of peace, and I worship you today.
Thank you for the gift of your peace that is mine. I pray that my eyes will be
focused on you and my steps will walk peacefully in your ways.

I HAVE STRAYED

Let me live that I may praise you, and may your
laws sustain me. I have strayed like a lost sheep. Seek your servant,
for I have not forgotten your commands.

PSALM 119:175–76, NIV

The cry and anguish of David after he has fallen short of God's will for him is expressed beautifully in the words of the prophet Isaiah. Let the beauty of this passage sink deep into your heart today as you celebrate God's salvation.

But the fact is, it was our pains he carried—our disfigurements, all the things wrong with us. We thought he brought it on himself, that God was punishing him for his own failures. But it was our sins that did that to him, that ripped and tore and crushed him—our sins! He took the punishment, and that made us whole. Through his bruises we get healed. We're all like sheep who've wandered off and gotten lost. We've all done our own thing, gone our own way. And God has piled all our sins, everything we've done wrong, on him, on him. . . .

Therefore I'll reward him extravagantly—the best of everything, the highest honors—Because he looked death in the face and didn't flinch, because he embraced the company of the lowest. He took on his own shoulders the sin of the many, he took up the cause of all the black sheep.

Isaiah 53:4–6, 12, THE MESSAGE

I am forever grateful that you bore my sins when
I had gone astray. Thank you for your redeeming love for me
and the entire world, O God.

SPIRITUAL JOYS

A Classic Devotion by Thomas Watson

*You will show me the path of life; in Your presence is abundant joy;
in Your right hand are pleasures forevermore.*

PSALM 16:11, HCSB

Spiritual joys are abiding joys. Worldly joys are soon gone. Such as bathe in the perfumed waters of pleasure—may have joys which seem to be sweet—but they are swift. They are like meteors—which give a bright and sudden flash, and then disappear. But the joys which believers have are abiding; they are a blossom of eternity—a pledge of those rivers of pleasure which run at God's right hand! "In your presence is abundant joy; in your right hand are eternal pleasures!"

If God gives His people such joy in this life, oh! then, what glorious joy will He give them in heaven! "Enter into the joy of your Lord!" God keeps His best wine until last. What joy will that be—when the soul shall forever bathe itself in the pure and pleasant fountain of God's love! What joy will that be—to see the orient brightness of Christ's face, and have the kisses of those lips which drop sweet-smelling myrrh!

How may this set us all longing for that place where sorrow cannot live—and where joy cannot die!

*Thank you for your gift of joy, my heavenly Father.
Thank you for giving me a joy that will last forever!*

RISEN ONE

JESUS CONQUERED THE GRAVE.
HE IS ALIVE!

JULY

Christ the Lord is risen today, Alleluia!
Sons of Men & angels say, Alleluia!!!
Raise your joys & triumphs high, Alleluia!
Sing, ye heavens, & earth, reply, Alleluia!!!

Lives again our glorious King, Alleluia!
Where, O death, is now thy Sting? Alleluia!!!
Once He died our souls to save, Alleluia!
Where thy victory, O grave? Alleluia!!!

King Jesus is risen! ✝

SUSTAINING ALL THINGS

The Son is the radiance of God's glory and the exact representation of his being, sustaining all things by his powerful word. After he had provided purification for sins, he sat down at the right hand of the Majesty in heaven.

HEBREWS 1:3, NIV

God has spoken to His beloved children in many ways throughout history. There have been prophets and other messengers who shared who God is and what He expects from His creation. But in Jesus Christ, "the radiance of God's glory," "the exact representation of his being"—the second person of the Godhead—God has given us His ultimate revelation. The Son was with the Father in the moment of creation and shines with His glory. He sustains all things. This is the same thought shared by Paul when he says, "He is before all things, and in him all things hold together" (Colossians 1:17).

Is it any wonder Jesus is worthy of all our praise? With God, as God, He is with His Father, the Creator and Sustainer of life. Through His death and resurrection He has purified us from our sins. He sits beside His Father in heaven. The name He has been given is not only precious to you and me; it is precious to the Father.

Hebrews is written to those living under the shadow of persecution. I pray your life is safe today. But I also know that at various times and various ways all of us come under attack. Never forget that the One who loves and created you is the One who sustains you—and everything else in the world—today.

Glorious Creator and Sustainer, I love and adore you.
I give you all my praise and thanksgiving.

ALIVE AND ACTIVE

For the word of God is alive and active. Sharper than any
double-edged sword, it penetrates even to dividing
soul and spirit, joints and marrow;
it judges the thoughts and attitudes of the heart.

HEBREWS 4:12, NIV

God is not distant and aloof. He doesn't give us the cold shoulder but speaks to us—through His Word and Spirit. We don't have to guess what is on God's mind or beg Him to tell us what His will is for us. His thoughts are recorded in the Bible, which is alive and active today. The Bible was written in antiquity, but it is no dusty tomb that is irrelevant to what is happening today.

As much as I pray that God's Word will be a huge part of your life, I must also warn you. Beware when you open your Bible. Like a mighty warrior's sword, it is razor sharp and cuts from both sides. Any of us who have read God's Word know firsthand what a source of joy and comfort it is. But we likewise know it cuts to the core. It cuts through excuses and attitudes of pride. God's Word always goes to the heart of the matter. God loves us enough to correct us and bring us back on course when we have gotten off His path for our lives.

Yes, it's true, God's Word can hurt. Never wield it carelessly. Read it in awe, knowing that God is penetrating your spirit and soul with wisdom, comfort, healing, correction—and all the truth you need in life.

Your word is a lamp unto my feet and a light unto my path.
Thank you, heavenly Father, that you speak words of life into my soul and spirit
through the pages of my Bible.

HOLD FIRMLY

*Therefore, since we have a great high priest who has ascended into heaven,
Jesus the Son of God, let us hold firmly to the faith we profess.*

HEBREWS 4:14, NIV

The book of Hebrews was written to Christians who were undergoing intense persecution. Just because you and I may live in relative peace and comfort, we must never forget that persecution is a present-day reality for many. It nearly breaks my heart to think of dear brothers and sisters who face hardship—and even death—because they lift up the name of our Lord Jesus Christ. We must continue to pray and take action where we can.

The writer of this magnificent letter reminds us what a wonderful Savior we have. As our "great high priest," Jesus is our bridge, the only way to God. The Hebrews reading these words would have understood the role of a priest as an intermediary between God and man, offering a blood sacrifice to cancel the people's sins in God's eyes. But Jesus was no ordinary priest. The next verse reads: "We do not have a high priest who is unable to empathize with our weaknesses, but we have one who has been tempted in every way, just as we are—yet he did not sin."

Remembering—praising and worshiping—our caring, compassionate, and perfect Lord is what gives us the strength to "hold firmly" to our faith, no matter what circumstances we face, whether dire need or plenty.

Hold firmly to the faith you have professed—and remember to pray for the deliverance of our brothers and sisters in Christ who suffer for His name.

*Father, with my every breath and every song I will profess my faith in you.
Even when I face trials I will hold firmly to you.*

HE SHARED OUR HUMANITY

Since the children have flesh and blood, he too shared in their humanity so that
by his death he might break the power of him who holds the power of death—that is,
the devil—and free those who all their lives were held in slavery by their fear of death.

HEBREWS 2:14–15, NIV

When a slave has been set free, our only response can be to praise God! Slavery was common in the first century of the Christian Era. But it has never gone away. In fact, there are more slaves alive today than in any time in history. We read and hear horrific stories of twenty-first-century slave trade, and our hearts are broken. I want to support my brothers and sisters in Christ who are at the forefront of exposing this trade that is straight from the pit of hell.

I cannot help but be reminded that much of the world is still trapped in spiritual slavery. The same evil force that steals the physical lives is at work in the spiritual realm. But we have a Savior who breaks the chains of death and destruction. He didn't do His work from afar. He entered the field of battle as flesh and blood, laying down His life as the ultimate sacrifice so that we could be free. And what a freedom we have. Not even the threat of death and the fear it produces can rob us of God's gift to us.

Let us pray for those who are still in slavery today, whether at the hands of evildoers or lost in their sins. But let's not stop with prayer. Let's work and give and speak up for the oppressed of the world. Let's pray for all those in battle on the front lines. And may we never take for granted the glorious gift of the One who left His rightful place in heaven to share in our humanity and bring ultimate freedom.

O God, you love us so much. Even when we had turned to our own ways,
you left your throne of glory in the person of Jesus Christ to break the chains
that bound us. I am forever grateful.

THE ANTIDOTE FOR DECEIT

See to it, brothers and sisters, that none of you has a sinful,
unbelieving heart that turns away from the living God.

HEBREWS 3:12, NIV

This Scripture makes it clear that even as a Christian, your heart can still become hardened if you don't tend to it well. And even as God's beloved children, we can rebel from Him, breaking the heart of our loving heavenly Father. And oh how such tragic rebellion hurts those who are friends and loved ones. We have all seen someone who was bold in their faith lose heart. Is it any wonder the writer to the Hebrews calls us to "encourage one another daily, as long as it is called 'Today,' so that none of you may be hardened by sin's deceitfulness" (v. 13).

Sin is deceitful. But we stand firm if we encourage each other and "hold our original conviction firmly to the very end" (v. 14). I want to stand firm to the end, and I know you do too.

Are you holding firm to the conviction that was yours in the moment of your salvation? And are you surrounded by brothers and sisters who encourage your faith—and whom you are called to encourage in kind?

People can disappoint us, and we can disappoint others. So ultimately our confidence must be in God alone. But God also calls us to be part of a fellowship of those who share our love for Him. There are times when I need to be alone to worship my God from the depths of my heart. But oh how I love the coming together of the church gathering to bring praise, sharing our common song that flows from the same conviction and love. I am so thankful for the love, community, and encouragement of those around me.

I praise you, my gracious and loving Father. Strengthen me in my convictions
and let me be an encouragement to those around me.

HE MEETS OUR NEED

Such a high priest truly meets our need—one who is holy, blameless, pure, set apart from sinners, exalted above the heavens. Unlike the other high priests, he does not need to offer sacrifices day after day, first for his own sins, and then for the sins of the people. He sacrificed for their sins once for all when he offered himself.

HEBREWS 7:26–27, NIV

What is your need? Do you struggle with a particular temptation that drags you down spiritually? Is there a damaged relationship in your life? Are there hurts from your past that seem to haunt you? Is your faith wavering? You are not alone. All of us have felt hopeless and weak at some time in our lives. But the real reason you are not alone is simply Jesus. He is near. And in Him is every provision to meet every need in your life.

Even our heroes of the faith have had times where they compromised their convictions. Moses murdered a man in rage. David fell into the sin of adultery and made a horrible situation worse when he had a trusted friend killed. Bold Peter denied Jesus out of fear in the presence of a servant girl. But Jesus was perfect. He never once fell into sin. And like priests before Him, He offered a sacrifice for the sins of the people. But His sacrifice was so much greater—in giving himself He provided the sacrifice that endures throughout all eternity.

Whatever your need, turn to the One who is exalted above the heavens. Turn to the One who loved you so much that He died for you. Such a high priest—such a Savior—truly meets even our deepest need.

Father, thank you for reaching down to me with a love that is sufficient for every need in my life, that goes beyond all my wrongdoing. Thank you for the gift of your Son!

WAITING FOR HIM

*Just as people are destined to die once, and after that to face judgment, so Christ
was sacrificed once to take away the sins of many; and he will appear a second time,
not to bear sin, but to bring salvation to those who are waiting for him.*

HEBREWS 9:27–28, NIV

One of the fruits of the Spirit is patience. There are many times we must wait
for the fulfillment of a hope or desire. In Proverbs 3:12, Solomon states,
"Hope deferred makes the heart sick, but a longing fulfilled is a tree of life." The
man with the wisdom of God noted that all of us want to see our hopes and dreams
come to fruition and grow heartsick when it seems like that is not happening.

I can't tell you when God's purpose for you will become manifest. But I can say
without reservation that the most important wait in your life, the hope of a Savior, is
over. Christ died for you and now appears before you to give you the deepest desire of
your heart: peace with God. Other plans and purposes might unfold over a schedule
that is hard to understand, but your need for salvation is fulfilled the moment you turn
to Jesus in faith and ask Him to forgive you of your sins.

God is doing a mighty work in His world and in your life. We can't always see it.
Sometimes it is like a seed that is buried beneath the ground. A miracle is happening,
but we won't see it until it bursts forth from the soil. But the foundational work—your
salvation and transformation into godliness—is present and visible right now. Let
that incredible truth guard your soul from any spiritual discouragement today.

*In Jesus' holy name, I thank you, Father, for what you are doing in and through me.
I don't always see the evidence of all I hope for, but I know you are working
and there will be a harvest in season.*

ENTER BOLDLY

*Therefore, brothers and sisters, since we have confidence to enter
the Most Holy Place by the blood of Jesus . . .*

HEBREWS 10:19, NIV

When the prophet Isaiah went to worship and truly saw the Lord high and lifted up, seated on His throne, he was awestruck. He saw a chorus of angels singing, "Holy, holy, holy is the Lord Almighty; the whole earth is full of his glory" (Isaiah 6:3). He fell in terror and all he could say was: "Woe to me! . . . I am ruined! For I am a man of unclean lips, and I live among a people of unclean lips, and my eyes have seen the King, the Lord Almighty" (v. 5). It was only after the Lord sent an angel to divinely anoint him that Isaiah could boldly respond to God's anointing on his life.

God is to be honored and respected above others. The first two commandments God gave to Moses were that He alone was to be honored as God, and His name was to never be taken in vain. That makes the invitation of Hebrews 10:19 all the more amazing and powerful. For the King of Kings, the mighty One, has commanded us to come into His very presence with confidence. *The Message* reads, "So, friends, we can now—without hesitation—walk right up to God, into 'the Holy Place.'"

Sometimes I feel a little bit like Isaiah. I am timid to walk into God's presence. I feel unworthy. But worship begins, and my heart is filled with His glory, the boldness that is commanded takes root in my heart.

Do you feel hesitant, unworthy, to enter God's presence? By Jesus' blood you have been given a grand invitation that is greater than any fear or inadequacy you might feel. Come boldly!

<hr />

*Thank you, God in heaven, for inviting me to come into your presence
as a beloved child, bold and confident that you are my loving Father.*

WORSHIPING TOGETHER

Let's see how inventive we can be in encouraging love and helping out,
not avoiding worshiping together as some do but spurring each other on,
especially as we see the big Day approaching.

HEBREWS 10:24–25, THE MESSAGE

*S*ometimes Jesus pulled away from the crowds so He could be alone to commune with His heavenly Father. I am thankful that my Jesus shares needs and feelings I have, just as He does with you. But the need for private time should never turn into the "avoiding of worshiping together." The great English evangelist John Wesley once said, "The Bible knows nothing of solitary religion." Our faith, our hope, our salvation is to share with the world in evangelism, and with our brothers and sisters in Christ as mutual edification.

We truly need one another in a relationship of giving and receiving. Do you have a place of worship, a local church family where you can turn to others? Are you in a place of worship where others can turn to you? Churches can come in all sizes and styles. What matters is that the Word is proclaimed, Jesus is lifted up, and there is a love for one another that makes it almost impossible to lose heart.

The Hebrews this letter was written to lived in a time of persecution and discouragement. The writer doesn't tell them that their troubles are almost over. They were to continue meeting "all the more as you see the Day approaching" (NIV). Was it the day of judgment? Was it a day of greater persecution? Either way, it was an urgent reminder that we can't fall out of the habit of meeting together: We need each other. Run to this house today. You never know what miracles await.

Thank you, Father, for the brothers and sisters in Christ
you have put into my life. Help me to always be an encourager and builder.
Help me to receive the blessings that come from others.

RICHLY REWARDED

So do not throw away your confidence; it will be richly rewarded.

HEBREWS 10:35, NIV

I love Paul's simple advice, "Do not be anxious about anything, but in every situation, by prayer and petition, with thanksgiving, present your requests to God" (Philippians 4:6). One can't help but sense the urgency the writer of Hebrews feels for this besieged Christian community.

In the verses leading up to our key verse he says: "Remember those earlier days after you had received the light, when you endured in a great conflict full of suffering. Sometimes you were publicly exposed to insult and persecution; at other times you stood side by side with those who were so treated. You suffered along with those in prison and joyfully accepted the confiscation of your property, because you knew that you yourselves had better and lasting possessions" (vv. 30–34).

He doesn't want them to lose their confidence. He wants them to know that their perseverance will result in rich reward. I confess that if I were in his place, I would probably have worried hard and prayed hard for my friends living in such tribulation.

As I've traveled to many places where there is such physical deprivation for proclaiming the name of Jesus, I am encouraged to see the church in all her diversity standing stronger, shining brighter, refusing to be afraid, understanding and declaring that nothing can separate us from His love.

This passage for me today is a call to pray for God's children all over the world—from those I know to those I will never meet on this earth. We pray for strength, courage, and joy in God's great presence.

My confidence is in you, O God. Even in good times, I have no other hope that is sure and true. I lift up my persecuted brothers and sisters so their confidence remains sure.

JESUS CHRIST IS RISEN TODAY

He is not here; he has risen, just as he said.

MATTHEW 28:6, NIV

Hallelujah! On the marvelous day of His resurrection, Jesus became our Victor and completed His work. That's reason to sing and praise.

Christ the Lord is risen today, Alleluia!
Sons of men and angels say, Alleluia!
Raise your joys and triumphs high, Alleluia!
Sing, ye heavens, and earth, reply, Alleluia!

Lives again our glorious King, Alleluia!
Where, O death, is now thy sting? Alleluia!
Once He died our souls to save, Alleluia!
Where thy victory, O grave? Alleluia!

Soar we now where Christ hath led, Alleluia!
Following our exalted Head, Alleluia!
Made like Him, like Him we rise, Alleluia!
Ours the cross, the grave, the skies, Alleluia!

Hymns of praise then let us sing, Alleluia!
Unto Christ, our heavenly King, Alleluia!
Who endured the cross and grave, Alleluia!
Sinners to redeem and save. Alleluia!

Thank you for your redeeming work, my God. Thank you that Jesus fought the fight and won, for my salvation and the salvation of the world.

YOU HAVE BEEN DISPLEASED

O God, You have cast us off; You have broken us down;
You have been displeased; Oh, restore us again!

PSALM 60:1, NKJV

*D*avid is ready to celebrate. He has just waged a great campaign from the northern point of his kingdom against Syria and won a mighty victory. But almost immediately after the fighting has ended, a messenger brings him word that Edom has invaded Judah from the south. David is shaken to his core. In verse 2 he says, "You have made the earth tremble." It's as if an earthquake has pierced his soul. He is shocked and confused. In verse 3 he declares, "You have made us drink the wine of confusion."

Most of all he is distraught. "You have cast us off; You have broken us down; You have been displeased."

Why would God allow such a terrible thing to happen? What had the people done to displease Him? Israel had been in inner strife and turmoil for such a long time as a legacy of Saul's leadership. David wanted something more for his nation. He wanted God's full approval and blessing. David knew that facing an army was one thing, but facing life under the displeasure of God was worse than all the armies in the world arrayed against the country.

David expressed the full gamut of emotions but then took a moment, a selah, and then returned to his dependence on God. "Oh, restore us again!" He knows where his help and hope come from. Do you have that sure confidence when all around you seems to be crashing in and an army is coming from the south?

Restore me again, O God. I thought everything was under control,
but there's a new battle waging in my life. Be pleased with me and bless me.
I know you have made a way.

A VICTORY BANNER

You have given a banner to those who fear You, that it may be displayed because of the truth. Selah.

PSALM 60:4, NKJV

*E*very battle we face in life represents a moment of decision. Read through the Psalms to see David himself faced over and over with the decision to despair or to trust. David could have given up and asked for terms of surrender. Undoubtedly many of his advisers urged him to do so. But what does this champion of the faith do? He unfurls a war banner and marches into battle. With God on his side, David knew that a war banner was already a victory banner.

Do you feel let down? Pressured from every side? Does it feel like life is a series of battles? Are you ready to rest? It is decision time for you. Do you brood on all the times you feel you've been let down and fall into despair? Or do you pick up the language of faith and dependence and talk of the unfailing promises of God? Do you give a shout and raise a victory banner or disappear into the shadows? I'll warn you that carrying the war banner makes you a target. That's why only the bravest men were entrusted to unfurl them in battle.

A banner signifies the Lord's favor, that God is with you in any fight. It is your guarantee of victory. So what will it be? Fight or flight? I say we stand in confidence that God is fighting for us. He has overcome.

Thank you for the favor you have shown me so many times in life, O God. Thank you for being the guarantee of my victory. Give me the faith of a champion.

BOLDLY REJOICE

*God has spoken in His holiness: "I will rejoice; I will divide Shechem
and measure out the valley of Succoth."*

PSALM 60:6, NKJV

Do we rejoice after our victory? Of course. But we also rejoice before and during the battle. I will rejoice. David knew the secret of success: complete dependence on the greatness of God. What did it take for him to recharge his batteries and head back into battle? He turned to God and His holy Word: "God has spoken in His holiness."

My friends, praise and worship don't begin when everything is fixed in life. It begins when we see the storm clouds blowing our way. It picks up fervency in the midst of the storm. It is a crescendo when the victory is ours. It is rooted in a vision of God and His holiness. Don't worry if you are strong enough for the fight ahead of you. Worship God!

David's faith is so bold that he begins dividing up the spoils of war and the lands before he even knows what he has to face. "I will divide Shechem and measure out the valley of Succoth."

There is a pride that leads to destruction. But David wasn't puffed up with pride. He was puffed up with God. He was bold in his faith because he had again seen and experienced God.

Whatever battle you face, let praise and worship overflow from your heart and lips.

*Thank you for the victory that is mine in and through you, O Lord.
Thank you for Jesus Christ, my Victor in whatever I face in life.*

Victor's Crown ♡

You are always fighting for us
Heaven's angels all around
My delight is found in knowing
that YOU wear the VICTOR'S crown

You're my Help & my Defender,
My Savior & my friend... by your
grace I live & breathe to worship
You.

THE WASHPOT

Gilead is Mine, and Manasseh is Mine; Ephraim also is the helmet for My head;
Judah is My lawgiver. Moab is My washpot; over Edom I will cast My shoe;
Philistia, shout in triumph because of Me.

PSALM 60:7–8, NKJV

I dug into this psalm at the beginning of one year and immediately wondered why I had started here. It was the phrase "Moab is my washpot" that honestly made me a bit squeamish. Not a very lovely word picture. But as I continued to read and reflect on these verses, even that image became a powerful teaching to me. I started to get excited about the principles from this psalm and how crucial these lessons are to each of our lives.

One of the things I learned is that even though some victories are won before they even commence, God still requires us to stand in faith as both an act of obedience and a witness to others. "Moab is my washpot." The washpot was where dirty feet were cleansed after a muddy battle or dusty journey. David is stating with total confidence that this nation coming against him would become his servant, washing his feet after losing to him in the battle. David would do more than go through the motions in the battle, but he already had dominion over enemies in his heart.

Was this foolish overconfidence? Was this a display of arrogance? Not at all. This was David expressing his absolute confidence in God. He had gone from a desperate fear in Psalm 59 to a bold confidence in Psalm 60.

How did he get there? It began when he worshiped God—not after the victory but before.

Dear God, you are my strength and salvation.
I thank you that victory is mine through the work of Jesus Christ my Lord.

THROUGH GOD

Who will bring me to the strong city? Who will lead me to Edom?
Is it not You, O God, who cast us off? And You, O God, who did not go out
with our armies? Give us help from trouble, for the help of man is useless.
Through God we will do valiantly, for it is He who shall tread down our enemies.

PSALM 60:9–12, NKJV

*B*ottom line, how will you do it? How will you win the victory? Whatever you are going through, you may feel like God is a long way away. But believe me, He is closer than your next breath and ready to intervene in His perfect time.

And that's exactly how you will be victorious—without compromise and living in a state of constant fear. You will win through Him. Gathering more armies to help you won't do it. The help of man is useless for certain battles. No, whatever you are facing, God is calling you to a bold and gutsy faith. If a mighty warrior like David knew he couldn't prevail without help from God, then it must be the same for us.

David asks, "Who will lead me?" He already knows the answer. He is simply making it clear that he needs God at every moment. Without the hand of God over his every move, he would be lost, whether in the midst of a battle or on a solitary mountaintop. There is no vanity in his actions, just a bold and simple trust.

Are you willing to trust God as never before today? Are you ready for God to take your heart from desperation to bold faith? Sing praises. Worship. Lift the victory banner. Call to God. He is always ready to deliver you.

❧

God, I am bold because you are with me. I am victorious
because you conquer my enemies. Thank you for your faithfulness to me.
I praise and worship you with all my heart.

HEAR ME!

Hear my cry, O God; attend to my prayer.
From the end of the earth I will cry to You.

PSALM 61:1, NKJV

*P*salm 61 was to be accompanied by stringed instruments. So if you play the guitar, piano, or another stringed instrument, add music to this reading!

In the first three verses we find David crying out to God with all his heart. "Hear my cry, O God; attend to my prayer." This is an earnest cry for help. It is not the prayer of a casual worshiper, but it is the cry of a man who has learned that in times of trouble he has nowhere else to turn and no one else to trust other than the Lord. I get the sense that he is not going to stop praying until he knows that he has the full attention of heaven. He was bold in battle and bold in prayer and worship!

Charles Spurgeon said, "Pharisees may rest in their prayers, true believers are eager for an answer to them. Ritualists may be satisfied when they have said or sung their litanies, but living children of God will never rest till their supplications have entered the ears of the Lord himself."

Can we do that? Can we demand that heaven hear us? If it is an expression of our absolute dependence on and faith in God, then Scripture tells us yes. I cry out, confident I am heard. Lord, thank you for the great privilege we have of being heard by you, always.

Thank you for hearing my cry, O Lord. Thank you for
your presence and help in all my situations of life!

LONGING FOR GOD

I will abide in Your tabernacle forever;
I will trust in the shelter of Your wings. Selah.

PSALM 61:4, NKJV

avid was far from home, and undoubtedly he was suffering a moment of feeling far from God. But David was never one to give up and fall into despair or disbelief. He never stopped praying.

As I have studied this passage and where it might fit in David's personal history, I have come to the conclusion that this was written when David's son Absalom led a revolt and had his father driven from Jerusalem. David had lost his home. But even more painful to him, he had no access to the tabernacle, the place of community worship. In these ancient times, to be absent from the place of divine worship was like having your breath taken from you. You were absolutely divorced from what mattered most. Forced exile from Jerusalem would have felt like being banished to the ends of the earth for David.

The opening of this verse can be interpreted as either longing or a statement. Both fit all we know about this man of faith! David seems to be telling us he longs for the tabernacle while at the same time declaring he in fact will dwell in the tabernacle forever.

Do you feel alone? Have you been separated from those you love? Don't lose hope. Hope is alive. Faith rests in the promises of God. God is close and promises to meet all your needs.

Thank you for sheltering me under your wings, O God.
Thank you for allowing me to worship in your presence now and forevermore.

A HIGHER PLACE

*From the end of the earth I will cry to You, when my heart
is overwhelmed; lead me to the rock that is higher than I.*

PSALM 61:2, NKJV

Though it sounds so contrary to say, there is great opportunity when we go through tribulation. If you open your heart to God during any painful experience, He will bring you close to Him even as He draws near to you. David seems to be the master of allowing difficult situations to walk him toward his heavenly Father. "Lead me," God's Word tells us. David isn't wallowing in misery. His faith is always active. Even in exile, he knows there is a better place for him, a rock that is higher and greater than his circumstances.

What do you do when your heart is overwhelmed? One popular saying advises us, "When the going gets tough, the tough go shopping!" You may laugh, but many people reach for temporary emotional fixes rather than reaching out to God and asking where He wants to take them. But our lovely Friend the Holy Spirit has the amazing ability to lead us to the Rock, that great towering Providential Rock that towers over any situation going on in our world.

When your heart is overwhelmed, come back to David's prayer in Psalm 61:2. Ask God to lift you higher than your situation.

*Lift me up, Lord, through your Holy Spirit. I am not willing
to wallow in self-pity. You lead me to a deeper love and understanding
of you in times of feeling overwhelmed.*

A HOPE AND A FUTURE

For You, O God, have heard my vows; You have given me
the heritage of those who fear Your name. You will prolong the king's life,
His years as many generations.

PSALM 61:5–6, NKJV

David has asked God to lead him to a place that is higher than any circumstances he is facing—even the betrayal of a family member and the loss of his position and possessions.

From the outside, some might say David is still defeated. But in the spiritual realm David is a victor, and it is only a matter of time before that is manifested in this world.

As he contemplates God's faithfulness, David takes up residence in a new place. David is now in the land of "God has heard me." Oh, God heard David even when all he could muster was a hoarse whisper. But David knows deep in his heart that he has been heard. His language has changed to a tone of confidence that God is with him—even in his state of exile and disgrace—and will lead him back to where he needs to be. His spirit is renewed as he regains his hope in the future: "You will prolong the king's life, His years as many generations."

What a promise from God. And David's faith was honored. We know firsthand because in Christ Jesus we are part of that spiritual heritage promised to David.

Even if today you feel completely unsure that things will work out, keep the faith. God is faithful to His promises.

Father God, thank you for protecting me when I felt all was lost.
Thank you for giving me a hope and a future, no matter what my circumstances.

PRAISE YOUR NAME FOREVER

So I will sing praise to Your name forever,
that I may daily perform my vows.

PSALM 61:8, NKJV

*W*hat a psalm. So many powerful life lessons. And what a testimony of faithfulness from David. He begins the psalm with a loud, desperate plea before God. He ends with a confident note of triumph, declaring that he will sing praises to God forever. It's so easy to take such a statement for granted. This was a man who had seemingly lost everything and was on the run for his life.

David teaches us that we worship God before, during, and after our battles. And this is exactly what he is doing in verse 8. David knows his strength is from God, so it is in worship that he receives the power to perform his vows. God has granted him his mercy and kindness on a daily basis, and David's response is praise and obedience, both of which are the worship God desires. This is his love song to God.

Dear friends, our God continues to wrap us in His grace that we may perform our vows and keep our hearts pure and passionate in complete humility and service for now and evermore. I follow David's example by praising God today. Worship Him in love and obedience, with your whole life.

Your mercy and kindness sustain and strengthen me, O God.
I am so pleased to praise you today. It is my joy to serve you.

EVEN WHEN YOU CAN'T SEE

*Now faith is confidence in what we hope for and assurance about
what we do not see. This is what the ancients were commended for.*

HEBREWS 11:1–2, NIV

I enjoy books and sermons on proofs that God exists. There are so many
evidences of a creator God and the life and ministry of our Savior Jesus
Christ—not just a literary symbol but as a real human who existed and revealed His
divine character. From the preservation of the texts and the unity of the themes and
message of manuscripts written over a duration of more than a thousand years to
archaeological support for the stories, God's Word has so much to commend it as a
miracle of revelation. We truly have a "reasonable" faith.

And yet we don't come to God through proofs, through what we can see. That
is not the nature of our relationship with Him. If God wanted it that way, He could
force us to see Him as He is and for who He is. He doesn't. He asks us to accept Him
without seeing Him, on the basis of faith. Our relationship to Him is spiritual and
must start in our spirit.

First Peter 1:8 says, "Though you have not seen him, you love him." I believe in
God with all my heart. I want the same commendation that the ancients received. I
want the praise of my Savior when He said to His disciples, "Because you have seen
me, you have believed; blessed are those who have not seen and yet have believed"
(John 20:29).

My dear friends, even when it seems so hard to perceive that God is near, believe!
Let your spirit connect with the Holy Spirit in faith and substance.

*Thank you for revealing yourself to me in so many ways, heavenly Father. Thank you for
planting the seed of faith in my spirit and that I can exercise that faith and know you.*

RUN THE RACE

Therefore, since we are surrounded by such a great cloud of witnesses,
let us throw off everything that hinders and the sin that so easily entangles.
And let us run with perseverance the race marked out for us, fixing our eyes on Jesus,
the pioneer and perfecter of faith. . . . Consider him who endured
such opposition from sinners, so that you will not grow weary and lose heart.

HEBREWS 12:1–3, NIV

*E*very four years the great athletes of the world come together to showcase their talents, to compete, to be the best of the best. All the years and countless hours of training will culminate in the chance to win a gold medal.

In our Christian life, we too are surrounded by a great cloud of witnesses—all the men and women of faith who ran the race before us. Now is not the time to be encumbered by the heaviness of regrets or hurts—we get rid of everything that hinders us and the sin that so easily entangles.

But sometimes there is a weariness and the temptation to lose heart. How can we compete? The good news, my friends, is that we put our focus on Jesus. This is not a competition against others, but a race set before us as individuals. We fix our eyes on what He has done for us when He endured the cross. We find our weary muscles strengthened and our spirits renewed.

Are you ready to race—not just talk about it but do it? What things are hindering your spiritual life? What sins have entangled you? Where are your eyes fixed? Look to Jesus. He has run the race and will lift you up and carry you each stride. A heavenly crown awaits you. Don't give up—run!

O God, thank you for Jesus, the author and perfecter of our faith.
Thank you that He is with me each stride of my spiritual race. Thank you for those
blessed saints that have gone before me and that are cheering me on.

WITH REVERENCE AND AWE

Therefore, since we are receiving a kingdom that cannot be shaken, let us be thankful, and so worship God acceptably with reverence and awe, for our "God is a consuming fire."

HEBREWS 12:28–29, NIV

The writer of Hebrews takes us back to Moses' burning bush encounter with God. He had run from Egypt in fear and shame. He was in a remote territory where all he wanted was to hide from his past—and from the burden God had placed on his heart for the plight of his people. Moses began his long journey back to Egypt to accept God's anointing on his life when he truly met God in worship. Nothing else would enable this stuttering and fearful man to boldly proclaim to Pharaoh, "Let my people go!"

What burden has God put on your heart? What assignment does He have for you that you know beyond a shadow of a doubt you don't have the ability to perform? Is it possible you are hiding from God's purpose for your life?

There is only one place to start: You must accept God's gracious invitation to meet Him face-to-face in worship. You must take off your shoes in humble acknowledgment that wherever God is is holy ground. He doesn't ask you to come before Him with everything figured out. He knows you aren't strong enough for the task ahead, so you don't have to pretend you have everything under control.

My dear friends, just worship. Worship the Almighty with reverence and awe. Let your praise and thanksgiving be all that you bring. He will provide everything else you need to face your past and accept the calling He has for you. These are great days of His power and grace.

I come before you, God Almighty, with no claim other than my love for you. I worship you with reverence and awe. Thank you!

KEEP ON LOVING

Keep on loving one another as brothers and sisters. Do not forget to show hospitality to strangers, for by so doing some people have shown hospitality to angels without knowing it. Continue to remember those in prison as if you were together with them in prison, and those who are mistreated as if you yourselves were suffering.

HEBREWS 13:1–3, NIV

I don't think we're on the same page. We have different visions. I feel strongly in my heart that I am on the right path. Maybe it's time to part ways. "Keep on loving."

I'm tired and just want some alone time. I really don't want to invite my neighbors over. Sometimes I feel awkward meeting new people. "Show hospitality to strangers."

I know God is loving and forgiving, but there are still consequences for sin. Some people end up in a bad place because of no one's fault but their own. "Remember those in prison."

I've got enough responsibilities with my own family. I know they need help, but there's only so much of me to go around. I can't take on any more. "Remember those who are mistreated as if you yourselves were suffering."

God's commands to us are simple. He hasn't created a complex system of laws and rules. His will is that we love Him through worship and love others through service. Doing His will and obeying Him don't diminish or burden us. They put us on paths of peace, joy, strength, purpose, and a never-ending source of renewal. When you live with joy, your strength is continual and the fruit of His Spirit is alive in you. When we share our lives with others, we open up the spiritual gates where God's love and blessings flow in us. Don't worry about running out of strength. Tap into the Giver of all grace and strength through loving others.

As I love others today, I know that you receive my service as love for you. I do love you and worship you with all my heart, soul, and strength.

HONOR MARRIAGE

Marriage should be honored by all, and the marriage bed kept pure,
for God will judge the adulterer and all the sexually immoral.

HEBREWS 13:4, NIV

*T*he writer to the Hebrews ends this wonderful book of worship and instruction by underscoring to us that marriage should be honored by all.

We live in a fallen world, and many have suffered a broken marriage. The whispering that comes from the enemy of our soul does not honor marriage, but treats it casually, as something that might be nice but is certainly not holy.

There are things that have happened in your life that you cannot undo. If a spouse has left you, there is no need to look back and feel your life is a failure. There may be sins in your past that brought consequences you never intended. Neither does that separate you from the love of God and His plans for your life. All you can do is walk forward in the light of God's will from this day on.

Pray for the purity of marriage. Whether single or married, honor marriage through your views and prayers. If considering marriage, commit your relationship completely to God and ask Him to confirm and bless this holy decision. If you are struggling in your marriage, don't give up and lose heart. Honor God by honoring your spouse, and let Him do His good work beyond anything you could plan or imagine.

When God calls us to be holy, He sets us apart in a special way for His use. Nowhere is that more true than in the bonds of marriage. Never forget that He will be with you every step of the way, as promised in verse 5: "Never will I leave you; never will I forsake you."

Thank you for the gift of marriage, God. Thank you for consecrating marriage
through the first miracle of Jesus. I give myself again today, heart and soul.

STOP CRITICIZING

Yes, each of us will give a personal account to God.
So let's stop condemning each other. Decide instead to live in such a way
that you will not cause another believer to stumble and fall.

ROMANS 14:12–13, NLT

There were several controversies in the early church about what was right and what was wrong. Perhaps the biggest was whether it was okay to eat meat that had been sacrificed to idols. After pagan religious ceremonies, the meat was taken to market to be sold. Some Christians said eating the meat was the same as participating in false worship. Others said that since the other religions were false religions and their own hearts were focused on Jesus, it meant nothing. It was just meat.

Interestingly, Paul says it is the ones who feel defiled by meat who are "weaker." The ones who realize that the meat means nothing are stronger. But he tells the stronger to be careful not to wound the consciences of the weaker.

To both groups he says emphatically, "Stop condemning each other!" There is room in the church for debate, for differences. We are human. We will see things differently. But when we waste so much time condemning each other over the most trivial things, we are forgetting about the real war going on. Loving one another sometimes means to keep quiet. Your opinion is not needed today! Remember, accusation is not from God, so the moment we hear from others and ourselves words of accusation and condemnation, we can know without a doubt our talk is not godly. At that moment we must immediately stop and follow God's will "to live in such a way that you will not cause another believer to stumble and fall." Where there is unity, God commands blessing (see Psalm 133). That is our promise from Him.

Father, help me to bring unity within the fellowship of believers. Help me to speak
boldly on what I believe, but always with love and grace in every word.

ALL TOGETHER

*May God, who gives this patience and encouragement, help you live
in complete harmony with each other, as is fitting for followers of Christ Jesus.
Then all of you can join together with one voice, giving praise and glory to God,
the Father of our Lord Jesus Christ.*

ROMANS 15:5–6, NLT

I love this call to worship. Paul is gathering the church to sing together. I see
this in visions all the time. The body, His body uniquely expressed across the
earth, gathered in unity, a song of faith and testimony flowing up from earth to the
King of Kings—His gathered picture of grace. He says the worship service will be in
complete harmony. I'm sure He knew someone might sing out of tune. But He is also
smiling because He knows if there is love for one another, the harmony will be just
fine and the music exquisitely beautiful.

This won't be a solo concert. It won't be one person singing for the rest of the
congregation to enjoy. It will be with one voice. Nothing is more wonderful than
a room filled to the brim with energy and passion and love because everyone is
singing together.

This worship service is going to change lives. People are going to be blessed and
grow in their faith and closeness to God. Why? The words and the music sung will
give praise and glory to God. Jesus will be lifted up. Each of us will experience the
deep and overflowing joy of honoring our Creator and Savior.

I can't wait. I want to be there now. Will you join me in a service of praise and
worship to our Victor? Let's be there all together!

*There is such joy in my heart when I lift my voice
with my brothers and sisters in Christ to give you all the praise and glory.*

TO SPAIN

I am planning to go to Spain, and when I do, I will stop off in Rome.
And after I have enjoyed your fellowship for a little while,
you can provide for my journey.

ROMANS 15:24, NLT

*I*t's a gross understatement to say that Paul was a man of energy and enthusiasm. He had physical problems. He had suffered shipwrecks. He had been beaten and left for dead. He had lived fast and hard and was getting up there in years. Time to retire and slow down, right?

You couldn't have told him that! He wasn't about to slow down. If you had said to him, "Paul, you are going to kill yourself with the pace you attack life," he might have smiled and said back to you, "Good! I'll see my Savior sooner." He wasn't winding down with aches and pains and age. In his mind, he was just getting started.

"I am planning to go to Spain. If there are people who haven't heard the good news of new life in Jesus Christ, my work isn't done. By the way, I'll stop by to see you on my way, and you can help make sure I have everything I need."

I am almost in tears when I think of this little man—Josephus said he was small in stature—ready to keep fighting for his Lord and Savior.

Most agree he didn't make it to Spain. His life ended in Rome, where he was executed. But he was ready. He was making plans. I pray that in every season of my life I will be ready. I pray for you today too, that you are energized from heaven itself, filled with joy and strength for all God has in store for you.

Thank you for your Word, your truth, your wisdom,
and those you inspired to record it for us. Thank you for Paul and this
marvelous book that teaches us tenacity through God's great grace.

THE MERCY OF JESUS

*I want mercy and not sacrifice. I want you to recognize me as God
instead of bringing me burnt offerings.*

HOSEA 6:6, NIRV

One of the most fascinating stories in the Bible is found in the life of the prophet Hosea. This prophet's life became a graphic drama that showed the relationship of God to His people.

Hosea married a prostitute. He loved and honored her, never holding her past against her. He blessed her with love and devotion. But Gomer refused to truly change her ways and heart, and after a time she began to meet other lovers. Despite her infidelity, Hosea loved her and would bring her back into his home when she would come to her senses. Finally, she left Hosea altogether. She loved the glamorous but debauched life she threw herself into. But as her beauty faded, her lovers were repulsed by her and rejected her. She ended up on the auction block as a common slave.

But Hosea still loved her. He paid the price for her freedom and brought her back to his home with all the honor and blessing she had before. What a story of unmerited favor and never-ending love. We recognize God in this drama and the people that forget the Most High God to fall in bed with other nations.

Yet God is faithful even when we are not. Jesus Christ paid the price to deliver us from bondage to sin and death once and for all. And He continues to offer that to us today even if we have been unfaithful. My friends, let's keep our devotion to God pure. What does He want from us? *Love me. Recognize me as God.*

*I do love you with all my heart, dear God. May I ever be faithful and true
to you with your grace and power sustaining my promises to you.*

A MORNING AND EVENING PRAYER

A Classic Devotion by Martin Luther

*The whole earth is filled
with awe at your wonders;
where morning dawns,
where evening fades,
you call forth songs of joy.*

PSALM 65:8, NIV

Morning

I thank you, heavenly Father, through Jesus Christ, your dear Son, that you have kept me safe from all evil and danger last night. Save me, I pray, today as well, from every evil and sin, so that all I do and the way that I live will please you. I put myself in your care, body and soul and all that I have. Let your holy angels be with me, so that the evil enemy will not gain power over me. Amen.

Evening

My heavenly Father, I thank you, through Jesus Christ, your beloved Son, that you have protected me, by your grace. Forgive, I pray, all my sins and the evil I have done. Protect me, by your grace, tonight. I put myself in your care, body and soul and all that I have. Let your holy angels be with me, so that the evil enemy will not gain power over me. Amen.

REDEEMER

JESUS REDEEMS US FROM OUR
INIQUITIES AND PURIFIES US.

AUGUST

Upon that Cross of Jesus
Mine eyes at times can see
The very dying form of One
who suffered there for me;
And from my stricken heart
with tears two wonders I confess:
The wonders of redeeming love
and my unworthiness.

♡ Redeemer, thank you!

QUIET LOVE

*Watch out! Don't do your good deeds publicly, to be admired by others,
for you will lose the reward from your Father in heaven. When you give to
someone in need, don't do as the hypocrites do—blowing trumpets
in the synagogues and streets to call attention to their acts of charity!
I tell you the truth, they have received all the reward they will ever get.*

MATTHEW 6:1–2, NLT

esus tells us: "In the same way, let your light shine before others, that they may see your good deeds and glorify your Father in heaven" (5:16, NIV). We are to be bold in serving Him through our worship and love. But then He tells us to do our good deeds in secret. Is this a contradiction?

Not at all! We let our light shine to glorify our Father in heaven—not to gain glory for ourselves. The religious leaders of Jesus' day loved showy displays of worship and service, but it was from a self-serving heart for their own glory and honor. What matters to Jesus is the motive of the heart. Paul, no shrinking violet when it came to boldness, echoed the same truth when he said, "May I never boast except in the cross of our Lord Jesus Christ, through which the world has been crucified to me, and I to the world" (Galatians 6:14, NIV).

Our world is desperate to see God's love revealed through His children. But even lovely acts of giving will ring hollow when done to lift oneself up. I am personally praying this prayer all the time, that the agenda of my heart will ring true before the Father. If I do not, I lose the only blessing and reward that truly matters—the reward of pleasing God.

Lift up the name of Jesus. Glorify God. Ask yourself the hard questions. His light shining through you is what turns hearts toward Him.

In everything I do, may I bring glory and honor to you, my gracious heavenly Father.

HAPPY NO MATTER WHAT

*God blesses you when people mock you and persecute you and lie about you
and say all sorts of evil things against you because you are my followers.
Be happy about it! Be very glad! For a great reward awaits you in heaven.
And remember, the ancient prophets were persecuted in the same way.*

MATTHEW 5:11–12, NLT

How is it possible to be happy when it feels like the world persecutes you? Is that even possible? In my humanness I almost think not. But then I meet people from countries where hardship and persecution for their faith are a way of life. I stand in awe of God's evident presence and joy flowing from their lives. Their smiles and spirit are contagious, and I am reminded in my soul that God gives us a joy and peace that is both deeper and more transcendent than any circumstance of life. Our gracious God always gives us a choice to respond and walk in response to His truth or to focus our attention on the difficulties that might surround us.

God is not cruel and does not bring temptation and trials into our lives. That is the result of our enemy and the fallen nature of the world in which we live, a world which God so loved that He sent His best for.

When God allows trials and tribulations—even persecution—in your life, know that His love and faithfulness is just as real and present. Focus on Jesus and the finished work of the cross, for His grace is sufficient for your every need. In fact, through every trial, I encourage you to lean into His grace. It reaches deep into your soul with the joy of knowing He is everything you need.

*I choose to walk in the happiness you bring to me through the Spirit, O God.
My eyes are fixed on you.*

A DIFFERENT RESPONSE

You have heard the law that says the punishment must match the injury:
"An eye for an eye, and a tooth for a tooth." But I say, do not resist an evil person!
If someone slaps you on the right cheek, offer the other cheek also.

MATTHEW 5:38–39, NLT

We sometimes think of this teaching as harsh and unforgiving. Actually, it was designed to be a statement of grace in a world where kingdoms and tribes practiced genocide, doing their best to utterly destroy anyone who had wronged them. Such outbreaks of incomprehensible violence and cruelty still happen every day in our world. Oh how the earth aches for Christ's answers.

But for the Christian, Jesus takes this grace to another level. Our Savior teaches us to love and treat the world in the same way God has loved and treated the world: with a redemptive kindness that goes beyond the demands of fairness and into the power of love.

And so we march forward in prayer, love, and action into the affairs of countries and international policy. But on a personal level, I know that when I was a sinner, lost in my sins, unconcerned with God and His ways, He looked beyond my rebelliousness with a patient love. He does the same for you. And He wants us to reveal and share this amazing love even with those who treat us unfairly.

Jesus' teachings are not always easy to instantly obey, but they are always filled with the wisdom of God. Are you willing to turn the other cheek to show someone God's love for them? My dear friend, may it be so for all of us.

O God, you loved me when I didn't love you. I am so grateful that you cared so much
for me. I need your grace, O God. Let me be a witness of that love in my world.

LOVE YOUR ENEMIES

You have heard that it was said, "Love your neighbor and hate your enemy."
But I tell you, love your enemies and pray for those who persecute you,
that you may be children of your Father in heaven. He causes his sun to rise
on the evil and the good, and sends rain on the righteous and the unrighteous.

MATTHEW 5:43–45, NIV

*S*urely God can't expect us to love those who hate us, can He? Wouldn't that make life too dangerous for us? Yet His Son declares it. His Word is true. It must be so. There is such peace and joy in following Jesus, but that doesn't mean that God's ways, God's paths, God's will for our lives will always be easy.

Just to agree with Jesus' words—"love your enemies"—takes some work. It goes against everything we are taught. But to then put Jesus' teaching into practice is even more difficult, perhaps the most difficult thing we will ever do. It requires complete surrender of our will and our ways, absolute trust, and an act of obedience. The way we respond is also an act of worship.

Never forget the One who has gone before us. Jesus Christ, the One who spoke the words and lived the words. What was the death on the cross if it wasn't His love for His enemies? Jesus never asks us to do what He wasn't willing to do himself. By dying on the cross, Jesus relinquished His will in obedience to His Father. In the same way, Jesus says that when we love our enemies, we show ourselves to be "children of your Father in heaven."

Father, even when it is hard to obey, I always want to do your will.
Thank you for always making a way. Give me the grace and the strength
to love my enemies as you have commanded.

FORGIVE AND BE FORGIVEN

For if you forgive other people when they sin against you,
your heavenly Father will also forgive you. But if you do not forgive
others their sins, your Father will not forgive your sins.

MATTHEW 6:14–15, NIV

God's love for us is unconditional, but far too often we put conditions on our response to God. I'll do anything you ask as long as you don't ask me to do this one thing. I'll love the world as you commanded, but there is one person I simply can't tolerate. I'll forgive others, but just hold on to a little bit of unforgiveness toward this or that person; they hurt me too badly.

Our lack of forgiveness blocks the flow of forgiveness we receive into our own life. It's not God being angry or withholding from us that stops the flow of forgiveness, but we ourselves who do the blocking.

Jesus has just given His disciples the model prayer, which includes much the same thought: "Forgive us our sins, just as we have forgiven those who have sinned against us" (v. 12, NCV).

Jesus is teaching all of us that forgiving and being forgiven are so tied together—two sides of the same coin—that it is impossible to separate them. These verses also remind us that when forgiving others is a struggle for us, we must quickly turn our eyes back to Jesus and reflect on His sacrifice of love that provided our own forgiveness.

I was in desperate need for forgiveness when I first met Jesus. Just as I need air to breath, I am still in desperate need of His forgiving power. He has been so gracious to me that I cannot help but be gracious with others.

Father, in an act of obedience and love, I do forgive those in my life who have wronged me. You know the name of the person I most struggle to forgive, and I give that name to you today with gratitude that you have truly forgiven me.

THE TREASURE OF YOUR HEART

*Don't store up treasures here on earth, where moths eat them
and rust destroys them, and where thieves break in and steal.
Store your treasures in heaven, where moths and rust cannot destroy,
and thieves do not break in and steal. Wherever your treasure is,
there the desires of your heart will also be.*

MATTHEW 6:19–21, NLT

We want to be secure. We want to be loved. But oh, how often we look for these needs to be met in all the wrong places.

God has placed each of us in the current place where we live, and it is His will that we do honest work and make wise decisions about our resources and finances, from always having a generous spirit to planning for our later years. But we cannot take our gold to heaven. Our possessions will not save us, for they do not endure. Moths eat, rust corrodes, and kingdoms rise and fall. What lasts forever is our spirit and soul. And that is where our greatest care must be given.

What we look at, think about, care for—that is our desire and where we discover our true treasure. Maybe today the things you truly treasure need some adjustment. It is no wonder that time in God's Word, a consistent prayer life, and a heart of worship and adoration for our great God puts our desires in a right place.

I love David's beautiful prayer: "I look up to the hills, but where does my help come from? My help comes from the Lord, who made heaven and earth" (Psalm 121:1-2, NCV). His treasure was the Lord—and He is the only eternal treasure we can desire.

*My help comes from you, my God and my Lord. You are the Creator
of the entire world and the One I can trust with my whole life.*

DON'T WORRY

So don't worry about these things, saying, "What will we eat?
What will we drink? What will we wear?" These things dominate the thoughts
of unbelievers, but your heavenly Father already knows all your needs.

MATTHEW 6:31–32, NLT

*L*iving in a developed country, it is hard for me to fathom the relentless hardship of poverty where securing the basic necessities of life is an everyday challenge. But in reading works by Mother Teresa, I've learned she often said she felt sorry for those living in the West. "The true poor," she would describe us, "cluttered by comfort, missing the miracle of provision."

Isn't it amazing that no matter what our surroundings, there is still a powerful temptation to worry? We worry about all sorts of things, but Jesus' words cover all circumstances. Simply put, worry is for unbelievers, not believers. Why? Because Jesus tells us so. Once you've put your trust in your heavenly Father, you should already know that He "already knows all your needs." Do you know that today?

Just a few verses later, Jesus adds this thought to our key verses: "So don't worry about tomorrow, for tomorrow will bring its own worries. Today's trouble is enough for today" (v. 34). Not only is worry for unbelievers, but He adds that a focus on present and future worries is too much for us to handle. It sucks the life and joy out of existence. That doesn't mean we are to be naïve and unaware of the issues in our world and our own lives. But there is a higher calling to trust, no matter what.

I turn my troubles over to you, O God. I acknowledge
with a grateful heart that you already know what I need.
That means I have nothing to worry about,
and I thank you!

SEEK FIRST

Seek first God's kingdom and what God wants.
Then all your other needs will be met as well.

MATTHEW 6:33, NCV

As we read through the Sermon on the Mount, the big topic is God's kingdom—its true nature, how we receive and how we live it. All the prophets through John the Baptist prepared for the coming kingdom. Jesus brought the kingdom of God.

Our key verse is an exclamation point to make sure we know how important the kingdom is. It is to be the controlling priority of our lives. Before we look to our desires, our own agendas, even our own needs, we are to seek the kingdom. It must become the burning desire of our lives. That's why when Jesus taught us to pray He included "your kingdom come. Your will be done on earth as it is in heaven" (v. 10, NKJV).

When we fall in love with Jesus, the One who ushered in God's kingdom, and have a passion for sharing this good news and making it a reality in our world, then all other fears and needs fade into the background. The great miracle is that "all your other needs will be met as well." When we make the kingdom our priority, God makes sure that our material needs are cared for.

What would happen in your life if your number one priority was seeking the kingdom of God? Would you have more worries or less? More joy or less? More peace and purpose and power or less? If you have not yet discovered firsthand and experienced the answers to that question, is today the day?

───~ⱺᴑⱺ~───

Not my will but thine. May what matters most to you matter most to me, O God. Today,
you are first and I am second in all my thoughts and plans, my life, my all.

DON'T JUDGE

Do not judge others, and you will not be judged. For you will be treated as you treat others. The standard you use in judging is the standard by which you will be judged.

MATTHEW 7:1–2, NLT

I know there is right and wrong. In the spiritual realm, there is good fruit and bad fruit. There are true teachers and false teachers. Jesus himself tells us "Not everyone who says to Me, 'Lord, Lord,' shall enter the kingdom of heaven, but he who does the will of My Father in heaven" (v. 21, NKJV).

What are we to make of Jesus' command not to judge? It would seem that sure and active judgment is needed every step of the way in life. But just as not forgiving others blocks forgiveness in our lives, so judging others brings forth greater judgment in our lives. Could it be that when we take on the task of judging, we are trying to assume what God reserves for himself?

When we become judgmental, we make the easy step to feeling self-righteous and forget how much we ourselves have been forgiven. We also make mistakes when we judge. We don't always get the facts straight, and we certainly can't see into someone's heart. We add anger and worry to our lives and lose focus on what matters. We even lose sight of our own shortcomings. Jesus says, "And why worry about a speck in your friend's eye when you have a log in your own? How can you think of saying to your friend, 'Let me help you get rid of that speck in your eye,' when you can't see past the log in your own eye? Hypocrite! First get rid of the log in your own eye; then you will see well enough to deal with the speck in your friend's eye" (vv. 3–5).

Father, you alone can judge the hearts of men and women. I know you want me to live wisely and righteously, but help my focus to be on sharing the good news of your kingdom and trusting you to bring conviction to the hearts of others.

PEARLS TO PIGS

Don't waste what is holy on people who are unholy.
Don't throw your pearls to pigs! They will trample the pearls,
then turn and attack you.

MATTHEW 7:6, NLT

We are, of course, called to share our testimony with the lost and dying of the world. But Jesus tells us not to "waste what is holy on people who are unholy." When he describes them as wild and savage pigs, He is telling us that some people have so hardened their hearts against God and His kingdom that it is sometimes unwise—and dangerous—to even approach them.

At first glance we don't always know who these people are, though some make their hostility to Jesus known and obvious to all. Jesus recognized that we might share His truth with people and only then discover their enmity when He told His disciples, "And if a home or town refuses to welcome you or listen to you, leave that place and shake its dust off your feet" (Matthew 10:14, NCV).

So who do we approach and who do we leave alone? And won't there be moments when even the most hardhearted person has a moment of openness to the love of God? The reality is we share too little of what God has done for us, even to those who are open and receptive to the gospel. Perhaps that is the right spot to start, asking God each day to bring someone across your path who needs to hear what Jesus has done for you and that He will do the same for that person. God speaks to us as we pray and listen to the Holy Spirit, and He will guide us toward the ready and away from those who are not ready.

Father, you brought witnesses of grace into my life to share how much you love me.
Let me be a word of grace to someone else today.

KEEP KNOCKING

*Keep on asking, and you will receive what you ask for. Keep on seeking,
and you will find. Keep on knocking, and the door will be opened to you.
For everyone who asks, receives. Everyone who seeks, finds.
And to everyone who knocks, the door will be opened.*

MATTHEW 7:7-8, NLT

God's Word is so rich. There is a treasure to be discovered in every chapter, on every page. In the Sermon on the Mount, the longest passage in Scripture that shares the very words of Jesus, there is a lifetime of truth and application.

A truth that touches my heart with such joy and wonder is that we are also to approach our Father in prayer just like little children that come to their parents with a request. Jesus had such a lovely way of explaining things so we can understand: "You parents—if your children ask for a loaf of bread, do you give them a stone instead? Or if they ask for a fish, do you give them a snake? Of course not! So if you sinful people know how to give good gifts to your children, how much more will your heavenly Father give good gifts to those who ask him" (vv. 9–11).

Is it any wonder the people who heard Jesus' words marveled at His teaching? It was the stories He told and the authority with which He spoke, but it was also the breathtaking truths He taught about the Father God. So many understood God as distant and severe. Jesus showed them—and you and me—just how kind and affectionate He truly is toward His children. Bring your requests to your loving Father, joyfully and persistently and with all the energy and enthusiasm of a child!

*Thank you for your kindness, O God, my loving Father.
Thank you for not only allowing me but inviting me to bring my requests to you.*

THE NARROW GATE

You can enter God's Kingdom only through the narrow gate.
The highway to hell is broad, and its gate is wide for the many
who choose that way. But the gateway to life is very narrow
and the road is difficult, and only a few ever find it.

MATTHEW 7:13–15, NLT

God's love is deep and wide. It reaches every nook and cranny of our lives—and of the entire world. Paul described it beautifully in one of his prayers: "And I pray that you, being rooted and established in love, may have power, together with all the Lord's holy people, to grasp how wide and long and high and deep is the love of Christ" (Ephesians 3:17–18, NIV).

And yet Jesus speaks of a narrowness in entering God's kingdom. As He teaches the people on this hillside, His stories and illustrations and precepts call for a joyful self-sacrifice, of pouring oneself out for others rather than seeking a life of comfort and ease. His words stir our hearts and minds, but will we truly embrace them? God's love toward us knows no hesitation. But what of our response to Him?

Following God with all your heart and strength will sometimes lead you on a lonely path. It will seem that everyone else in the world is rushing in another direction. But His grace and blessings mean that living for Him leads to no regrets. As the martyr-missionary Jim Elliott said: "He is no fool who gives what he cannot keep to gain what he cannot lose."

My friends, never fear to follow God's will for your life. You will never be alone—He will be with you each step of the way. I would rather have one day with Him than a thousand days anywhere else.

Dear God, I enter your gate, as narrow as it might seem,
to live the fullest life possible to me.

BUILD ON ROCK

Everyone who hears my words and obeys them is like a wise man who built his house
on rock. It rained hard, the floods came, and the winds blew and hit that house.
But it did not fall, because it was built on rock. Everyone who hears my words and does
not obey them is like a foolish man who built his house on sand. It rained hard,
the floods came, and the winds blew and hit that house, and it fell with a big crash.

MATTHEW 7:24–27, NCV

Of this conclusion to the Sermon on the Mount, Charles Spurgeon wrote: "Our Lord closes not by displaying his own powers of elocution, but by simply and affectionately addressing a warning to those who, having heard his words, should remain satisfied with hearing, and should not go forth and put them into practice. What a mercy there is a rock to build on! We could not have made one; but there is the rock."

The wise man is obedient, but humble enough to know that his obedience does not save him. It is a response to God's mercy. Spurgeon was right. We can't build the rock, but we can build on it. This is a familiar theme throughout all of Scripture. Moses said of God, "He is the Rock, his works are perfect, and all his ways are just. A faithful God who does no wrong, upright and just is he" (Deuteronomy 32:4, NIV). Through obedience we build our life on a foundation that will withstand all floods and winds. The world may feel uncertain at times, but if our life is built on the foundation of God, our life is safe in His hands.

Don't miss that the same message was given to both the wise and foolish builder. The difference is their response. My prayer is that even today, all who read Jesus' words will build their home—the entirety of their life—on the only sure foundation.

O God, I both hear and obey you this day. I enter through the narrow gate.
I trust my life into your hands, no matter where you lead or what you ask.

A TEACHER'S AUTHORITY

*When Jesus finished saying these things, the people were amazed
at his teaching, because he did not teach like their teachers of the law.
He taught like a person who had authority.*

MATTHEW 7:28–29, NCV

THE MESSAGE translation of the Bible has a powerful way of expressing these two verses: "When Jesus concluded his address, the crowd burst into applause. They had never heard teaching like this. It was apparent that he was living everything he was saying—quite a contrast to their religion teachers! This was the best teaching they had ever heard."

His disciples often called Jesus "Teacher." As a person of God, he literally carried the wisdom of God. As a man who lived without sin—His every word, thought, and deed gave glory to His Father in heaven—He was unique in that He fully lived what He taught. David understood the power of right living when he said, "Blessed are those whose ways are blameless, who walk according to the law of the Lord" (Psalm 119:1, NIV).

The lessons of the Sermon on the Mount are powerful and intense. We are to pray for God's will to be expressed on earth; we seek His kingdom first and foremost as the driving priority of our life; we serve with humility so that God gets all the glory; we love our enemies, even those that persecute us; we treat what is in our heart with the same import as our actions; we don't judge others.

My prayer for you and for me is that, like Jesus, we share these truths with the authority that comes from living what we teach.

*Dear God, grant me the power to not just hear your words of wisdom but to walk in them.
Make me a teacher through my words and my actions.*

BENEATH THE CROSS OF JESUS

May I never boast except in the cross of our Lord Jesus Christ,
through which the world has been crucified to me, and I to the world.

GALATIANS 6:14, NIV

When we are weary and discouraged, when we are tempted, when we are lonely, when things are uncertain, when we are challenged . . . isn't it wonderful to know there is a place we can take our stand?

> Beneath the cross of Jesus I fain would take my stand,
> The shadow of a mighty rock within a weary land;
> A home within the wilderness, a rest upon the way,
> From the burning of the noontide heat, and the burden of the day.
>
> Upon that cross of Jesus mine eye at times can see
> The very dying form of One who suffered there for me;
> And from my stricken heart with tears two wonders I confess:
> The wonders of redeeming love and my unworthiness.
>
> I take, O cross, thy shadow for my abiding place;
> I ask no other sunshine than the sunshine of his face;
> Content to let the world go by, to know no gain nor loss,
> My sinful self my only shame, my glory all the cross.

Heavenly Father, thank you for being the Mighty Rock,
the Home, the place of rest I need in life.
I am so grateful for your redeeming love.

Victor's Crown ♡

You are always fighting for us
Heaven's angels all around
My delight is found in knowing
That YOU wear the VICTOR'S crown

You're my Help & my Defender,
My Savior & my friend... by your
grace I live & breathe to worship
YOU.

WORSHIP HIS NAME

Elohim

In the beginning, God created the heavens and the earth.

GENESIS 1:1, NIRV

*I*f we want to understand God better, one of the great areas of study should be His names as found throughout Scripture. They reveal His nature and His purpose and describe in perfection what our relationship with Him is to be. His names point us to the full revelation of who Jesus Christ is and the breadth of His glory and power. I pray His name will be revealed to you today in a new and deeper way as you praise God for all He really is.

Elohim is the first word for God we encounter in the Bible. The name means mighty or strong. And yes, this mighty and strong God is the creator God. The very same God who flung the stars into space knows us in the most finite detail, since before one of our days even came to be. That's the God of heaven and earth, our mighty and strong God, the God we love and the God we worship.

And because of His crazy love, incredible kindness, and patience for and toward rebellious and sinful children, He continues to stand with arms open wide and calls us to himself, even though many do not recognize Him as God or even understand that there is a God of all.

As Christ lives in us, we are called to also stand and reflect Christ wherever we find ourselves, to anyone who is in our sphere of influence.

My friends, let's go back to the creation of the universe and meditate upon the mighty works of our God. No other power can compare.

You are my mighty God. By your incomparable power you created a beautiful world for us to live in. I put my life in your hands and totally depend on you.

WORSHIP HIS NAME

El Elyon

*May God Most High bless Abram. May the Creator of heaven and earth
bless him. Give praise to God Most High. He gave your enemies into your hand.*

GENESIS 14:19–20, NIRV

*I*n Genesis 14 Abraham meets the king of Salem, a powerful and mysteri-
ous figure who was known not only as a king but a priest of the one true
God. Though God did not give us His holy Word through him, God did give to
Melchizedek special revelation of just who He was so that he taught our fathers
of faith a true understanding of God and became part of our Scripture through
that help.

Abraham has just won a victory over those who would keep him from the land of
promise, and his desire is to worship God. He meets with Melchezedek and brings
him a tithe. He asks to be blessed, and in that beautiful moment of worship he is
taught that God is the Most High God, sovereign over all the universe. He lived in
a time when it was taught that there were many gods that led certain tribes and had
power in certain lands. Now Abraham is learning there is a Most High God who is
not one of many but the greatest and only.

Our Most High God is not just a good option to be considered in our world
filled with many "gods." He is the only true God. No matter how fluent the speech
and persuasive the words, flee from any teaching that would tell you otherwise. Jesus
Christ is not *a* way to God. He is *the* way to God Most High.

*God Most High, I proclaim you alone are worthy of our praise. You alone have created
the world and saved us from our sins. I worship you in spirit and truth today.*

WORSHIP HIS NAME

El Roi

The angel of the Lord found Hagar near a spring of water in the desert.
The spring was beside the road to Shur. He said, "Hagar, you are
the servant of Sarai. Where have you come from? Where are you going?"
"I'm running away from my owner Sarai," she answered.

GENESIS 16:7–8, NIRV

The name *El Roi* tells us that God sees everything. He never rests or sleeps. He is everywhere. There is nothing that can hide from His gaze.

In this story from Genesis, Hagar has fled from Abraham's presence, discouraged and afraid of Sarah's jealousy and anger toward her. Better to brave the wilderness than be mistreated by her master. But as she wanders aimlessly, she realizes she is lost. In exhaustion, she finally lays herself down to die along with her unborn baby. She has given up ever being found.

But God's angel knows right where she is. He is sent by El Roi, the God Who Sees. God's angel asks her where she came from and where she is going, not because he doesn't know but so that she would be honest with her situation.

No matter how lost you feel, no matter how cut off and alone you feel, El Roi, the God Who Sees, knows exactly where you are. You are not lost and alone. You aren't abandoned in whatever wilderness you are passing through at this moment.

Thank you, Father, that when I felt utterly lost and alone, you saw
just where I was. You knew where I had been and you had wonderful plans
for my future. Thank you, God Who Sees all.

WORSHIP HIS NAME

El Shaddai

He said, "I am the Mighty God. Walk with me and live
without any blame. I will now put into practice my covenant
between me and you. I will greatly increase your numbers."

GENESIS 17:1–2, NIRV

*E*l *Shaddai.* He is the almighty and all-sufficient God, capable of doing and providing anything. He is all that we need in the world, for He meets our every need. This is the mighty God who takes care of His own. The name proclaims His power—but not a power that is warlike. In fact, the image of God that we gain from this word is that He gently feeds us as if from a woman's breast. Just as a mother provides all the food and nourishment a baby needs from her own body, so God imparts from himself everything we need in this life.

Abraham has heard God's call to be the father of a vast and mighty people. He will be given a son and a land to establish God's chosen people, His people of faith. But Abraham is discouraged. He has no son and has not yet taken possession of the land. God speaks directly to him to establish a covenant—a vow, a marriage, a binding contract—that He, God himself, will ensure from His all-sufficiency. Abraham will be given the child of promise, for God is able to do anything and He will make it so.

Is there an impossible situation in your life? Is there something you need to do but have absolutely no means to accomplish? Don't lose heart. Don't give up. Realize you serve an all-sufficient God who can do the impossible.

Thank you, El Shaddai, for meeting my every need.
Thank you for doing for me what I cannot do myself.

WORSHIP HIS NAME

Adonai

*Moses answered the people. He said, "Don't be afraid. Stand firm.
You will see how the Lord will save you today. Do you see those Egyptians?
You will never see them again. The Lord will fight for you. Just be still."*

EXODUS 14:13–14, NIRV

Adonai tells us that our God is Lord and Master. He is to be served.

God has delivered His people from Egypt through His servant Moses. The Pharaoh, a stubborn man if there ever was one, has finally relented after ten plagues struck his people, culminating in the death of his son. But his heart never really softened, and now he repents of his decision. He leads his army to bring the slaves back. The Hebrew children cry out in terror. They complain to Moses that he has brought them into the desert to die. Slavery is better than death.

When Moses answers them to say God will fight for them, he doesn't use a word for God that emphasizes His might and strength. He tells them their Master God will fight their fight. Why would Moses have chosen that word for God?

I believe he is telling this fearful and grumbling mob that it is time to be quiet and obedient to their Master. God is their Deliverer, but He is their Lord. Hush. God has freed you from an evil master, so now is the time to serve a kind, gracious, loving Master God with obedience.

It is wonderful to be reassured with God's might and power, but sometimes it is good to simply trust our Lord. El Shaddai tells us our God is all-sufficient. Adonai tells us He is our Lord and to be obeyed.

---

*I serve you, Adonai, with a glad and obedient heart.
My obedience is my worship to you today.*

WORSHIP HIS NAME

Yahweh

⌇

*"Do not come any closer," God said. "Take off your sandals. The place
you are standing on is holy ground." He continued, "I am the God of your father.
I am the God of Abraham. I am the God of Isaac. And I am the God of Jacob."*

EXODUS 3:5–6, NIRV

The most frequent name for God in the Bible is *Yahweh* or *Jehovah*. The word
means God's essence or being. Because it was considered blasphemous to
utter the name of God, it was only written and never spoken. It is God's way of saying
I AM. All other attributes and descriptors are wrapped up in His being. We have
all at one time said something to the effect of, "I want you to love me not for what I
do but for who I am." That describes in small measure what God is getting at here.

We love and worship Him because He is faithful, good, kind, and every other
wonderful thing we can say about Him. But don't just love Him for what He does.
Love Him for who He is. God is so faithful that it seems impossible to separate
who He is from what He does, but the idea is that He is always and ever worthy of
our worship and praise. It is good for us to daily take the time to stop and adore
the Almighty.

Moses, a murderer, is hiding in the wilderness. All he wants to do is live out his
days far from the court of Pharaoh. The great I AM has other ideas. He calls Moses
before Him for a purpose.

Have you stood on holy ground? Have you encountered the great I AM? I pray
you encounter Him afresh today.

*I stand in reverence and awe before you, Yahweh.
You are eternal, before creation and time.*

WORSHIP HIS NAME

Yahweh-jireh

So Abraham named that place The Lord Will Provide.
To this day people say, "It will be provided on the mountain of the Lord."

GENESIS 22:14, NIRV

*Y*ahweh-jireh. The great I AM will provide. Our God is the provider God. He doesn't meet our needs because He feels sorry for us. He desires to provide everything we need to live victoriously.

No story in the Old Testament is more gripping than when Abraham hears God's call to sacrifice his son Isaac. How could this be? Isaac was the son of promise. He came to Abraham and Sarah in their old age. He was the fulfillment of God's call to Abraham that he would be the father of many peoples. But Abraham had such an amazing trust in God that he took Isaac to the mountain to sacrifice him in obedience and worship.

Later God would sacrifice His own Son to take our sins away from us, but for Abraham He provides a ram. Abraham's faith and courageous obedience are rewarded. This blood sacrifice is not necessary—and would not have been sufficient to fulfill God's purposes anyway. Only God can provide everything we need to live.

We sometimes cling to and fear for our resources. We look at our money, our belongings, our food and see a finite supply. The great news is that's not how it works in God's kingdom. God is our provider and is always renewing what we have—particularly when we are willing to give it away. Don't cling. Don't hoard. Trust Yahweh-jireh, your provider God.

All that I need is supplied by knowing you, Yahweh-jireh.
Thank you for the unlimited resources that you lavish on me.

WORSHIP HIS NAME

Yahweh-rapha

He said, "I am the Lord your God. Listen carefully to my voice. Do what is right in
my eyes. Pay attention to my commands. Obey all of my rules. If you do, I will not send
on you any of the sicknesses I sent on the Egyptians. I am the Lord who heals you."

EXODUS 15:26, NIRV

*Y*ahweh-rapha. The great I AM is our healer God. God is truly the Great
Physician. He is able to heal all of our ailments in life, whether physical,
emotional, or spiritual. One of the great promises for eternity is that when we see
Him and live with Him in heaven, we will be glorified—we will be given bodies that
are perfect. That is the ultimate healing!

What has just happened with God's children when Moses introduces Yahweh as
our healer? They have escaped a country that is under divine siege. Egypt is wracked
with illness. No corner of the kingdom has gone untouched. Now the Hebrew children have passed through the Red Sea to begin a whole new life. Moses reminds them
that their God is a healing God. He will heal their emotional scars of slavery and
deliver them from all the sicknesses that visited Egypt.

When we think of Jesus' life and ministry, one of the most dominant thoughts
we have of Him is His many healings. Blind received sight; the lame walked again;
leprosy disappeared without a blemish. He even raised the dead back to life.

Are you in need of healing today? Bring your illness, your damaged body, or your
damaged psyche to Him, and rest in the finished work of Jesus.

Thank you for the various ways you bring healing into my life,
Yahweh-rapha. Most of all, thank you for being my true healer God.
You heal me now and ultimately in eternity.

WORSHIP HIS NAME

Yahweh-nissi

Then Moses built an altar. He called it The Lord Is My Banner.

EXODUS 17:15, NIRV

The Lord is my Banner. It is He who goes before me in battle against our enemies. After a tremendous victory over the Amalekites, a godless tribe that represented the worst in cruelty and evil, Moses knows it wasn't he and the people who won the battle. It was Yahweh-nissi, our Banner, our warrior God.

We know full well that God loves sinners but hates sin. But in the case of the Amalekites, their hearts were so hardened and depraved that to fight their army was to fight evil itself. God wants us to win the world to Him with a persuasive love, His love. But sometimes we have to stand up and fight against ideas and agendas and practices that are based on evil. We don't stand up in anger but in love. Our heart is intent on defending the innocent and helpless.

We need to be aware of what evil is up to, be alert to plans that would succeed in the exploitation of the innocent, and be ready to participate in the fight against injustice. But we do so with a bold humility, the utmost confidence that it is God who goes before us in battle as our mighty Banner.

❧

Yahweh-nissi, help me to never turn my eyes from the acts of evil
that exploit and enslave the helpless of our world.
Give me courage and faith to do what I can, knowing that when I act,
it is you who goes to battle on my behalf.

WORSHIP HIS NAME

Yahweh-mekoddishkem

⁓ꞔꝏꞔ⁓

*He said, "Tell the people of Israel, 'You must always keep my Sabbath days.
That will be the sign of the covenant I have made between me and you for all
time to come. Then you will know that I am the Lord. I make you holy."*

EXODUS 31:13, NIRV

*Y*ahweh-mekoddishkem. This is the righteous God who sanctifies us, who makes
us righteous.

To sanctify something is to set it apart for service—like something you reserve
for special use, something valuable, precious. God sets apart His people—you and
I—to be at His service, to be different from the world in ways that make a difference.
We don't give ourselves to sinful desires but to serving our God. For God's chosen
people, the sign that they were set apart for Him was their observance of the Sabbath.

The important thing to notice here is that we don't sanctify ourselves. Only God
does that. When we respond to all He has done for us in Christ Jesus and offer
ourselves completely to Him, he does a miraculous work in us. We are "transformed
by the renewing of [our] mind" (Romans 12:2, NIV).

Let's never lose sight of the truth that we love Yahweh-mekoddishkem, the righteous God who desires for us to grow in righteousness. We are called to be holy, to
grow in Christlikeness. Beautifully, His presence is made evident in and through us
as we simply love and serve Him with all we have and all we are.

*Make me more like Jesus, O Yahweh-mekoddishkem. Transform me by a renewing
of my mind. Give me the righteousness that can only come from you.*

WORSHIP HIS NAME

Yahweh-shalom

—⁂—

So Gideon built an altar to honor the Lord there.
He called it The Lord Is Peace. It still stands in Ophrah to this very day.
Ophrah is in the territory that belongs to the family line of Abiezer.

JUDGES 6:24, NIRV

*Y*ahweh-shalom. God of peace. The Israelites were under bondage to the Midianites. This was God's judgment on them for their lack of faithfulness. Sin always carries a price. But when they turned their eyes back to God and cried for deliverance, He raised up a deliverer named Gideon. He wasn't famous and wasn't known as a great warrior. But against incredible odds he led Israel to a decisive victory over their oppressors and established an altar that he named God of peace.

When do we most need peace? That becomes the cry of our heart when our life is in turmoil and battles are being waged against us. It is God who gives us a peace that passes all human understanding. It is He who gives us a supernatural calm when everything around us is in chaos.

No matter what turmoil or chaos is in your life right now, the God of peace will give you a calm to get through it with poise and grace—and to give you the ultimate victory that results in peace. And not just peace at the end of the storm, but peace along the journey. The Lord is peace. And He offers that peace to you.

I don't feel at peace right now, Yahweh-shalom. There are conflicts and confusion
in my life. I cry out to you, my God of peace. Restore peace in my mind. I trust you to be
the peace in my family, my life. I will be still and know that you are my God of peace.

WORSHIP HIS NAME

Yahweh-sabaoth

*David said to Goliath, "You are coming to fight against me with a sword, a spear
and a javelin. But I'm coming against you in the name of the Lord who rules over all.
He is the God of the armies of Israel. He's the one you have dared to fight against."*

1 SAMUEL 17:45, NIRV

*Y*ahweh-sabaoth. The Lord of Hosts. God is commander of the heavenly army.
David knew that full well. So what did it matter that he was but a boy facing
a giant? He had the commander God at His side. He wasn't alone with five smooth
stones. The armies of heaven were arrayed all around him. Goliath, a giant and
warrior who had been trained in the "arts of war" since his youth, laughed and scoffed
at David. David never backed down. He boldly called out that it was God himself
Goliath had dared to fight. We all know how David's words came true.

When the odds are against us, when evil seems bigger and stronger and has us
outnumbered, when deliverance seems impossible, let's never forget that our Lord is a
warrior. We are called to show a courageous faith—though we don't have to be particularly tough ourselves. That's not what matters. That's not who wins the victory.
The Lord of Hosts goes before us, fights our battles for us, and giants are slain with
one smooth stone.

David never lost his youthful and energetic belief in God's deliverance. In Psalm
46:7 he declares, "The Lord who rules over all is with us. The God of Jacob is like a
fort to us." Is your trust completely in Yahweh-sabaoth, the Lord of Hosts?

I place my confidence completely in you, Yahweh-sabaoth.
Thank you for providing deliverance for me when deliverance did not seem possible.
I trust in your strength and wisdom today, O God.

WORSHIP HIS NAME

Yahweh-raah

The Lord is my shepherd. He gives me everything I need.

PSALM 23:1, NIRV

Yahweh-raah. The Lord is my shepherd. Perhaps the most famous of all of David's psalms gives a beautiful description of the shepherd God who would lay down everything to care for, provide for, and love His sheep.

Our Lord is both shepherd and friend. I love how this passage reminds us that just as the shepherd leads and guides his flock to fields of safety and well-being, so does our shepherd King guide us in ways that lead us to absolute security. That at the very center of this psalm, His rod—His heavenly hand of protection and authority—is there, an instrument of support, giving great confidence and incredible comfort.

The Reverend Derek Kidner says about verse 4, "Only the Lord can lead a man through death; all other guides turn back, and the traveler must go on alone."

The Lord is my shepherd. He gives me everything I need. He lets me lie down in fields of green grass. He leads me beside quiet waters. He gives me new strength. He guides me in the right paths for the honor of his name. Even though I walk through the darkest valley, I will not be afraid. You are with me. Your shepherd's rod and staff comfort me. You prepare a feast for me right in front of my enemies. You pour oil on my head. My cup runs over. I am sure that your goodness and love will follow me all the days of my life. And I will live in the house of the Lord forever. —Psalm 23

You give me everything I need, O Yahweh-raah. I will fear no evil. You hold and lead me through every moment. I thank you with all my heart and love.

WORSHIP HIS NAME

Yahweh-tsidkenu

*"A new day is coming," announces the Lord. "At that time I will raise up
from David's royal line a true and rightful Branch. He will be a King
who will rule wisely. He will do what is fair and right in the land.
In his days Judah will be saved. Israel will live in safety. And the Branch
will be called The Lord Who Makes Us Right With Himself.*

JEREMIAH 23:5–6, NIRV

*Y*ahweh-tsidkenu, the Lord Our Righteousness. On our own merits we have
no righteousness. On our own we would only receive what we deserve. But
through our righteous God we are made pure, free, whole. God's perfection provides
the righteousness we need to have an authentic relationship with God. He loves us so
much He is willing to do whatever it takes to have fellowship with us.

I am amazed that the prophets were able to predict the coming of our Savior
so perfectly. Even when it seemed that God's redemptive plans would be thwarted
through the continued disobedience of His people, Christ's coming could not be
stopped. His work on our behalf would be completed because Yahweh-tsidkenu
declared it so and made it so.

Do you feel unrighteous? Do you feel you have failed God so many times that
there is nothing that can be done to save you now?

All that might be true were it not for the God who is Our Righteousness. His
love and plans for you cannot be thwarted. Believe and rest in this truth today!

*You are the righteous One, O God, and you are my righteousness.
I have no other pleas and hope. I only trust in you and your name today.*

WORSHIP HIS NAME

Yahweh-shammah

❦

The city will be six miles around. From that time on,
its name will be The Lord Is There.

EZEKIEL 48:35, NIRV

*Y*ahweh-shammah. The Lord Is There. Ezekiel had a divine revelation of heaven and saw God sitting on the throne, high and lifted up. That's why he could call on the name of God as The Lord Is There. But this name of God is a promise for all circumstances in our life.

When we are alone and isolated, God Is There.

When we have failed Him, God Is There.

When we come before Him in worship, God Is There.

When we pray, God Is There.

When we face temptation, God Is There.

When our life is in danger, God Is There.

When we share the gospel, God Is There.

When we go through the everydayness of our lives, God Is There.

My friends, have you caught on? No matter where you are right now in life, God Is There because He loves you and is on your side. What a glorious promise!

Thank you, Yahweh-shammah, for your constant presence
in my life, when times are good and when times are tough.
You are my faithful and ever-present help.

JOYFUL SUBMISSION

A Classic Devotion by Oswald Chambers

You call Me Teacher and Lord, and you say well, for so I am.

JOHN 13:13, NKJV

Our Lord never insists on having authority over us. He never says, "You will submit to me." No, He leaves us perfectly free to choose—so free, in fact, that we can spit in His face or we can put Him to death, as others have done; and yet He will never say a word. But once His life has been created in me through His redemption, I instantly recognize His right to absolute authority over me. It is a complete and effective domination, in which I acknowledge that "you are worthy, O Lord" (Revelation 4:11). . . .

If our Lord insisted on our obedience, He would simply become a taskmaster and cease to have any real authority. He never insists on obedience, but when we truly see Him we will instantly obey Him. Then He is easily Lord of our life, and we live in adoration of Him from morning till night. The level of my growth in grace is revealed by the way I look at obedience. We should have a much higher view of the word obedience, rescuing it from the mire of the world. Obedience is only possible between people who are equals in their relationship to each other; like the relationship between father and son, not that between master and servant. Jesus showed this relationship by saying, "I and My Father are one" (John 10:30). "Though He was a Son, yet He learned obedience by the things which He suffered" (Hebrews 5:8). The Son was obedient as our Redeemer, because He was the Son, not in order to become God's Son.

It is my privilege to submit to you, my God and Redeemer.
I joyfully trust my life to your will!

BREATH OF LIFE

JESUS IS THE WAY, THE TRUTH, AND THE LIFE.

SEPTEMBER

Breathe on me, breath of God,
Fill me with life anew,
That I may love
        what thou dost love,
And do what thou wouldst do.

Breathe on me, breath of God,
So shall I never die,
But live with thee the perfect life
Of thine eternity.

♡
        Amen, Lord! Amen, Jesus!♡

GOD GOES BEFORE US

*When you, God, went out before your people, when you marched
through the wilderness, the earth shook, the heavens poured down rain,
before God, the One of Sinai, before God, the God of Israel.*

PSALM 68:7–8, NIV

Psalm 68, a psalm of David, is an absolutely glorious psalm of praise that reveals to me the power of worship. It is composed of nine stanzas, each expressing the triumphant rule of the God of Israel. David takes us on a journey from the days of Moses to his own rule as king of Israel. But he doesn't stop there. Woven into the words are glimpses of Jesus, our ultimate Victor.

David feels particularly blessed by what God is doing in his life, and his mind and heart go back to how God blessed His people in past days. He delivered the people from Egypt with a miraculous crossing of the Red Sea and then safe passage through the wilderness. "The earth shook, the heavens poured down rain." God's deliverance and protection were marked by stunning events that announced and confirmed the birth of the kingdom of God. Earlier in this psalm it is noted that the wicked live in a parched land. The heavy rains God gave to His people were just as much of a physical manifestation of His power as the earthquakes.

When I start to speak this psalm out loud, I can see the Lord walking through the path of history and all His enemies falling at His feet, with no power to stand against Him. In the footsteps of the Lord establishing His people, I see the triumphant rule of the Lord Jesus Christ. I see everything that is not right in our fallen world being made right in Him. In these words of remembrance and praise, I see again our ultimate triumph.

*Mighty God, thank you for always providing for and protecting your children.
Thank you that the victory of Jesus Christ ensures our victory for all eternity.*

GOD GIVES US A FAMILY

Sing to God, sing in praise of his name, extol him who rides on the clouds;
rejoice before him—his name is the Lord.

PSALM 68:4, NIV

This psalm of praise continues to impart such hope into my soul. I see God at work throughout all of human history. I continue to see my Lord Jesus Christ make the wrongs of fallen humanity right. Is it any wonder we are called to sing to God, praise His name, give Him all glory and honor, and rejoice in Him? What other response could we have? Our Victor rides on His great white horse and creates a new world filled with peace and joy for us.

The fatherless find refuge in the shadow of the Almighty. They are not only given a safety and comfort they have never known before, but God miraculously gives them a true sense of home, of belonging, which is what we all need. I see once-vulnerable widows become strong with Jesus as their first line of defense. No longer are they living in fear, but standing strong on the arm of the Most High God.

As we continue to sing this song of triumph and praise, God sets every lonely one in a place of security and nurture. They are given a family of their own. They are not "taken in," but God himself sets them there. Oh, friends, can you see it? Can you see what David saw seven hundred years before Christ's coming? It's the rule of Christ making all things right as He makes His way through all of life.

Have you allowed Him the rule of your life that He so kindly requests? Are you ready to join in His march across our broken world to bring salvation and healing?

Dear God, I am so honored to follow you into a battle to bring
redemption and healing to a lost and hurting world.

PRISONERS SET FREE

He leads out the prisoners with singing.

PSALM 68:6, NIV

David sees prisoners emerge from captivity with a song of praise on their lips rather than a life sentence. Can there be a more powerful and beautiful act of redemption than a murderer or a thief finding God?

I wonder if Jesus had this verse in mind when He said to His disciples: "Then the King will say to those on his right, 'Come, you who are blessed by my Father; take your inheritance, the kingdom prepared for you since the creation of the world. For I was hungry and you gave me something to eat, I was thirsty and you gave me something to drink, I was a stranger and you invited me in, I needed clothes and you clothed me, I was sick and you looked after me, I was in prison and you came to visit me'" (Matthew 25:34–36).

I find it fascinating that on judgment day God will remember what we did for the hungry and thirsty, the sick, the naked, and the prisoner. Do you think we put enough time and emphasis on ministry to prisoners? I have ministered in many prisons across the planet, and we always sing "Amazing Grace" together. The sound of the sacred and humanity coming together . . . there is nothing like it.

In this psalm we see the marvelous and miraculous ways the Lord takes care of the people He loves so much—including widows, orphans, the lonely, and prisoners. God just might be suggesting to us where we need to spend more of our time!

Heavenly Father, I ask for a special grace on prisoners all over the world.
Some guilty of their crimes, some falsely imprisoned. I pray for a miraculous
revealing of Jesus to all of them.

HE BEARS AND HEALS OUR BURDENS

Praise be to the Lord, to God our Savior, who daily bears our burdens.

PSALM 68:19, NIV

*L*et me ask you a personal question. When the Lord came into your world, did you allow Him into all the places of your heart? Even the damaged places, the lonely places, the cold places? All of us have areas of our lives that are shut off from the eyes of others. But what about with God? Have you given Him access to your entire being, even those burdens you never knew how to deal with?

My friends, read back through Psalm 68 and see what God's heart is toward us. He is so loving. There may have been others in your past you couldn't trust, but God is absolutely trustworthy. Will you unlock the door to even those uncomfortable areas of your life? Let your heavenly Father in to tend to the soil and provide water for parched and scorched areas. Let him into all the areas of your inner life to bring such a gentle healing and renewal that you will know once and for all what it means to be free. He is waiting at the gate now. He is able to do what He promised. But there is an action of willingness required. You must open the door. You must be willing to say, "Yes, I make way for the Risen Lord."

I encourage you to continue reading this entire psalm, and spend time meditating and seeing the Lord walking through the corridors of your own heart—putting right that which is out of place, bringing healing to those areas that are still sore to the touch. God is Father, Defender, Provider, Healer. He is exactly what you need in your heart.

Lord Jesus, I pray your healing rain over the very core of my life and the lives of all who read this. Heal us and work inside us that we may in turn serve and love you with all we are!

HIGHER THAN THE HIGHEST MOUNTAIN

Mount Bashan, majestic mountain, Mount Bashan, rugged mountain,
why gaze in envy, you rugged mountain, at the mountain where God chooses
to reign, where the Lord himself will dwell forever?

PSALM 68:15, NIV

Psalm 68 is filled with the exhilarating language of victory. He brings victory over our enemies. He brings victory to widows, orphans, and prisoners. He is even victorious over high and lofty mountain peaks. Perhaps you have had opportunity to view the vista of all that is below from the lookout point of a majestic mountain. Maybe your breath was taken away as you looked at everything below you. David has fun with words as he speaks to these mountains and "teases" them. "You thought you were highest. But now you feel small and envious—in fact, I think you are mad—because God is so much greater and higher than you." Next to God's throne and presence on Mount Zion, Bashan was a little hill!

David may have had a smile on his lips with these words, but he certainly understood the age-old problem of feeling so much smaller and insignificant compared with those around him. After all, he was the youngest son of an insignificant family in Bethlehem. When Samuel approached his father in search of the next king of Israel, his father didn't even think to call for him to stand before the man of God!

I love this about our Lord: When He challenges mountains, He is really challenging us. As you recognize the greatness and grandeur of God, He will continue to restore to you the full dignity and sense of worth you desire! Feeling forgotten? Worship God and discover your true worth.

Most High God, when I see you in your greatness and majesty—above all others—
you restore to me a sense of dignity and worth I thought I had lost forever.

THE PLUNDER

When you ascended on high, you took many captives;
you received gifts from people, even from the rebellious—that you,
Lord God, might dwell there.

PSALM 68:18, NIV

his victory song continues to be sung as David quotes from the words of Deborah (see Judges 5:12) after God had used her and Barak to deliver His people from an army of enemies. The scene David is describing is one of plunder. As one commentary said, "God shares with them the booty of His victory."

When a city, tribe, or country was defeated, they had no choice but to give gifts to the victors. In this case, David has painted such a vivid picture of the wicked who have exploited and robbed the poor that this becomes a beautiful expression of God's justice. The wicked have lived off of plundering the helpless, but God will not allow such wickedness to continue forever. With God leading our army, we get back that which was stolen. It is returned with interest. Wicked strongholds will fall before God. No walls or defenses can stand against Him. He will take what is His. He will dwell in His place of glory forever.

Don't lose sleep with resentment when it seems the wicked prosper while the righteous suffer. First of all, that is a temporary state of injustice. But second, the righteous have had more than the wicked all along, based on the presence of God. Even if their spiritual wealth is not fully manifest in the human realm, it is still here in our faith and worship.

I proclaim that I am wealthy beyond measure because of the riches
you have given me in Christ Jesus my Lord.

OUR GOD SAVES

Our God is a God who saves; from the Sovereign Lord comes escape from death.

PSALM 68:20, NIV

"Praise be to the Lord, to God our Savior, who daily bears our burdens" (v. 19). That comes just before today's verse. But stop there. Reflect on it before moving on. How often do we rush through life, forgetting the daily benefits that our God so generously lavishes on us? Count your blessings—your daily blessings. God isn't there for you some of the time; He is there for you all of the time. Every day.

Is it any wonder that the call to worship God is so imperative? We praise and worship our God to acknowledge who He is and all He has done on our behalf. I can't imagine a life without worship.

Never forget that in the midst of hardship and trial is the grace of God. Even now, so many benefits are lovingly given to you, His beloved child. Not all of God's blessings and work are immediately recognized. Take comfort in knowing that more is happening beneath the surface—like the seed that has not yet sprouted—than you see in this moment.

From the Sovereign Lord comes escape from death. What more can be said? What a powerful statement and obvious foreshadowing of what Jesus has done for us in defeating the power of sin and death. Not feeling blessed? Our God saves. He gives us eternal life so that we never die but live with Him forever. When my own father was very sick with cancer, I asked him, "Why are we not seeing your healing?" He said, "My love, I have everything I need and more. I know Jesus."

Thank you for all your precious gifts and provision in my life. You bless me every day. And you have made a way for me to live forever, basking in your glory.

THE DESTRUCTION OF HIS ENEMIES

Surely God will crush the heads of his enemies,
the hairy crowns of those who go on in their sins.

PSALM 68:21, NIV

The very first Old Testament prophecy of the coming Savior is right after Adam and Eve have sinned and are about to be booted from the garden home that God made for them. Life is about to get harder, but there is still a glorious hope. God's first hint that a Savior is coming is said to the Serpent: "And I will put enmity between you and the woman, and between your offspring and hers; he will crush your head, and you will strike his heel" (Genesis 3:15).

David understood clearly that God fights our battles for us. Notice that he doesn't claim that he and his armies crushed the heads of their enemies. God did that for them. We get so intent on defending ourselves and making things right that we play God ourselves and forget to let Him do the work only He can do!

The word picture is ugly and bloody. All we need to take from this is the promise that God will destroy our enemies. His enemies and our enemies are the same—those who persist in their sin and take pride in rejecting the grace and kindness of the One who gave them life and being. They truly are the offspring of the Serpent, for he too was created in the image of God and, in fact, was made most beautiful in heaven. What led to his banishment? He decided he would be God. The root of all evil and personal destruction is the desire to be God of our own lives and world.

God's enemies may seem to prosper for a season, but spiritual death and destruction await them.

God, thank you for fighting the battles I cannot win on my own.
Thank you that you sort the goats and the sheep and reward each of us in view
of whether we accepted your gift of salvation.

THE VICTORIOUS KING

*Your procession, God, has come into view, the procession of my God and King
into the sanctuary. In front are the singers, after them the musicians;
with them are the young women playing the timbrels. Praise God in the
great congregation; praise the Lord in the assembly of Israel.*

PSALM 68:24–26, NIV

We move from the ugly aftermath of war to the beauty of God's sanctuary as the victorious King marches to His throne with all the people singing His praise. It's fascinating and a bit heartbreaking to think about the thing David most wanted to do for God: to build God's temple. God did not allow it due to the blood on David's hands. But David never resented that rebuke and always cherished the vision of the place where God would sit in splendor and rule His people. Yes, David was a man after God's heart, for he saw the true nature of God—which allowed him to point his people's faces to the coming of Jesus.

If there is one thing that I truly treasure whenever I enter the house of God, it is simply His presence. God's presence is a constant source of strength and hope for His people. In fact, it is what defines us as His. In Psalm 68 we are reminded that our mighty Lord is not an aloof, austere King who stands far off and is unconcerned for the needs of His people. He daily bears our burdens, provides us a way of escape.

I can just picture this scene of triumph. The ark of the covenant is being carried through the streets to the entrance of the tabernacle. The singers are out front and the musicians are behind. All announce the presence, the victory, and the fullness of God. Yes, when David worshiped God, he saw deep into the future. Let your worship of God bring hope and life to the very heart of who you are.

*Thank you, God, for revealing yourself to us as we worship you.
Thank you for the gift of Jesus, the Victor over all our enemies and battles in life.*

YOU ARE AWESOME

Sing to God, you kingdoms of the earth, sing praise to the Lord. . . .
Proclaim the power of God, whose majesty is over Israel, whose power
is in the heavens. You, God, are awesome in your sanctuary; the God of Israel
gives power and strength to his people. Praise be to God!

PSALM 68:32–35, NIV

The reality of God's power is on full display to the very end of Psalm 68. God, our conquering King, pulls His enemies out of the shadows and into full view of all those they have terrorized. Wickedness will be cast in the depths forever. Righteousness will reign. The victory is forever ours.

After any victory in your life, always remember to say thanks to God. Sing praise to the Lord. How often have you gone to God with a great need, received a mighty victory, and then just gone on your way as if life were normal? When you forget to say thank-you, you lose out on the blessing of thanksgiving and worship—but so do others who need to hear that God is the answer to their every need!

I love the picture painted here of nations that were once in rebellion witnessing the glory of God and unable to resist joining in with the multitudes praising His name.

Yahweh's power is manifest in His temple, and His presence literally imparts power and strength to His people. If you feel the lack of strength in your spirit, ask yourself if you are taking yourself to those places where you experience His presence. Draw near to Him, for He will draw near to you. Don't hesitate. Don't get too busy. Run to see the King of Kings lifted up!

Thank you for your presence that gives me the power
to live the victorious life—always and ever in the name of Jesus.

BREATHE ON ME

And afterward, I will pour out my Spirit on all people.
Your sons and daughters will prophesy, your old men will dream dreams,
your young men will see visions.

JOEL 2:28, NIV

With the Spirit in our lives, we see things with new eyes—spiritual eyes. As you praise God for His gift of the Holy Spirit in song, ask to see the world with His eyes and vision!

Breathe on me, breath of God,
Fill me with life anew,
That I may love what thou dost love,
And do what thou wouldst do.

Breathe on me, breath of God,
Until my heart is pure,
Until with thee I will one will,
To do and to endure.

Breathe on me, breath of God,
So shall I never die,
But live with thee the perfect life
Of thine eternity.

I want your will to be my will, God.
Let my life glow with your divine fire!

COMMISSIONED

One day as they were worshiping God—they were also fasting
as they waited for guidance—the Holy Spirit spoke: "Take Barnabas and Saul
and commission them for the work I have called them to do."

ACTS 13:2, THE MESSAGE

*I*t's interesting that this commissioning takes place in Antioch, not Jerusalem, which is where you would expect such a monumental event to take place. The Jerusalem church has faithfully kept the faith under intense persecution. Key leaders and members have been scattered throughout the world now. So it's not surprising that strong leadership has risen up. But I would also carefully add that sometimes a great work and vibrant move of God can grow stale over time through holding on to traditions and a spirit of "that's how we've always done it" rather than asking, "Are we following God's way?"

Don't get me wrong. I love traditions. I don't love change for change's sake. I definitely don't want to ever compromise on the absolutes of our faith. But sometimes our past success can stifle new ways God is working today. Let's not hold on tightly to what isn't working—and let's never discourage young sons and daughters who are taking the gospel to their world in bold and creative new ways. Encourage and pray for them. It's the message that is sacred, not the method. Thank God that He is raising up men and women everywhere to bring the gospel to this generation.

Are you willing to be led outside of your comfort zone? Bottom line, we need to keep our eyes open to what God is wanting to do today.

❧

Thank you that you are always creating a new work in the world.
Direct me where you want me to go and what you want me to do—even if
it is outside of my comfort zone.

BRIMMING WITH JOY

Some of the Jews convinced the most respected women and leading men
of the town that their precious way of life was about to be destroyed.
Alarmed, they turned on Paul and Barnabas and forced them to leave.
Paul and Barnabas shrugged their shoulders and went on to the next town,
Iconium, brimming with joy and the Holy Spirit, two happy disciples.

ACTS 13:50–52, THE MESSAGE

The gospel was being spread. There were new believers every day. But as is the case today, there were those who rejected the gospel. When Paul and Barnabas traveled to Pisidian Antioch, they were first invited to speak in the Jewish synagogue there. They became an instant success, with crowds overflowing the synagogue like never before. In their final preaching they had to move outside because there wasn't enough room to hold everyone who came out to hear them.

Why did this wonderful start end in the two men being booted from the city? Luke tells us there was jealousy to begin with. But what really stirred the hearts of the people against them was that they were willing to accept Gentiles directly into the church. Some of these devout Jews were open to the gospel—as long as new converts became observant Jews first and then Christians.

Let's never compromise on our faith, my friends. Let's make sure we aren't asking new believers to jump through hoops that God doesn't require or ask of them. God is the God of humanity, where all are welcomed home.

Paul knew that the gospel had been planted and the church would grow, so he left town with a smile and a song on his lips. Are you rejoicing today?

Thank you for empowering me to share your gospel everywhere I set my foot.
Even when there is resistance and rejection, may I never lose the joy
of my salvation as I share that hope with others!

GODS OR MEN

When the crowd saw what Paul had done,
they went wild, calling out in their Lyconian dialect,
"The gods have come down! These men are gods!"

ACTS 14:11, THE MESSAGE

We love and admire those who do God's work with grace and power. The Bible teaches us to honor those who share the Word of God with us. But it is possible to give man glory that is God's alone—and to receive glory for what we do that is God's alone. You don't have to be called a god to grow addicted to the praise of men. But we were never designed to receive glory, only to give glory to our awesome God.

What an amazing scene—almost humorous, were the people not so serious. "They called Barnabas 'Zeus' and Paul 'Hermes' (since Paul did most of the speaking). The priest of the local Zeus shrine got up a parade—bulls and banners and people lined right up to the gates, ready for the ritual of sacrifice" (vv. 12–13).

Before their very eyes they had been made into gods, and a parade was being led in their honor. "When Barnabas and Paul finally realized what was going on, they stopped them. Waving their arms, they interrupted the parade, calling out, 'What do you think you're doing! We're not gods! We are men just like you, and we're here to bring you the message, to persuade you to abandon these silly god-superstitions and embrace God himself, the living God'" (vv. 14–15).

Paul turns this comedy of errors into yet another opportunity to declare the greatness of God. We don't worship the created. Our worship is reserved only for the Creator!

You are the creator God who loves us so much and blesses us
in so many ways. My worship is always for you, O God!

GOD BE WITH YOU!

It seemed to the Holy Spirit and to us that you should not be saddled with
any crushing burden, but be responsible only for these bare necessities:
Be careful not to get involved in activities connected with idols;
avoid serving food offensive to Jewish Christians (blood, for instance);
and guard the morality of sex and marriage.

ACTS 15:28–29, THE MESSAGE

St. Augustine said, "In essentials, unity; in non-essentials, liberty; in all things, charity." What a wonderful principle for the church in all ages. It must break God's heart when we allow differences to turn us against one another.

The early church was at risk of a civil war over the issue of Judaism. Was the Christian responsible to keep the Jewish law? As more and more converts came from non-Jewish backgrounds, Jewish believers became ever more intent on insisting on total adherence to the law.

The answer was obvious to Paul: If they returned to a religion based on legalism, Christ's death and resurrection were in vain. But he was also sensitive to not trample on the feelings of others. So he traveled to Jerusalem for a church meeting to make sure everyone was on the same page. There was direct honesty but also a beautiful harmony. Out of that meeting they reaffirmed salvation as an unmerited gift from God, not a matter of good works.

It is very appropriate to have boundaries, but never as a means of salvation—and with the strong caution that they not become crushing burdens. Unity, liberty, love. Let's ask God to give us the wisdom to live within those three guidelines.

Thank you, God, for leading me into paths of peace with my brothers and sisters
in Christ. Let love be our ultimate rule based on your free gift of salvation.

SEPARATE WAYS

Barnabas wanted to take John along, the John nicknamed Mark. But Paul wouldn't have him; he wasn't about to take along a quitter who, as soon as the going got tough, had jumped ship on them in Pamphylia. Tempers flared, and they ended up going their separate ways: Barnabas took Mark and sailed for Cyprus; Paul chose Silas and. . . went to Syria and Cilicia to build up muscle and sinew in those congregations.

ACTS 15:37–41, THE MESSAGE

The church was growing by leaps and bounds, but growth often brings more challenges. Mark was a member of Paul and Barnabas's first missionary journey and party. We don't know why it was too much for this young minister, but he abandoned the mission and went home. Paul proclaimed and lived by grace, but in this particular situation he didn't yet trust Mark to get the job done. Barnabas—the consummate encourager—felt Mark was ready for this second chance.

Paul and Barnabas were spiritual brothers through and through. But tempers flared, and they elected to go separate ways.

Praise God that this split ended up doubling the missionary efforts out of Antioch. Instead of one powerful team taking the gospel, there were two. And praise God that there was total reconciliation among those involved. At the very end of his life, Paul specifically mentioned what a help John Mark had been in his ministry.

We're human. We're imperfect. We're emotional. If there is tension in your relationships, ask God to forgive you, and then do all in your power to make peace. "Blessed are the peacemakers, for they will be called the children of God" (Matthew 5:9). Watch and see the miracle that only God can do!

*Thank you, Father, that you can work in us even when we disagree.
I pray that my life would reflect your love and forgiveness in all my encounters.*

A BOLD NEW VENTURE

*That night Paul had a dream: A Macedonian stood on the far shore
and called across the sea, "Come over to Macedonia and help us!"
The dream gave Paul his map. We went to work at once getting things ready
to cross over to Macedonia. All the pieces had come together. We knew now
for sure that God had called us to preach the good news to the Europeans.*

ACTS 16:9–10, THE MESSAGE

*O*ur mission is to reveal Jesus to the entire world. There will always be a bold new venture that God has in His heart and mind. That means He will always be looking for faithful servants to fulfill those plans. Is your heart open to God's voice? Are you willing to change direction to align yourself with His will? Are you ready to say yes to something new and outrageous that God would ask of you?

Paul had been hitting Asia Minor with all his heart and energy with the gospel. No one would ever think to say to him, "There's something more you can do." But God did. He met Paul in a dream and showed him a Greek man pleading for help. Who would have thought that a whole new continent was praying for the gospel? Paul changed his own plans to experience his greatest days of ministry.

God's call to us comes in many ways. But one of the best ways to know that God has something new for you is when you see a need and feel a burden on your heart.

Have you felt a burden for a special need in your world? Could it be God is calling you to bold new work? Nothing will bring you greater joy and satisfaction in life than knowing that God has a mission for you to fulfill. What are you waiting for?

*Thank you that you still speak to us today, God. My ears and eyes
are open to anything you ask me to do. Thank you for the empowerment
of the Holy Spirit to fulfill any call you put on my life.*

A PRISON WORSHIP SERVICE

*Along about midnight, Paul and Silas were at prayer and singing
a robust hymn to God. The other prisoners couldn't believe their ears.
Then, without warning, a huge earthquake! The jailhouse tottered,
every door flew open, all the prisoners were loose.*

ACTS 16:25–26, THE MESSAGE

Paul and Silas had cast demons out of a deranged and tortured young girl who was a moneymaking freak show for her heartless master. It was an incredible cause for celebration. But her owner only saw a loss of income. He took the case before the authorities, and they took the side of money-grubbing over deliverance. The two men were cast in prison.

Were they discouraged and defeated? Did they curse their bad luck and plot how to get revenge on this man? That would be the natural response. But these two missionaries had a supernatural trust in God. So they began to worship, praying and singing with loud voices. They weren't afraid. In fact, this was a great opportunity for them. Any other prisoner within earshot had no choice but to hear the gospel!

There is such joy and power that comes to us when we worship. Their chains were broken and the door flew open. The jailer was ready to fall on his sword rather than face the punishment that would have awaited him over their escape. Before the evening was over, he and his entire family were baptized.

The church is unstoppable—you are unstoppable—when you worship the risen Savior in any circumstance, with a loud voice, with prayer and singing, in stillness or simply by pouring out your life in service before God.

*Father, your unmerited grace saved me from my sins, and your undeserved favor
gives my life such fulfillment and joy. I will worship you all of my days!*

THE DIVIDING POINT

*At the phrase "raising him from the dead," the listeners split: Some laughed at him and
walked off making jokes; others said, "Let's do this again. We want to hear more."*

ACTS 17:32, THE MESSAGE

*P*aul and Silas were now in the center of Greek culture, the great city of
Athens. Philosophers, priests, and orators held court all over the city, but
the people were drawn to these two strange men who talked of a God who was both
killed and risen from the dead.

Paul was willing to be all things to all men that some might be saved, but he wasn't
willing to present Jesus Christ as just another nice religious option to consider. He
knew Jesus' words, that He is "the Way" and not just "a way" to God the Father.

He presented Him as the crucified and risen Lord of all. Some scoffed. Their
belief in their own wisdom and philosophical systems would not allow them to take
this claim seriously. Is it any different with the "wise" of our day? Others were willing
to hear more and consider Paul's words more carefully. But ultimately, we read little
about the gospel taking hold in Athens.

When man insists and persists in self-sufficiency and wisdom to discover his
own path of salvation, the gospel will be rejected. We receive salvation not by being
smarter than others but through a faith that is infused with humility before God.

The spirit of Athens is alive and well today: brilliant thoughts but no understanding of salvation and godly wisdom. Study, think, learn, grow in your understanding
of the world. But never forget that man's wisdom is not God's wisdom. His wisdom
trumps all others. We enter the kingdom of heaven with the simple faith of a child!

*Father, thank you for the gift of salvation that goes below and above any human
understanding of being saved. I place my confidence and faith in you and you alone.*

STICK IT OUT

In the course of listening to Paul, a great many Corinthians believed and were baptized.
One night the Master spoke to Paul in a dream: "Keep it up, and don't let anyone
intimidate or silence you. No matter what happens, I'm with you and no one is going to
be able to hurt you. You have no idea how many people I have on my side in this city."
That was all he needed to stick it out. He stayed another year and a half,
faithfully teaching the Word of God to the Corinthians.

ACTS 18:9–11, THE MESSAGE

*P*aul ended his second missionary journey in Corinth, where he stayed for a year and a half. It was a major city politically and economically. He didn't want to give even the appearance of preaching the gospel for gain in this jaded city, so he worked as a tentmaker. In previous cities he had started by preaching to the Jews—which had been both successful and a source of concentrated rejection and persecution—so in Corinth he focused on sharing the gospel with Gentiles.

God visited Paul again in a dream—He knew that even this man with an irrepressible personality and enthusiasm was growing weary of constant opposition. God both commanded and encouraged Paul by telling him not to be afraid and to never stop speaking. Paul is considered to be the twelfth apostle by many Bible teachers, but he wasn't present when Jesus gave the Great Commission. So God reminded him of Jesus' promise that He would be with him always, even to the very ends of the earth.

Are you discouraged? Have you grown weary with the challenges of ministry? Don't give up. Stick it out. Even now, Jesus is with you.

Thank you for the precious promise that Jesus is with me no matter
where I am in the world. Thank you for casting out fear and giving me the resilience
to never remain quiet about your goodness.

FRESH HOPE

With things back to normal, Paul called the disciples together and encouraged them to keep up the good work in Ephesus. Then, saying his good-byes, he left for Macedonia. Traveling through the country, passing from one gathering to another, he gave constant encouragement, lifting their spirits and charging them with fresh hope.

ACTS 20:1–2, THE MESSAGE

Each of us has been uniquely gifted to do what only we can do in this world. But I think that each one of us carries the responsibility and ability to be an encourager to one another. All it takes is a listening ear and a kind word. We don't have to be trained in counseling or have a special way with words. Sometimes words aren't even necessary to offer encouragement. A simple hug can be the most powerful communication we can deliver to a friend who is discouraged.

Keep in mind that Paul was on his way back to Jerusalem for his final meeting with the church there. But every mile of his journey was contested by those who wanted to stomp out this growing movement based on faith in Jesus Christ. There were sweet times too, as he got to spend time with his beloved children who came to know Jesus Christ through his preaching. But it was hard to be under constant siege.

What an amazing man. His first thought was always on others. Is it any wonder that he revealed Jesus with such power? People were able to see God's grace on his life under fire. I am convinced that thousands would never have listened to his sermons had they not seen his passionate and godly life.

I can promise you this, my friends. If you will focus on encouraging others—even when you feel discouraged and weary yourself—God himself will draw near to you and renew your heart and mind.

Dear God, you are my source of encouragement. You are my Friend and Counselor. You lift me up when I feel like I've hit rock bottom. Thank you for your love for me.

IT HURTS

Then Paul went down on his knees, all of them kneeling with him, and prayed.
And then a river of tears. Much clinging to Paul, not wanting to let him go.
They knew they would never see him again—he had told them quite plainly.
The pain cut deep. Then, bravely, they walked him down to the ship.

ACTS 20:36–38, THE MESSAGE

When Shakespeare wrote that "parting is such sweet sorrow" in Romeo and Juliet, he might have been describing this farewell scene between Paul and his friends in Miletus. Two opposite emotions were present: joy and sorrow. Paul felt joy that a new generation of spiritual leaders was now assuming their place in the church, but knowing he would never see them again was heartbreaking. In the same way, the elders knew Paul had important work in Jerusalem, including a love offering he had collected for them. But this was their spiritual father they were saying good-bye to for the last time. Together they cried a river of tears.

How beautiful. How sad. There are people who keep others at arm's length in life to protect themselves from this kind of sorrow. But if you think about it, it's only the people who bring us great joy who can bring us great sorrow. If we are to have the kinds of deep and abiding relationships God has created us to experience, then this will be a bittersweet pattern in life.

I for one would not trade one tear I've shed for the joy of Christian love I have for brothers and sisters all over the world. Open your heart to true love. I would rather live with the risk of pain than to live without the joy of love.

Thank you for the precious bonds of love you have given me
through fellowship with those who share my love for you.

WHAT A STORY TO TELL!

After a time of greeting and small talk, Paul told the story, detail by detail,
of what God had done among the non-Jewish people through his ministry.
They listened with delight and gave God the glory. They had a story to tell, too:
"And just look at what's been happening here—thousands upon thousands
of God-fearing Jews have become believers in Jesus!"

ACTS 21:18–20, THE MESSAGE

I love the church, in all her forms—tiny, large, and everything in between. I also love when the church at large gathers together, putting aside differences and taking a stand for unity—across a city, a nation, a people group. I have led worship in many settings where denominations and generations have gathered together to lift up the name of Jesus, and there is nothing quite like it. There is something powerful about seeing that the body of believers is bigger than our local place of worship. It opens our eyes to even more ways God is at work in the world.

When Paul finally arrived in Jerusalem, I can just see this group of leaders staying up all night, laughing and crying, asking questions and sometimes interrupting as they told of the marvelous things God was doing all over the world. What a story Paul had to tell. It filled the Jerusalem leaders with amazement. But oh what a story they had to tell him. He could not have been happier.

When we arrive in heaven, we will be amazed at how many are there that we didn't even know existed. Gathering together in larger settings is just a taste of what we will experience in eternity.

Thank you, Father, for my local church. And I thank you for making me part
of a fellowship that crosses centuries and countries and languages and cultures.

LIKE HIS MASTER

The people in the crowd had listened attentively up to this point, but now
they broke loose, shouting out, "Kill him! He's an insect! Stomp on him!"
They shook their fists. They filled the air with curses.

ACTS 22:22, THE MESSAGE

From this moment on, Paul would spend the rest of his life in prison. The religious leaders were infuriated with someone who challenged their prejudices, which weren't an expression of true faith and certainly brought no glory to God.

My heart's desire is to be true to the teachings of God's Word, and my responsibility to that end is to study, to remain teachable, and to be always listening for revelation. For Paul, this ultimately cost him everything. But his joy was complete in serving his King.

Just as Jesus' arrest and trial and death were part of God's plan, so the next steps of this dear apostle were ordained. Paul knew that to spread the gospel far and wide he had to preach in the largest and most influential cities. What other city in the world could compare with Rome? The arrest and trials that followed ensured that Paul would carry the gospel of Jesus Christ to the city that was not *a* hub but *the* hub of communication in the Greco-Roman world.

The wonderful reminder for us is that God can use us no matter what circumstances swirl around us. When you are experiencing smooth sailing, thank God for His blessings. When life is filled with storms, thank God for His blessings and His plans to reveal Jesus through your grace and poise. I pray that our lives would be a great example of God's beauty and kindness in our lives.

Father, protect your servants under opposition, persecution, and imprisonment.
Thank you for the grace you bestow upon them and their testimony of that grace
that touches the hearts of even their enemies.

MY WITNESS IN ROME

That night the Master appeared to Paul: "It's going to be all right.
Everything is going to turn out for the best. You've been a good witness for me
here in Jerusalem. Now you're going to be my witness in Rome!"

ACTS 23:11, THE MESSAGE

God confirmed in Paul's heart what he already knew was his destiny. Paul knew what was coming and stayed his course with determination and joy. Here are just a couple of the predictions and foreshadowing of what would happen to him in Jerusalem:

"The Holy Spirit has let me know repeatedly and clearly that there are hard times and imprisonment ahead. But that matters little. What matters most to me is to finish what God started" (20:23-24).

"After several days of visiting, a prophet from Judea by the name of Agabus came down to see us. He went right up to Paul, took Paul's belt, and, in a dramatic gesture, tied himself up, hands and feet. He said, 'This is what the Holy Spirit says: The Jews in Jerusalem are going to tie up the man who owns this belt just like this and hand him over to godless unbelievers.' When we heard that, we and everyone there that day begged Paul not to be stubborn and persist in going to Jerusalem. But Paul wouldn't budge: 'Why all this hysteria? Why do you insist on making a scene and making it even harder for me? You're looking at this backward. The issue in Jerusalem is not what they do to me, whether arrest or murder, but what the Master Jesus does through my obedience. Can't you see that?'" (21:10-13).

Are we ready and willing to complete the work God has given us to do? No matter what the cost?

Father give me the courageous faith to do whatever
you would ask of me to reveal Jesus in my world.

ALMOST PERSUADED

But Agrippa did answer: "Keep this up much longer
and you'll make a Christian out of me!"

ACTS 26:28, THE MESSAGE

*L*ike Pilate, the Roman governor who had no idea what to do with Jesus, so
Festus, the current Roman governor over Palestine, was perplexed by this
man Paul. He too wanted to hand him back to the religious authorities because he
felt it was a religious matter. But Paul demanded his right to a Roman trial. He was
intent on preaching in Rome, after all, and this meant his way was paid!

Festus called for King Agrippa to join him to discuss the case. Agrippa observed
Jewish religious customs and had beheaded James and other early church leaders. But
he was intrigued by what Festus told him about Paul. He asked to speak to him, and
not surprisingly, Paul delivered a powerful sermon. It's possible he was being sarcastic,
but most Bible scholars believe Agrippa was sincerely touched by Paul's words. He
told Paul, "Keep this up much longer and you'll make a Christian out of me!"

Paul, chained as a common prisoner but always quick on his feet, responded,
"That's what I'm praying for, whether now or later, and not only you but everyone
listening today, to become like me—except, of course, for this prison jewelry!" (v. 29).

Did Agrippa become a Christian? Later accounts from Josephus suggest probably not. But the importance of this passage is clear. Paul preached the gospel to
Agrippa. He gave him a poignant opportunity to follow Jesus. But the choice was
Agrippa's. Our obedience to God will not always achieve the results we want, but our
ultimate call is not to be successful, but to be faithful!

Keep me faithful so that I serve you joyfully and obediently all my life, O God.

ALL DAY AND ALL NIGHT

*They agreed on a time. When the day arrived, they came back
to his home with a number of their friends. Paul talked to them all day,
from morning to evening, explaining everything involved in the kingdom of God,
and trying to persuade them all about Jesus by pointing out what Moses
and the prophets had written about him.*

ACTS 28:23, THE MESSAGE

Paul's "ministry in chains" was coming to an end. Soon he would be executed. He was an old man. His body was a wreck from beatings, stonings, and thousands of miles on foot. If ever anyone deserved the opportunity to slow down and enjoy some ease and rest at the end of life, it was Paul. But try telling him that.

His body was not his own. He wasn't preserving it for anything better in life. So he welcomed everyone into the house prison he rented out—another opportunity to reveal Jesus. "Paul talked to them all day, from morning to evening."

Do you feel a little worn out and beat up yourself? Paul's admonition to you is the same he had for himself: "So let's not allow ourselves to get fatigued doing good. At the right time we will harvest a good crop if we don't give up, or quit. Right now, therefore, every time we get the chance, let us work for the benefit of all, starting with the people closest to us in the community of faith" (Galatians 6:9–10).

He preached day and night. He knew that at the right time he would reap a bountiful harvest for his efforts, and that many would come to know about God's amazing love and grace. He is such a fine example to us all.

*Thank you for the joy and privilege of serving you. Thank you
for changed lives—and that others are saying yes to the call of the gospel.*

RESPECT AUTHORITY

Everyone must submit to governing authorities. For all authority comes from God,
and those in positions of authority have been placed there by God.

ROMANS 13:1, NLT

I believe with all my heart that God has planted greatness in all of us. There are times all of us are called to be leaders and take charge of a situation.

But I also fully believe we are called—commanded—to recognize and respect those who are in authority in our lives. We are to do this even when those authorities aren't perfect. And we all know that no one and no system is perfect.

Though there are many places where brutal dictators still do their evil, in much of the world there are limits on authority, and systems have been set in place for respectful discourse and even disagreement. So we aren't living in the world of the Roman Empire that Paul toiled in. But let's not give the freedoms we cherish and the invitation for input and participation to allow us to think that God's principles of respect and submission aren't still binding on us.

We honor God when we honor authority. God asks us to pray for those in authority—in our homes, churches, governments, nations. . . .

So let's participate, using our influence based on godly understanding, but always with the utmost respect. And let's teach our children the same. We honor others by showing respect, and we can honor the Word of God today by following His Holy Spirit wisdom. Will you pray today for someone who has influence over your life as a leader?

If my people, who are called by my name, will humble themselves and pray
and seek my face and turn from their wicked ways, then will I hear from heaven
and will forgive their sin and will heal their land.

THE DEBT OF LOVE

Owe nothing to anyone—except for your obligation to love one another.
If you love your neighbor, you will fulfill the requirements of God's law.

ROMANS 13:8, NLT

We all know that too much financial debt is a burden that brings great stress into our lives. If you are under such a dark cloud, act now in prayer and by seeking wise counsel and making the changes you need to make.

But there is a debt that Paul says is wonderful—the obligation to love. Throughout the New Testament, the various writers have clearly heard and clearly revealed Jesus' teaching that the law can be summed up by loving God and loving others.

Whom do we owe this debt to? Our neighbor? Even though we are to love our neighbor, that is not who we owe the debt to. The debt is based on what Jesus Christ did for us in His death and resurrection. It is in view of the mercy, because He first loved us, that we love others.

Even if there is someone in your life you find difficult to love, you can do it. Not necessarily because you feel warmth and affection for them, but because of how much you love God. Matthew 5:43–45 puts it like this: "You have heard that it was said, 'Love your neighbor and hate your enemy.' But I tell you, love your enemies and pray for those who persecute you, that you may be children of your Father in heaven. He causes his sun to rise on the evil and the good, and sends rain on the righteous and the unrighteous."

Love God, and show Him love by doing your best as you pray for those who challenge you, allowing the Holy Spirit to work in your heart today!

Thank you, heavenly Father, for your gracious kindness to me. I can never repay
the debt I owe you for what Jesus did for me. I will express my love to you
as I love others—even the ones who are difficult for me to love.

THE LORDSHIP OF JESUS

A Classic Devotion by A. W. Tozer

*We must pay the most careful attention, therefore,
to what we have heard, so that we do not drift away.*

HEBREWS 2:1, NIV

We are under constant temptation these days to substitute another Christ for the Christ of the New Testament. The whole drift of modern religion is toward such a substitution. . . .

The mighty, revolutionary message of the early church was that a man named Jesus who had been crucified was now raised from the dead and exalted to the right hand of God. "Therefore let all the house of Israel know assuredly, that God hath made the same Jesus, whom ye have crucified, both Lord and Christ" [Acts 2:36, KJV]. . . .

He is the way to God, the life of the believer, the hope of Israel and the high priest of every true worshiper. He holds the keys of death and hell and stands as advocate and surety for everyone who believes on Him in truth.

With Him rest the noblest hopes and dreams of men. All the longings for immortality that rise and swell in the human breast will be fulfilled in Him or they will never know fulfillment. There is no other way (John 14:6).

Salvation comes by believing on the Lord Jesus Christ, the whole, living, victorious Lord who, as God and man, fought our fight and won it, accepted our debt as His own and paid it, took our sins and died under them and rose again to set us free. This is the true Christ, and nothing less will do.

*O God, I embrace Jesus Christ as you have revealed Him in Scripture
and confirmed through the presence of the Holy Spirit in my life!*

PEACE

JESUS HIMSELF IS OUR PEACE.
HE BRINGS UNITY.

OCTOBER

When peace, like a river,
   attendeth my way,
When sorrows like sea billows roll;
   Whatever my lot, thou has taught me to say,
It is well, it is well, with my soul.

And Lord, haste the day
   when my faith shall be sight,
The clouds be rolled back as a scroll;
The trump shall resound,
   and the Lord shall descend,
Even so, it is well with my soul.

THE STORY CONTINUES

*Dear Theophilus, in the first volume of this book I wrote on everything that
Jesus began to do and teach until the day he said good-bye to the apostles,
the ones he had chosen through the Holy Spirit, and was taken up to heaven.*

ACTS 1:1, THE MESSAGE

*I*f we want to reveal Jesus to our world, who better to look to for guidance than
the very first group of "Jesus Revealers," the small band of early Christians
that shared Jesus to the four corners of the Roman Empire and beyond.

In the New Testament, Luke and Acts are separated by the gospel of John. But
these two books are bound together. The physician Luke makes clear they are part
1 and part 2 of the story of Jesus and the birth of the church. With the crucifixion
of Christ, one might expect a decline in this fledgling faith. But His resurrection
ensures that the story of Jesus is just beginning—the story continues!

Acts is written to Theophilus, which literally means "friend of God." There may
have been a real Theophilus, or that may have been the way Luke liked to address
his fellow Christians. Either way, the point is clear: If you are a friend of God, then
this book is written to you. Yes, my friends, God has things he wants to share with
us today.

Savor this fabulous narrative that shows how Jesus was revealed to His earliest
followers and how they in turn revealed Him to their world. Put yourself in these
stories. You may not be beaten, prosecuted, or shipwrecked for your faith, but you will
discover that your faith in Jesus Christ is revealed in every area of your life.

*Open my eyes to your Word, to your story, to the miracle
of your reality in our lives. May all of us recapture the mission
of taking you to the four corners of the earth.*

A TIME TO WAIT

As they met and ate meals together, he told them that they were on no account to leave Jerusalem but "must wait for what the Father promised: the promise you heard from me. John baptized in water; you will be baptized in the Holy Spirit. And soon."

ACTS 1:4–5, THE MESSAGE

I am not the most patient person in the world. When God puts something on my heart to do, I want to start yesterday. But sometimes God calls us to wait. It might be that the time isn't right for us to launch what is in our heart. It might mean that we need more time to prepare.

Jesus didn't begin His public ministry until He was thirty. After Paul's conversion on the road to Damascus, he went into the desert to study Scripture for two whole years. Yes, you heard that right. Paul, the man who was driven to get things accomplished, delayed his work that long.

The resurrected Jesus, our Victor, tells His disciples they need more before they begin their ministry. They need the Holy Spirit. That was God's special promise to them and is His special gift to us today when we receive Jesus into our lives. He becomes our Teacher, our Guide, our Empowerer. He is God, so literally He is the presence of God in our lives.

God may still ask us to wait before we begin a great undertaking. But wait in faith and expectation that God's timing is perfect and His ways are higher than our ways. Know and rest in the presence of the Holy Spirit in your life. With His power, nothing is impossible for you!

Thank you for the promise and the gift of the Holy Spirit.
I submit myself to His guidance and teaching and power in my life today.

CHANGED LIVES

That day about three thousand took him at his word, were baptized and were signed up. They committed themselves to the teaching of the apostles, the life together, the common meal, and the prayers.

ACTS 2:41–42, THE MESSAGE

*W*ow. What a sermon. What an anointing. Peter, once afraid to make his faith known in front of a teenage servant girl, is now a bold and passionate preacher. Of course, he's received the gift of the Holy Spirit that has given him power from on high for Christian living and service. Now thousands are accepting the good news of Jesus Christ.

The need for Jesus is just as desperate in our world today as it was when Peter drew a crowd in Jerusalem. Pray with all your heart that we will all stand and declare that God is here, that we can speak with a power and clarity that rings true in the hearts of nonbelievers—even among those who are most resistant to God.

We must check our own hearts and ask ourselves if we are allowing the power of the Holy Spirit to flow in us and through us, spilling over with the love of Christ to those around us.

Peter preached in the open air, and thousands were drawn to Christ. I am praying that in arenas and convention halls, on television and radio, in the open air, in churches, in our schools and universities—wherever people are gathered—we will all take our place in sharing the good news of Jesus Christ. Nothing is more important in our day than revealing Jesus to the whole world.

Thank you, heavenly Father, that you empower me to share Jesus Christ. I pray for all who read this prayer, young and old. The harvest is ripe. Here we are, Lord. Send us.

WHAT I HAVE I GIVE

Peter said, "I don't have a nickel to my name, but what I do have, I give you: In the name of Jesus Christ of Nazareth, walk!" He grabbed him by the right hand and pulled him up. In an instant his feet and ankles became firm. He jumped to his feet and walked.

ACTS 3:6–8, THE MESSAGE

*H*e was a crippled beggar brought to a busy spot where he would be seen by Jewish worshipers approaching the temple. He was there to ply the only trade he knew—appealing to the generosity of others. Little did he suspect that he was about to receive so much more than he could ever dream of.

It is emphasized that Peter looked him right in the eyes and demanded that the man look at him in the same way. This was no casual encounter for Peter. He wasn't trying to get away from the beggar as fast as he could without being embarrassed by eye contact. Peter was engaged on this man and his real need. If we're too busy to listen to someone in need—to stop and engage—then we are just too busy.

Peter obviously did not have much to give in the natural, but he gave the man something so much better—complete healing. Peter declared the healing in the name of Jesus of Nazareth. I love this! He gave out of what he did have. To be honest, that's all God ever asks of us. Our prayers go up to our heavenly Father, but even they are sealed in Jesus' name.

I think it's significant that Peter reached out his hand to help the man up. No, it wasn't Peter who healed him. Jesus did that. But he still offered what he had, including a helping hand. That wasn't just an isolated event two thousand years ago. Miracles happen every moment of every day . . . when we pray, believe, serve, and give a hand in Jesus' name.

Thank you that you use me to bring salvation and healing to those around me when I offer what I have in the beautiful name of Jesus.

GOD KNEW

And now, friends, I know you had no idea what you were doing
when you killed Jesus, and neither did your leaders. But God, who through
the preaching of all the prophets had said all along that his Messiah would be killed,
knew exactly what you were doing and used it to fulfill his plans.

ACTS 3:17–18, THE MESSAGE

Peter, a common fisherman, is preaching to huge crowds everywhere he goes. He is now in the temple gate and preaching from Solomon's porch. Despite his humble beginnings, he is being honored and shown respect as a man of learning and wisdom. Friends, don't ever feel inadequate in sharing God's truth to others because you feel you don't have enough formal education. Wisdom begins in humility, knowing that God is to be respected and feared above all.

Peter doesn't pull any punches. He tells it straight to the crowd. *You killed the Messiah.* He adds that it was in ignorance, which probably made some of them madder. But before calling the people to repentance, he makes a bold declaration. "God knew what you were doing and used it to fulfill his plans." Not even the worst misunderstanding and mistake in human history was outside of God's plans.

Romans 8:28 says, "And we know that in all things God works for the good of those who love him." He works all things together for good. If you love Jesus, rest in this promise. Even when you make mistakes thinking you are doing the right thing.

God knew. God knows! He knows what's going on in your life right now. Give your heart to Him in humility and commitment and see what great things He can do through you. It's time to trust God with a brand-new understanding of His commitment toward you.

Thank you for the marvelous plans you have for my life. Thank you for guiding
my steps even when I don't fully understand the direction you are taking me.

ONE HEART, ONE MIND!

The whole congregation of believers was united as one—one heart, one mind!
They didn't even claim ownership of their own possessions. No one said,
"That's mine; you can't have it." They shared everything. The apostles gave powerful
witness to the resurrection of the Master Jesus, and grace was on all of them.

ACTS 4:32–33, THE MESSAGE

Greek culture was still a huge influence throughout the Roman Empire. Going back to Aristotle, they had a most interesting description of friendship: a single soul dwelling in two bodies. Much of Luke's audience had Greek backgrounds, and they would have immediately understood his application. I love and thrive on the sweet fellowship I find in my church family. It's very imperfect, full of individuals who are as different as can be, but committed to a greater purpose.

I pray you find yourself in a congregation saturated with grace that spills over into love for one another that is deep and affirming. I pray that you are in a place where there is such a sense of common purpose that differences of opinion melt into nothingness. Nothing hurts the testimony of the church more than bitter strife. That doesn't mean there won't be disagreements on strategies and every decision—keep reading through Acts and you will find that was the case in the early church—but this must never turn into contempt or dislike for one another.

Pray for your pastor. Pray for your brothers and sisters. Pray for your own spirit and attitudes. Ask God for an outpouring of grace that will make your place of worship a powerful ministry where all pull together with one heart and one mind!

Thank you for my church, O Lord, where you have planted me. May we open
our hearts to your unlimited supply of grace, where our love for one another will grow
even more as we work together to reveal Jesus in the place you have gathered us.

WE WILL OBEY GOD

Peter and the apostles answered, "It's necessary to obey God rather than men. The God of our ancestors raised up Jesus, the One you killed by hanging him on a cross. God set him on high at his side, Prince and Savior, to give Israel the gift of a changed life and sins forgiven. And we are witnesses to these things. The Holy Spirit, whom God gives to those who obey him, corroborates every detail."

ACTS 5:29–32, THE MESSAGE

In his first letter, Peter reminds us to respect and honor authority. God has instituted government to promote safety and prosperity. But in Acts this same apostle shows us there is a limit to our obedience to civil authorities. The religious rulers had ordered him and John to stop preaching the gospel of Jesus Christ or face imprisonment and possibly even death. The two disciples of Jesus knew these weren't idle words. After all, they were witnesses to the crucifixion.

But when it came to the task of revealing Jesus, their own personal safety was of no concern to them. They were fearless. And Peter establishes the supreme rule of obedience: "It's necessary to obey God rather than men." This cannot become an excuse for taking the law of the land lightly.

But when government asks us to disobey God and dishonor our Christian convictions, we are called to obey God first—not in anger, but with love in our hearts.

Are you being asked to violate your conscience? Pray for God's wisdom and guidance. Then obey Him with humility and respect.

Father, thank you for establishing me as a person of character and conviction. I pray that all my words and thoughts would be seasoned with grace and love. Make me a witness to your truth through the way I live and move and have my being.

THE FACE OF AN ANGEL

*As all those who sat on the High Council looked at Stephen, they found
they couldn't take their eyes off him—his face was like the face of an angel!*

ACTS 6:15, THE MESSAGE

The first martyr of the Christian faith was Stephen, a young man filled with grace and wisdom. He preached with such power and conviction, was so effective in revealing Jesus in what had become "enemy territory" for Christians, that it focused on him the anger the Jewish religious leaders were feeling toward followers of Jesus Christ. "That stirred up the people, the religious leaders, and religion scholars. They grabbed Stephen and took him before the High Council. They put forward their bribed witnesses to testify: 'This man talks nonstop against this Holy Place and God's Law. We even heard him say that Jesus of Nazareth would tear this place down and throw out all the customs Moses gave us'" (vv. 12–14).

The pattern is so similar to the arrest and accusations made against Jesus. Everything was untrue, and people had to be bribed to testify against this young man of God. As the trial began, even Stephen's accusers could not pull their eyes off him. Stephen was so full of the Spirit—so full of wisdom, faith, grace, light, and power—that the glory of God shone from his face.

This man had seen and experienced Jesus Christ so deeply and fully, there was a physical glow that radiated from him. Have you ever seen someone you have never met and known in your heart he loves God? When we walk with love for Jesus and His joy is on our face, we make Him known to a broken and hurting world.

They weren't able to convict Stephen of wrongdoing, but it is obvious he was "guilty" of loving his Savior. I pray we would all be convicted on the same charge!

*Thank you, Father, for filling my heart with the power and the joy of knowing Jesus
as my Savior and my Friend. May it overflow to all around me today.*

DON'T BLAME THEM

As the rocks rained down, Stephen prayed, "Master Jesus, take my life."
Then he knelt down, praying loud enough for everyone to hear,
"Master, don't blame them for this sin"—his last words. Then he died.

ACTS 7:59–60, THE MESSAGE

*S*tephen is given his chance to speak in his own defense and delivers a beautiful sermon. He walks through the promise made to Abraham and how it was preserved in Joseph; he reminds them of Israel's redemption and ongoing rebellion, including in the present day—something that made his accusers very unhappy. He also reveals himself to be a man of worship, not based on a physical building, the temple, but based on the majesty and glory of God. The Jewish leaders are infuriated. They can't see what is right in front of them: Stephen is a man of God. Let's never let tradition become a poor substitute for open and faithful hearts before God.

Like his Lord, Stephen dies with a supernatural peace. He is praying for his murderers with his last words: "Master, don't blame them for this sin."

For any of us that have held a petty grudge or harbored unforgiveness in our heart, this verse forever destroys any excuse for holding on to grievances.

Stephen was so filled with God's peace that the Scripture tells us he fell asleep. God was taking care of him in death, and Stephen woke to be with Him in glory! My own grandfather in his final days said, "These are the greatest days of my life, the veil between me and heaven so very thin."

Forgiveness to all who have hurt us on any level is the only way to living a life that is truly free. Follow Stephen's example today.

Father God, if I am harboring even a trace of anger or resentment toward anyone—
even if they truly have sought to harm me—I offer full forgiveness now
through your peace and strength. I speak blessing over their lives in Jesus' name.

NOT FOR SALE

When Simon saw that the apostles by merely laying on hands conferred the Spirit, he pulled out his money, excited, and said, "Sell me your secret! Show me how you did that! How much do you want? Name your price!" Peter said, "To hell with your money! And you along with it. Why, that's unthinkable—trying to buy God's gift!"

ACTS 8:18–20, THE MESSAGE

The church continues to thrive and spread like wildfire despite severe persecution. Peter and John are sent into Samaria. It is now their moment to receive the Holy Spirit. God's plan to save the whole world is unfolding.

Filled with the Spirit, Peter and John's words are anointed with power, and people accept Jesus by the thousands. They heal the sick and perform miracles. A magician named Simon sees this and wants this authority for himself. He offers them whatever amount of money it takes. He sees this as an investment to gain an even bigger financial gain.

Simon was not the first nor the last to corrupt true faith for financial gain. I don't stand in judgment of any Christian minister who has been blessed abundantly in service to Jesus Christ. But I remind myself and anyone who is supported financially for full-time ministry to never let power and gain become their motive for service. Everything we do is to be out of love and worship for God and the building of His kingdom! Many years ago while I was praying over my future, God spoke clearly to my heart: "Daughter, you are not for sale. You have already been bought with a price." Remember today how valuable you are, bought with the precious blood of Jesus, made in the image of God himself. You are not for sale. Period.

Clean hands. Clean hearts. Keep us pure in our service to you, O God. I do everything I do for your glory, not mine. I love you with all my heart today!

BLINDED BY THE LIGHT

He set off. When he got to the outskirts of Damascus, he was suddenly dazed by a blinding flash of light. As he fell to the ground, he heard a voice: "Saul, Saul, why are you out to get me?"

ACTS 9:3–4, THE MESSAGE

*S*omething happened when Saul witnessed Stephen's martyrdom. The change did not come into his heart and life immediately—in fact, he tried to block the vision by going on a murderous rampage against followers of Jesus—but his heart was under conviction. When he saw Stephen, he caught a glimpse of Jesus. When you reveal Jesus to others, some will accept Him immediately. Others will reject Him. Don't give up on the rejecters.

God had set up an appointment with Saul, and Jesus appeared when he was ready to listen. God is so faithful to us. We might not encounter Jesus in a blinding light, but God is still trying to get our attention. He found you in salvation. He continues to seek you to renew your spirit and service. Keep your eyes and heart open. You don't know when God has a special revelation for you.

"Saul, Saul, why are you out to get me?" Jesus' words are meant to make Saul's decision crystal clear. He is asking Saul the ultimate question all of us must answer: "Why are you rejecting God, who loves you so much?"

When we reveal Jesus, many will come up with reasons they can't accept Him. They'll point fingers at parents or hypocrites or bad experiences. But the question must always come back to Jesus and their decision to receive or reject Him.

I lived far away from you, God. My heart was not open. My eyes could not see. I was rebellious. But you love me so much you broke through all my defenses and excuses, and my life has never been the same. I am forever grateful.

A NEW VISION

So Ananias went and found the house, placed his hands on blind Saul, and said,
"Brother Saul, the Master sent me, the same Jesus you saw on your way here.
He sent me so you could see again and be filled with the Holy Spirit." No sooner were
the words out of his mouth than something like scales fell from Saul's eyes—he could
see again! He got to his feet, was baptized, and sat down with them to a hearty meal.

ACTS 9:17–19, THE MESSAGE

I bet our first response wouldn't have been so different from that of Ananias. God spoke to him and told him to bring Saul, the great persecutor of the church, to his home. "What, me? Did you say Saul? Are you playing a joke on me, God? Did you mistake me for someone else, someone more spiritual than I?" But despite his protests, Ananias simply obeyed. He might have felt that he was walking to his death, but he obeyed.

Fast-forward a few hours. This godly man has laid hands on Saul and blessed him. "He sent me so you could see again and be filled with the Holy Spirit." Saul regains his sight, he is baptized into fellowship with Jesus Christ, and the two share a meal together as if they have been friends for ages.

That's really how it happens, my friends. The Holy Spirit convicts someone's heart, and it is amazing how God will make sure the right people are around at the right time. Maybe God is sending you to someone today. You may feel inadequate. Don't worry! When we are weak, our God is strong. What matters is that we obey— even when it doesn't seem to make sense. Your boss, a neighbor, a client, a shop owner, a stranger . . . Has God put someone on your heart? Simply obey!

Thank you for the people you sent into my life when I was far away from
you and fighting against your love for me. I pray that I would be that person
for others who need to know you!

NO FAVORITES

Peter fairly exploded with his good news: "It's God's own truth, nothing could be plainer: God plays no favorites! It makes no difference who you are or where you're from—if you want God and are ready to do as he says, the door is open. The message he sent to the children of Israel—that through Jesus Christ everything is being put together again—well, he's doing it everywhere, among everyone."

ACTS 10:34–36, THE MESSAGE

Persecution couldn't stop the church. In fact, many of those who fought the church at every turn were being saved; most notable the young scholar and teacher named Saul, who became know as Paul. Jesus tells us that not even the gates of hell can prevail against the church.

But there was something slowing the growth of the church. Sadly, it was the church itself. Almost all of the new converts were from the Jewish faith. Many thought the church was to be the new Judaism. They had not yet grasped Jesus' words that the gospel was to be shared in Jerusalem, Samaria, and then on to the ends of the earth. Even Peter was reluctant to break bread with Gentiles to the point that Paul confronted him on it. But now Peter is given a dream and realizes Jesus is not just for the Jews but for the entire world.

The church will never be stopped by persecution. But is there anyone you are reluctant to have fellowship with, anyone you would withhold the gospel from? My friends, we must say no to prejudices and yes to God's love for all mankind. The Word asks us to remove the log from our own eyes before we try judging anyone else's issues! It's pretty plain.

❧

Thank you for bringing me the glorious news that through Jesus Christ my sins were no longer held against me. I am so undeserving of your great love. May I never withhold what you have given to me from anyone else.

SLEEPING LIKE A BABY

Then the time came for Herod to bring him out for the kill. That night, even though shackled to two soldiers, one on either side, Peter slept like a baby. And there were guards at the door keeping their eyes on the place. Herod was taking no chances!

ACTS 12:6, THE MESSAGE

Herod Agrippa was the grandson of Herod the Great—the mad and bloody ruler who had babies slaughtered and was not averse to killing his own children. He was the nephew of Herod the Tetrarch, who beheaded John the Baptist. He inherited a healthy measure of their cruelty. He practiced the Jewish faith, but most of all he wanted to maintain a peaceful rule on behalf of Rome. He was probably looking for his next promotion.

So he jumped into the persecution of the church with both feet. First he had James executed. Next he took Peter prisoner.

Peter was terrified and filled with doubts. Right? Wrong! Chained to two soldiers in a dungeon, he showed his absolute trust in the sovereign will of God by sleeping like a baby. The church was awake, praying desperately and tearfully on his behalf. He sang a few songs of praise and went to sleep with a content heart. When an earthquake freed him from prison, it seems he was not surprised. When he found where his friends were praying for him, they didn't believe Peter could be there.

I want to sleep like that! I want to live my life with a calm and cool grace even when the bullets are flying. And when we let the love of God drive out fear because we trust Him completely, that is exactly the peace that is promised to us. Perfect love casts out all fear.

Thank you for the peace that comes from knowing that no matter what I face today, you have already delivered me!

Victor's Crown ♡

You are always fighting for us
Heaven's angels all around
My delight is found in knowing
That (YOU) wear the VICTOR's crown

You're my Help & my Defender,
My Savior & my friend... by YOUR
grace I live & breathe to worship
YOU!

Hallelujah!
Jesus ♡ You have
overcome the WORLD. Amen

IT IS WELL WITH MY SOUL

The peace of God, which transcends all understanding,
will guard your hearts and your minds in Christ Jesus.

PHILIPPIANS 4:7, NIV

*P*raise is not just for the easy days, but must be proclaimed even in the midst of storms. Nothing gives us victory over the storms of life more than our praise!

When peace, like a river, attendeth my way,
When sorrows like sea billows roll;
Whatever my lot, thou has taught me to say,
It is well, it is well, with my soul.

Refrain
It is well, with my soul.
It is well, with my soul.
It is well, it is well, with my soul.

My sin, oh, the bliss of this glorious thought!
My sin, not in part but the whole,
Is nailed to the cross, and I bear it no more,
Praise the Lord, praise the Lord, O my soul!

And Lord, haste the day when my faith shall be sight,
The clouds be rolled back as a scroll;
The trump shall resound, and the Lord shall descend,
Even so, it is well with my soul.

In the midst of any trials or storms, I know that you are good and that you
love and keep me. Thank you for saving my soul. I give you all praise.

CLEAN HANDS, CLEAN HEART

Do you indeed speak righteousness, you silent ones?
Do you judge uprightly, you sons of men? No, in heart you work wickedness;
you weigh out the violence of your hands in the earth.

PSALM 58:1–2, NKJV

his is another of the great Psalms. It is a mighty cry against injustice. I love that the psalmist does not allow any of us to get complacent when it comes to being just and speaking and working for justice in our world. All we have to do is look around to see what an incredible need this is in the world today. Maybe you experienced an unjust judge, if not in the legal system then in everyday life. Most of us have had wrongful complaints brought against us at some point. One of the great promises of Scripture is that God, the supreme Judge, will always judge rightly.

The injustice David calls out is fascinating. It begins in their hearts as a wicked scheme and then is expressed in actions. I'm sure some were making excuses when called to account: "It was an innocent mistake." "I didn't mean to take advantage of anyone." "My motives were innocent." David knows that is not the case. Their false judgments are a result of calculated and deliberate ruthlessness.

They take advantage of others for personal gain and then head for church. David is echoing what he said in Psalm 24: "Who may ascend into the hill of the Lord? Or who may stand in His holy place? He who has clean hands and a pure heart" (vv. 3–4).

Clean hands and a pure heart. That's the true way to prepare ourselves for worship! Don't read this and feel condemned. Read this and thank God that He is the ultimate in new beginnings. Let's hold on to the promise of God for today.

If I am ever tempted to take advantage of others for personal gain,
check and correct my heart immediately, O righteous God!

CLEAN LIPS

The wicked are estranged from the womb; they go astray as soon as they are born, speaking lies. Their poison is like the poison of a serpent; they are like the deaf cobra that stops its ear, which will not heed the voice of charmers, charming ever so skillfully.

PSALM 58:3–5, NKJV

I'll never forget the first time my daughter told me a lie. My cherub, my treasure, my perfect little long-awaited daughter, the child of my heart was telling me a lie. I asked her, "Honey, what do you have behind your back?" Her reply wasn't so sweet and innocent when she nearly yelled, "Nothing!"

Well, of course, she had candy nicely tucked behind her back. It didn't help her plea of innocence that she also had candy firmly planted in her cheek.

So angelic and innocent she seemed that I was shocked at how easy it was for her to say something not true. What would happen if that behavior was never confronted by the Spirit of God—and expressed through her mom? Imagine if she was left to make up her own set of rules to live by. We all know examples of how what was cute as a baby becomes ugly and dangerous as an adult.

David is confronting those who may have gotten away with things their whole lives. There was now nothing pleasant about those whose words were as poisonous as the venom from a snake.

Sin and dishonesty begin early because we are born with a sin nature. That's why we need a Savior! No matter what age you are in life, now is the time to allow God's correction to give you clean and honest lips.

May all my words be honest and filled with grace, my Savior.
Give me a clean heart, cleans hands, and clean lips.

A TIME TO FIGHT

Break their teeth in their mouth, O God! Break out the fangs
of the young lions, O Lord! Let them flow away
as waters which run continually; when he bends his bow,
let his arrows be as if cut in pieces.

PSALM 58:6–7, NKJV

When David says, "Break their teeth in their mouth, O God!" I have to admit, to me it sounds very harsh. But before assuming David is too strong in his words, look who he's describing—poisonous snakes, ferocious lions, and enemy warriors armed and ready to kill. Is this who you want running loose in your neighborhood? These are dangerous predators. They might be young now, but they are already capable of much damage and will only grow stronger in doing wrong. If they can't be convinced to speak truth and be just toward others, David wants their weapons taken away so they have no ability for evil.

David is a poet and a warrior—and now the warrior in him is speaking loud and clear in his poetry. He is ready to go to battle to protect the innocent and weak from the unjust. Our God is a God of peace, but that doesn't mean there isn't a time to fight for what is right.

As a heartfelt note to parents with children in the home, sometimes it seems too hard and unpleasant to stand up and correct bad behavior in our children. But you bless and show love to your children by not letting that which is wrong and evil to take root. They will thank you later.

God, grant me the courage and wisdom to know when it is right to fight.
Give me boldness to stand up for you when evildoers exploit the innocent and weak.

THE FALL OF THE WICKED

The righteous shall rejoice when he sees the vengeance;
he shall wash his feet in the blood of the wicked.

PSALM 58:10, NKJV

*N*othing is quite so discouraging as seeing the wicked not only get away with their sins but actually prosper from their wrongdoing. Many have been led astray when they see the wicked with plenty of money and status. They aren't convinced that doing right is the best path for their lives. And so without fear of repercussions, they live without restraint. The Word says sin is pleasurable for a season, but long-term effects are disastrous for us and others.

We all need to be reminded of David's words that violence will visit the wicked and they will be destroyed: "Let them be like a snail which melts away as it goes, like a stillborn child of a woman, that they may not see the sun. Before your pots can feel the burning thorns, He shall take them away as with a whirlwind, As in His living and burning wrath" (vv. 8–9).

All that could have been is like a stillborn child for the wicked. David's word pictures of God's wrath and judgment are so graphic, but they make the point we all need to hear: In the end, the wages of sin is death.

I know most reading these words are loving and serving God. Amen. But before any of us feel puffed up, we must remember where we came from. That same sin nature that brought the wicked to ruin is at work in all of us. We celebrate when evil is exposed and brought low, but we never forget that all of us have fallen short of the glory of God and need our Savior! Find yourself in prayer for humanity. We are all in need of a Savior.

I need you as much today as the first day I met you, O God.
Thank you for being my Savior all the days of my life.

THE REWARD OF THE RIGHTEOUS

So that men will say, "Surely there is a reward for the righteous;
surely He is God who judges in the earth."

PSALM 58:11, NKJV

David continues to speak against every lie and every wrong that the enemy tries to throw his way. When injustice is dealt your way, you too have the right to defend yourself. But what we usually find is that when we push back and confront evil, evil tends to push right back. Knowing who you are in Christ is absolutely crucial if you want to tackle injustice head on. We fight wickedness with the Word of God, understanding that this battle is not of flesh and blood but of principalities and powers.

The greatest reward of the righteous is not that others are destroyed but that we know we are saved in this life and the life to come. God actually promises us persecution—not a perfect life but a life on the front line. But He also promises us that He will never leave us or forsake us.

The great news—the great reward—for us is that the righteous will never be forsaken and given over to their enemies, even if it seems to be the case in a particular moment. Don't lose heart. Even the wicked will be forced to acknowledge God in the final judgment. And we will receive the ultimate reward of life.

Even if you have doubts and things don't seem fair, never give up. What you have affirmed in your heart through faith in Jesus Christ will be proven true to your eternal reward.

I will not give up, even when things are unfair, O God. I know you are righteous
and will give me reward now and in eternity for my faithfulness to you.

NEVER DESTROYED

To the Chief Musician. Set to "Do Not Destroy." A Michtam of David
when Saul sent men, and they watched the house in order to kill him.

PREFACE TO PSALM 59, NKJV

*I*n the original text this psalm is titled "Destroy Not." As you look deeper into the meaning of that title, you find it literally means, "Cannot destroy!" What a promise! What God preserves, neither the devil nor wickedness can destroy.

Don't read that as a nice little slogan or platitude. Remember who is writing it.

David is under siege, trapped in his home, surrounded on all sides by his enemies. And not just any enemies. These men have been sent by King Saul, the man David loved and faithfully served.

So when David tells the chief musician to set it to music that is titled "Destroy Not," it is powerful. When David cries out to God for rescue in the following verses, it is not just figurative language. It is literal. He literally needs God to take him to a high place of safety where the enemy cannot get hold of him.

Oh, don't miss what is right in front of our eyes. David is surrounded. What does he do? He prepares for worship. When you hear yourself crying out in frustration and fear, turn your words into worship, your petitions into praise. Doubts and fears will flee in the presence of our Most High God.

No matter how tough your situation seems to be, no matter how many enemies are surrounding you, no matter how hopeless you feel, never forget that what God preserves cannot be destroyed. That means you. He will preserve you.

Mighty God, thank you for being my Deliverer.
Thank you that no matter how many forces are arrayed against me,
with you I will be saved and live in your presence forever.

INTIMACY WITH GOD

Deliver me from my enemies, O my God;
defend me from those who rise up against me.
Deliver me from the workers of iniquity,
and save me from bloodthirsty men.

PSALM 59:1–2, NKJV

*H*ave you noticed how David addresses God in this verse and throughout Psalm 59? Take a look in particular at verses 9 and 17. There are many ways he describes God, but what I love to read is that he addresses Him as my God. David had such respect and reverence for God, but he never saw Him as distant and aloof from him, a God in heaven who was unapproachable. David's view of God is so intimate and personal and loving. "My God." Is it any wonder that he was known as a man after God's own heart? Is it any wonder Jesus quoted David's words so many times in His understanding that He was one with God the Father?

When you talk to God, do you speak to *my* God? Do you feel a closeness and friendship that lifts your spirit and gives you ultimate security?

"For God is my defense. My God of mercy."

Surrounded by enemies, David affirms that whatever God preserves cannot be destroyed. He lifts his heart in worship. And he talks to God with words that express his love and the closeness of their relationship.

Deliver me from my enemies, O my God.
I love you with all my heart. Thank you for desiring fellowship with me,
for letting me know how much you love me and want to know me.
Thank you that you are my God!

SOMETHING BEAUTIFUL

*But I will sing of Your power; yes, I will sing aloud of Your mercy in the morning;
for You have been my defense and refuge in the day of my trouble.*

PSALM 59:16, NKJV

*R*ead through Psalm 59 again today. What beautiful words. Such exquisite expressions of faith in God. I would love to have been present the first time this psalm was sung as part of worship!

I've already mentioned that in the face of adversity, David begins to worship. He doesn't moan and complain. He lifts his voice in praise. Isn't it fascinating that all of David's troubles and conflicts have released to us such beautiful words of worship? These rich psalms express prayers and simple cries of the heart that were wonderful in his day but are preserved for us to hold fast to today. They are just as beautiful today as when he wrote them.

Even a quick glance at history shows us that the great artisans of the world have always created culture-altering works during or after great personal trials. In fact, the music of the house of God is in no small degree indebted to the trials of the saints and God's faithfulness to them. God blessed them—and us—through their faithfulness.

There is no need for us to go out looking for troubles. Because we live in a fallen world, trouble will find us with little or no help. But when we do experience hardship and even persecution, let's never forget that a special blessing awaits us—and our grace under fire leaves something special and beautiful for those that follow us. You don't have to write songs to leave a legacy of God's grace to future generations!

*Thank you for the faithfulness of your saints, O God. They have left me
with such a richness of faith and beauty. When I face trials and tribulations,
give me the grace to bless those who follow me.*

GOD IS AWAKE

Awake to help me, and behold! You therefore, O Lord God of hosts, the God of Israel, awake to punish all the nations; do not be merciful to any wicked transgressors.

PSALM 59:4–5, NKJV

avid describes the enemies as dogs who prowl the city, looking for their prey. Their howls are a chilling reminder of just how near they are. Danger is not far off. It is close. Loud shrieks and cries from the enemy have always been used to strike terror in our hearts. Let's never forget that any noise of the enemy, no matter how loud and shrill it seems, is actually pitiful compared to the victorious roar of the Lord!

When Jesus slept in the midst of a storm and His disciples awoke Him, was He unaware of the danger? Of course not. And when David cries out, "Awake to help me—look what is happening all around me!" God is not asleep. David's words are for his own benefit. He is telling himself that God already is awake. Everyone else may have fallen asleep in exhaustion, but not our mighty God.

I love this truth and love to pray it. God is all-knowing and never misses anything. It gives me great confidence in the midst of a particular trial to pray, "Father, I thank you that even while we sleep, you are still working on our behalf. I see no way in the natural to fix this, but even while I sleep you make a way." I love how this prayer leaves me—and you—with stress-free sleep. The Bible promises sweet sleep for the righteous. God's vigilance gives us rest!

⸙

Thank you for protecting me and carrying my burdens for me, O God. You know those situations in my life right now that I have no solutions for. Thank you for making a way for me—even when I sleep!

GOD WILL MEET ME

My God of mercy shall come to meet me.

PSALM 59:10, NKJV

I have noticed that the longer I have known Christ, the more my prayer language has changed. I used to worry that my prayers would not be right or not be beautiful enough to be heard in the heart of God. I did not want to disappoint my Savior with my lack of skill when it came to addressing the Author of life. As time has gone on, however, I have learned that the best way to approach the Lord in prayer is through honest, heartfelt conversations.

It's not your style, it's your heart. Flowery words won't get God's attention any more than simple everyday language. The promise that David gives us here is that "my God of mercy shall come to meet me." That's what you need to know. Then talk to God like you believe it. He is present, right there, listening and talking to you.

Yes, God is most holy, but He is also our Abba Father—our Daddy-Father.

David's raw emotion and honest words show me that he knew God as the ultimate Daddy. I hear David's total trust in his Daddy as I read this. He teaches me that I too can have a real relationship with the Most High God who is my Daddy.

My friends, if you are struggling to pray, just be honest. Speak what is on your heart and mind. Don't hide behind rhetoric or sophisticated words. Realize God is right there in the room with you. It is true. Your God of mercy shall come to meet you.

Thank you for loving me so much I can call you Daddy.
You are the Creator, you are all-powerful, you are all-knowing,
and yet you invite, me—yes me—to come into your presence as your child.
Thank you for loving me more than I can fully comprehend.

I WILL GIVE YOU THE SIGN

*All right then, the Lord himself will give you the sign. Look!
The virgin will conceive a child! She will give birth to a son
and will call him Immanuel (which means "God is with us").*

ISAIAH 7:14, NLT

*I*t is quite miraculous that we are able to utter the phrase "God is with us." To think that the Maker of heaven and earth actually dwells with His people is one of the greatest gifts in our lives. As the prophet Isaiah announced the soon-coming king, Jesus Christ was revealed yet again. The hope of the world, Immanuel, was on His way.

When Jesus himself announced His ministry at His hometown of Nazareth, He quoted from Isaiah (see Luke 4:17). Isaiah was a member of the royal family of the southern kingdom of Judah. He saw the destruction of the northern kingdom of Israel at the hands of the Assyrians—God's punishment for their lack of faithfulness.

His heart yearns for his people to turn their hearts completely to God so they will not suffer the same fate. He is called to be a prophet in worship, and it is in worship that he sees that even if judgment comes, there is hope. God begins to reveal Jesus to him, and he begins to reveal the coming Messiah to his people. The first sign is that the coming Savior will be born of a virgin. To see that seven hundred years before it happened is a miracle of revelation born in worship. Worship God with all your heart today, and you too will begin to see Jesus more clearly!

*Immanuel, O God who is with us, thank you for the promise of a deliverer
from our sins. Thank you for the precious signs pointing to Jesus.*

I WILL SEND A LIGHT

The people who walk in darkness will see a great light.
For those who live in a land of deep darkness, a light will shine.

ISAIAH 9:2, NLT

God's chosen people had lost their way. They had turned from faith in the one true God to worship gods that were diametrically opposed to the nature and teachings of Yahweh. They made treaties with nations that God had clearly commanded them to stay clear of because of their wickedness. When Isaiah speaks of "a land of deep darkness," he is describing Judah.

It is tragic and heartbreaking to see someone who was once on the path of godliness set a new course on a path to destruction. Living life your own way may feel good for a minute, but ultimately, we were never designed for life without Christ. I pray we never become a people who sit around judging those who walk in darkness, but that we would continue to rise as people who know how to pray and intercede on behalf of broken humanity.

It is beautiful to see that even in the midst of deep darkness, Isaiah sees what others ignore. He knows God so well that he discovers God has plans to redeem His people. He is sending a light that John celebrated when he said, "The Word gave life to everything that was created, and his life brought light to everyone. The light shines in the darkness, and the darkness can never extinguish it" (John 1:4–5).

We might still live in a world of deep darkness, but never lose hope, my friends. There is a Light that no darkness can ever extinguish. We have the promise of eternal life in heaven, where the glory of God himself will be our light.

Thank you, Father, for bringing light to my dark world through Jesus Christ.
Thank you for the promise of eternity without darkness.

I WILL SEND A CHILD

*For a child is born to us, a son is given to us. The government will rest
on his shoulders. And he will be called: Wonderful Counselor, Mighty God.
Everlasting Father, Prince of Peace.*

ISAIAH 9:6, NLT

Apparently the people of Jesus' day were expecting the Messiah to come as a mighty ruler. And according to Isaiah that would indeed be the case: "His government and its peace will never end. He will rule with fairness and justice from the throne of his ancestor David for all eternity. The passionate commitment of the Lord of Heaven's Armies will make this happen!" (v. 7). Christ is the Victor and His eternal reign has begun. But the people of Jesus' day missed the preceding verse from Isaiah where he prophesied that Jesus would come to us as a child.

David's prayer was that his eyes would be open to God at work. I pray that for my own life today, that I would not be too busy to see the lost and to bring the love of Christ at every opportunity, revealing Jesus—just as was begun in the work of Isaiah—for who He is: the Victor who rules by His love and mercy.

There are countless people all around you who won't open their eyes to see the glorious Savior without seeing His love modeled and expressed through our lives. All of us have been called to reveal Jesus in our places of influence—in our homes, our cities, and beyond. We don't do that by cursing the darkness, but only by showing the Light. Hear Jesus' words again today: "In the same way, let your good deeds shine out for all to see, so that everyone will praise your heavenly Father" (Matthew 5:16).

*Father, help me to let my light shine to people whose eyes are closed
to you right now. Help my love and good deeds be a beacon that is irresistible
to those living in darkness around me.*

I WILL GATHER THEM

*The Spirit of the Sovereign Lord is upon me, for the Lord has anointed me
to bring good news to the poor. He has sent me to comfort the brokenhearted and
to proclaim that captives will be released and prisoners will be freed.*

ISAIAH 61:1, NLT

This is the Scripture that sits like wildfire in my spirit. Jesus fulfilled this prophesy when He announced His ministry. In these words Jesus announced a new kind of kingdom. No longer would the powerful be free to exploit the powerless. He was bringing the precious gift of God's love and salvation to the poor, the brokenhearted, the captives, and the prisoners. This was quite a shock to His hearers. They thought their accomplishments and knowledge, their success and accumulations would merit God's gift.

They had completely missed the wisdom of God throughout the Old Testament. They forgot that as a people they were redeemed from slavery. They forgot that all their victories were based on God's power, not theirs. They forgot that God is Creator and man is the created, that no one can stand beside Him.

Isaiah sought God with all his heart, and God revealed His heart to this prophet. He gave him a message for the people of his day, Jesus' day, and our day! Grace has come. Recognize your need of God, and understand you don't have it all under control and you can't handle life on your own.

My dear loved ones, we can never accumulate enough wisdom, wealth, and worthiness to earn God's unmerited favor. Isaiah reveals that Jesus is recognized first by the one who realizes his need for a Savior. Let's open our eyes in humility today.

*Thank you for meeting me when I was lost, O God. Thank you for loving me when
I was unlovable. I am poor in spirit and in need of you and your grace all of my days.*

I WILL HEAL MY PEOPLE

But he was pierced for our rebellion, crushed for our sins.
He was beaten so we could be whole. He was whipped so we could be healed.

ISAIAH 53:5, NLT

*T*he religious leaders missed so many of Isaiah's prophecies concerning the coming of Jesus that they undoubtedly missed the magnificent passage from Isaiah 53 as well. For after all, wasn't it the Sanhedrin who called for Jesus' arrest, torture, and crucifixion? When Pilate washed his hands of the trial and said it was on "their heads," they accepted that judgment blindly and gladly.

Isaiah saw seven centuries earlier what the ones who should have recognized Jesus immediately entirely missed. We must always guard our hearts and minds from being closed to the glorious new things God is doing among us. Let's never let traditions or preferences turn us into those who would protest and reject the stunning "new" that God is always bringing to the table.

Isaiah sees the judgment against sin that is to crush his people. But he sees even more clearly that God will always be faithful to his children. He sent His one and only, His very best, to suffer what the sinner deserves. You were spared the punishment for your sin because our gracious loving Savior took the sins of the entire world upon His shoulders.

Never forget where you came from. For no matter how much we grow spiritually, we must always return to the promise of Isaiah that Jesus came to accomplish what we could not do ourselves. What a glorious Savior.

Thank you for no longer holding my sins against me. Thank you for suffering
the punishment for my rebellion in my place. May I never forget where I came from.
Jesus, be revealed in my life more and more, I pray.

A PSALM OF THANKSGIVING

On your feet now—applaud God!
Bring a gift of laughter,
sing yourselves into his presence.
Know this: God is God, and God, God.
He made us; we didn't make him.
We're his people, his well-tended sheep.
Enter with the password: "Thank you!"
Make yourselves at home, talking praise.
Thank him. Worship him.
For God is sheer beauty,
all-generous in love,
loyal always and ever.

PSALM 100, THE MESSAGE

God, it is so sweet to be in your presence,
to know that you are with me at all times.
I bring you my praise and worship.
Thank you for your faithfulness to me.

FRIEND OF SINNERS

JESUS CALLS US FRIENDS, NO LONGER SLAVES.

NOVEMBER

What a friend we have in Jesus,
all our sins & grief to bear!
What a privilege to carry
everything to God in prayer!
O what peace we often forfeit,
O what needless pain we bear,
all because we do not carry
everything to God in prayer.

Praise Jesus, our Friend!

NEVER FORGOTTEN

This is a revelation from Jesus Christ, which God gave him to show his servants the events that must soon take place. He sent an angel to present this revelation to his servant John, who faithfully reported everything he saw.

REVELATION 1:1–2, NLT

Just as David was known as "a man after God's heart" (Acts 13:22), John was "the one Jesus loved" (John 20:2) and "the beloved disciple" (John 21:24). The youngest and most tenderhearted of all the apostles, his emotional attachment to the Savior was evident, as he never left his side. All the disciples loved their Master and Savior, but John wore his feelings on his sleeve.

But as he inks the words of this book in response to a divine revelation, as the only apostle still living, he is now the oldest and the last known eyewitness. He never lost his tender heart through the years as he cared for Mary as if she were his own mother, through all the time he planted and pastored churches in Asia Minor. What memories he must have had as he spent time on the rocky island of Patmos, his prison and place of exile. When authorities exile someone as a punishment, it is their intention to cut that person off from all their connections. Someone in Rome might have thought this would be not only the end of John but the end of the church.

But that was not to be. Jesus had not forgotten His young friend—though now in the winter of his life. On spiritual and physical levels He gave "the beloved disciple" a most amazing experience of worship, one that reached all the way to heaven. For the book of Revelation is at its core a book of worship.

Do you feel cut off? Separated from others? In exile? Don't believe the enemy's message that you are forgotten. Your Savior is ready to meet you in worship.

Father, your love reaches me wherever I am physically and emotionally. I thank you that you know where I am.

I AM THE LIVING ONE

When I saw Him, I fell at His feet like a dead man.
And He placed His right hand on me, saying, "Do not be afraid;
I am the first and the last, and the living One; and I was dead, and behold,
I am alive forevermore, and I have the keys of death and of Hades."

REVELATION 1:17–18, NASB

*J*ohn was not the first to fall like a dead man when he received a vision of the last days: "I, Daniel, was the only one who saw the vision; those who were with me did not see it, but such terror overwhelmed them that they fled and hid themselves. So I was left alone, gazing at this great vision; I had no strength left, my face turned deathly pale and I was helpless. Then I heard him speaking, and as I listened to him, I fell into a deep sleep, my face to the ground" (Daniel 10:7–9, NIV).

Readers of John's revelation who knew the Old Testament might have wondered if the same angel that visited Daniel was appearing to John. But then, to their astonishment, they would have read, "Do not be afraid; I am the first and the last, and the living One; and I was dead, and behold, I am alive forevermore, and I have the keys of death and of Hades."

The elder statesman of the church, exiled to a remote rock in the middle of the Mediterranean Sea, John wasn't being visited by an angel. His Friend, the One he left everything to follow, spoke words to drive out fear and bring peace to John's heart.

Isn't that just like Jesus? Appearing to us when we feel abandoned and need Him most. My heart is moved, comforted, and encouraged that He was there for John. Jesus is always there for me. I want to always be there for Him.

You have been my closest Friend, dear Lord. Thank you for being there when I needed you most. I want to always be there for you, to do whatever you would ask me to do.

WORTHY IS THE LAMB

Worthy are You, our Lord and our God,
to receive glory and honor and power;
for You created all things, and because of
Your will they existed, and were created.

REVELATION 4:11, NASB

Heaven sings praises to our Lord Jesus Christ. John's vision included living creatures too magnificent to describe, along with elders whose faith had carried them from death to life, all falling down and worshiping Him "who sits on the throne" and "who lives forever and ever" (vv. 9–10). The elders cast their crowns before the throne. They know full well that no honor or accomplishment they have received or achieved compares to the glory and honor of our Lord.

Oh that we would worship with the zeal of heaven. Nothing changes our attitudes, actions, and spiritual vitality like worship. It is the moment when we realize that we were created to serve, honor, and glorify the Creator. Beginning in the garden of Eden, all folly and tragedy flows from missing this simple connection. The Creator is to be worshiped.

If you are ever tempted to feel small and unimportant, never forget that it is by God's will that you exist and were created. He knows who you are—He knows your name. He loves you and has fabulous plans for your life. That's reason to give Him all glory and honor from the depths of our being.

Thank you that you know me and every circumstance of my life, O Lord.
You created me and sustain me. I give you all of my life, my spiritual act of worship.

OUT OF THE TRIBULATION

I said to him, "My lord, you know." And he said to me,
"These are the ones who come out of the great tribulation, and they have
washed their robes and made them white in the blood of the Lamb."

REVELATION 7:14, NASB

There is a great tribulation, but every generation has its own tribulations. So many of us live in relative peace and safety that we can't fully comprehend the number of Christians living under severe persecution today. It seems like a thing of the past—or the future. Yet there have been more Christian martyrs in the past ten years than all previous centuries of the Christian Era combined. Pray for our brothers and sisters who are willing to lay down their lives for the name of Jesus.

John's vision paints a beautiful picture of God's love and care for martyrs past, present, and future—and their ultimate reward: "For this reason, they are before the throne of God; and they serve Him day and night in His temple; and He who sits on the throne will spread His tabernacle over them. They will hunger no longer, nor thirst anymore; nor will the sun beat down on them, nor any heat; for the Lamb in the center of the throne will be their shepherd, and will guide them to springs of the water of life; and God will wipe every tear from their eyes" (vv. 15–16).

The revelation given to John is written about things to come—but is also written to us right now today. Hold fast to the truth that no matter what the cost of your faith, a day will come when God will wipe every tear from your eyes. You will be washed white as snow in the blood of the Lamb. Blessings today and the joy of His presence throughout eternity!

God, whether my world is filled with peace or tribulation, I put my trust in your hands,
knowing you are my shield, my strength, and my reward in eternity.

HE WILL REIGN

Then the seventh angel sounded; and there were loud voices in heaven, saying,
"The kingdom of the world has become the kingdom of our Lord and of His Christ;
and He will reign forever and ever."

REVELATION 11:15, NASB

*I*n John's magnificent book of worship, trumpets of judgment have sounded, followed by the announcement of the coming of Christ and the establishment of God's kingdom. That's what we've prayed for since Jesus taught us to pray for the coming of His kingdom in the Lord's Prayer. That's reason for praise and worship in every age.

All throughout Scripture—all throughout human history—there is a cycle of man's rebellion and God's acts of redemption. In the divine revelation from the heart of God to the "beloved disciple," we find the ultimate end of this cycle. Oh what a glorious moment, when evil will be judged and put to an end, and God's kingdom of love and righteousness prevails in all of life. Think of that. The end of evil and evil influence.

Our prayers must be joined with the elders that stand before the throne: "We give you thanks, O Lord God, the Almighty, who are and who were, because you have taken your great power and have begun to reign" (v. 17). God has allowed free will and choice, which has allowed evil to do its work, but there is an appointed time when God says "no more" to that which destroys. His reign will begin not just in the hearts of believers, but in all things.

Lord, even as I wait for your kingdom to come, I pray that my life and faith
and obedience will make your kingdom real in all the situations of my life.

THE ACCUSER THROWN DOWN

*Now the salvation, and the power, and the kingdom of our God
and the authority of His Christ have come, for the accuser of our brethren
has been thrown down, he who accuses them before our God day and night.
And they overcame him because of the blood of the Lamb and because of the word
of their testimony, and they did not love their life even when faced with death.*

REVELATION 12:10–11, NASB

*D*on't lose heart. Even if it feels like evil has its way, the blood of Christ has broken the chains of sin and death through His blood. This is already reality. But there is a moment coming when satan will be expelled completely from our world. What brings about the victory? Grit and determination? Better weapons? Of course not. Our victory—satan's defeat—is based solely on the blood of Jesus Christ.

The Hebrew word for *satan* literally means "accuser." Jesus teaches us not to stand in judgment of others—our job has never been to accuse others of their sins. Satan's name, and his banishment from heaven, are based on arrogant pride. He somehow felt he could do God's job better than God could. Is it any different for humans? When we demand "not His will, but mine," and determine that we can do God's job for Him as Lord of our own life, tragedy always follows.

All authority is God's. And all humanity will discover that through redemption or through judgment. My prayer is that we will continue to overcome in the total confidence in the blood of the Lamb.

*Father God, you gave all authority to Christ to throw satan down.
Thank you that through Christ's blood we can overcome
the accuser who would destroy us.*

A NEW SONG

And they sang a new song before the throne and before the four living creatures and the elders; and no one could learn the song except the one hundred and forty-four thousand who had been purchased from the earth.

REVELATION 14:3, NASB

As most songwriters and worship leaders understand, part of our role is to bring new songs. In the Psalms alone, over forty times we are asked to sing new songs. New represents life. Songs help us to pray those deepest prayers, giving voice to human expression like nothing else.

There is a new song that will be sung in heaven that contains everything I love—and it will be sung by a special choir made up of the faithful that endured the tribulation, surviving under the cover of God's protection. We aren't given the words for that song, but in the next chapter of Revelation, there is another choir that sings the ancient hymn of Moses and expresses his heart of praise: "And they sang the song of Moses, the bond-servant of God, and the song of the Lamb, saying, 'Great and marvelous are your works, O Lord God, the Almighty; righteous and true are your ways, King of the nations! Who will not fear, O Lord, and glorify your name? For you alone are holy'" (15:3–4).

I want to hear that choir of voices and experience the awe of those who stood true for God. I want to sing that kind of song in heaven—and on earth today. Whether or not you are a talented singer, your voice is at its finest when it expresses praise and honor to the King of nations. Sing a new song today!

Every song I sing, I sing to you, as praise and thanksgiving for your marvelous works, King of the nations and my Lord.

MARRIAGE OF THE LAMB

"Let us rejoice and be glad and give the glory to Him, for the marriage of the Lamb has come and His bride has made herself ready." It was given to her to clothe herself in fine linen, bright and clean; for the fine linen is the righteous acts of the saints.

REVELATION 19:7–8, NASB

Very few occasions are as joyful as a wedding. What a wonderful time when a couple makes their spiritual vows of love and devotion before God and friends. But there is a marriage that is beyond all others, when Christ, the bridegroom, takes His pure bride in a union that will last forever. In verse 6 we are told that the praise of heaven is so loud at this moment that it is like the sound of "many waters." Some picture heaven as a quiet place, but throughout the book of Revelation we discover it is a loud and joyful place to be, indeed.

In the Old Testament, Israel was considered the bride of God. Twice in the New Testament Paul describes the church as the bride of Christ (see 2 Corinthians 11 and Ephesians 5). In Jewish custom, once a couple was engaged, they were considered married, even though the ceremony was not yet held. That's the word for "bride" here; the saints are already Christ's wife. But now that relationship is sealed in eternity.

Is it any wonder that heaven rejoices? Loudly! The promise of eternity is fulfilled. What a time of happiness and joy. Christ tells John, "Write, 'Blessed are those who are invited to the marriage supper of the Lamb'" (v. 9). You know who is invited? We are. You and I. We are both the bride and those who come to celebrate. Salvation is through Jesus Christ alone, but our response to this love is acts of righteousness, and it is our obedient service that makes what we wear pure and spotless.

I worship you, O God, for all your blessings, most of all that you have chosen me to be yours throughout all eternity.

NO MORE DEATH

*And I heard a loud voice from the throne, saying, "Behold, the tabernacle
of God is among men, and He will dwell among them, and they shall be His people,
and God Himself will be among them, and He will wipe away every tear
from their eyes; and there will no longer be any death; there will no longer
be any mourning, or crying, or pain; the first things have passed away."*

REVELATION 21:3–4, NASB

When John describes a new heaven and a new earth, it is beyond our ability to grasp its beauty and wonder. But most magnificent of all is that God will walk among us. John is told that there will no longer be the need for the temple— or even the sun. God's radiance is all we need: "I saw no temple in it, for the Lord God the Almighty and the Lamb are its temple. And the city has no need of the sun or of the moon to shine on it, for the glory of God has illumined it, and its lamp is the Lamb" (vv. 22–23).

The world we live in is filled with wonders and blessings of many kinds. There is the beauty of nature, the fellowship with our brothers and sisters, and the presence of Jesus in our lives through the Holy Spirit. I want to savor every moment of the life God has given us. But I know that what we have now cannot compare to what heaven will be like.

And for anyone who has a heavy heart due to the loss of a loved one, heaven is a place where there will be no more mourning, no more crying, no more pain. Death has been defeated and all that is fallen has passed away. All things are new—no more nighttime, no more dangers. Heaven is for real—and it is a glorious place.

*You are the God of all comfort. I thank you that you comfort me now
and that there will be no more death and mourning in eternity.*

MY SON

And He who sits on the throne said, "Behold, I am making all things new."
And He said, "Write, for these words are faithful and true." Then He said to me,
"It is done. I am the Alpha and the Omega, the beginning and the end. I will give
to the one who thirsts from the spring of the water of life without cost. He who overcomes
will inherit these things, and I will be his God and he will be My son.

REVELATION 21:5–7, NASB

When God reached down and saved me, He planted in my heart such a profound sense of gratitude for His love, His sacrifice, the person of Jesus, that my life since that day has been given to worship. What an amazing thing to discover one's ministry in the moment of salvation. Oh, I had no idea what God had in mind for me in that instant, but the revelation that I was to spend the rest of my days saying thank-you was like an explosion in my heart.

Revelation is filled with so many fantastic images. One theme that I can't miss and that resonates with my soul is worship. Even if I can't teach the meaning of every verse, I can appeal to you to come before the throne, fall on your face with respect, and to stand and praise the King who is over all kings.

What does He offer us? Like the woman at the well, like the revelation of John, He offers the "water of life without cost." We won't buy or earn our way into heaven. He has made all the provision we need.

My friend, if there is anything that is holding you back from experiencing the fullness of Christ today, I pray that you would drop to your knees, ask for His forgiveness, give Him your thanks and worship, and stand up as one who is called His son.

God, you truly are my Father. Thank you for making me your child.
Thank you for making me a home in eternity.

WHAT A FRIEND

*I no longer call you servants, because a servant does not know
his master's business. Instead, I have called you friends, for everything
that I learned from my Father I have made known to you.*

JOHN 15:15, NIV

I am truly amazed that God, my Lord and King, should call me His friend.

What a friend we have in Jesus,
all our sins and griefs to bear!
What a privilege to carry
everything to God in prayer!
O what peace we often forfeit,
O what needless pain we bear,
all because we do not carry
everything to God in prayer.

Have we trials and temptations?
Is there trouble anywhere?
We should never be discouraged;
take it to the Lord in prayer.
Can we find a friend so faithful
who will all our sorrows share?
Jesus knows our every weakness;
take it to the Lord in prayer.

*You are my Lord and King, and I give you all honor and respect.
But I am so grateful that you call me your friend. Thanks for such love and kindness.*

WE HAVE SEEN AND HEARD

We announce to you what we have seen and heard,
because we want you also to have fellowship with us.
Our fellowship is with God the Father and with his Son, Jesus Christ.
We write this to you so we may be full of joy.

1 JOHN 1:3–4, NCV

A funny thing happens in modern culture. An amazing claim is made, and because of the Internet it travels around the world faster than a forest fire. But in a short while people start fact-checking and find it never really happened. It was a hoax, an urban legend.

We aren't the first generation to get carried away with a story that isn't true, but in the past it took a lot longer for stories to spread and then get corrected.

John, the beloved disciple, is now an old man. He is writing a letter to the churches he has planted and helped oversee. It is so difficult to stay in touch that he doesn't want there to be any question as to what he has to share. So he stresses that when he talks about Jesus, it is not a secondhand account based on a rumor he heard. He was there. He is an eyewitness. This is not just a mythical tale. "We announce to you what we have seen and heard."

The modern world is full of skeptics and cynics. If someone insists on doubting God's Word, it is only through a revelation that they will see Jesus for who He is. But I do want to say to you, my friends, God's Word is true and can be depended on. What we read in John's letter is based on personal testimony. When you read and ponder these verses, affirm in your heart that this is not just from man, but from the heart of God.

Thank you for the truth and dependability of your Word, dear God.

FROM THE BEGINNING

We write you now about what has always existed, which we have heard,
we have seen with our own eyes, we have looked at, and we have touched
with our hands. We write to you about the Word that gives life.

1 JOHN 1:1, NCV

Jesus was born in a manger and appeared to us as a baby. But that is not His beginning. He is not part of creation; He was with God in creation. He is God. Fully human and fully God, He was and is able to save us from our sins.

There is a very simple truth I don't want us to miss in this verse. Our salvation was not a desperate plan B that God came up with after humanity fell into sin. Our salvation was designed in eternity, before the world and all that is in it was created. Even if there had been no need for forgiveness of sins, we still would have needed a bridge between our humanity and God's divinity. Jesus was that bridge before the foundations of the world were laid.

Don't miss that God loved you before you and all your ancestors were born. God's desire for you and each of us has always been fellowship. Jesus God suffered and died for our sins, but He was our Creator and has always been our access to the fullness of fellowship with God. He was the Victor in creation, incarnation, crucifixion, and resurrection. Is it any wonder that when we truly see Him, our only response is to fall to our knees in worship? Let's worship Jesus the Creator today.

God, even when I can't understand the depths of your being,
I am always stirred by your eternal love for me. Thank you for Jesus.

THE JOY OF REVEALING JESUS

We write this to you so we may be full of joy.

1 JOHN 1:4, NCV

What motivates you to do what you do? What brings you the most joy in life? For the apostle John it was sharing the truth of Jesus to his brothers and sisters in Christ—and to a lost and dying world.

If your heart doesn't yearn and burn to make Jesus known to the world, my goal is not to heap condemnation or a sense of guilt on you. I would simply urge you to look again at our Savior. Read Scripture about His life and ministry. Reflect on what He did and what He said. Think about all He has done for you. Talk to Him in prayer. Ask Him to reveal himself to you. Go straight back to the source. I promise you that as you seek Him, He will make himself known to you.

Once that happens, there is little anyone needs to say to you or any of us about sharing our faith, about revealing Jesus to the world. It becomes natural. Not sharing our Savior would be like keeping a fountain of life and joy and healing a secret all to ourselves.

John writes about Jesus so that his joy will be complete. Share Jesus with your world and see just how joyful you become!

Thank you, Lord, that you have revealed Jesus to me.
Thank you for the privilege of revealing Jesus to my world.

A LIGHT HAS APPEARED

Here is the message we have heard from Christ and now announce to you:
God is light, and in him there is no darkness at all.

1 JOHN 1:5, NCV

Once light is introduced to a place, darkness is forced to leave. Light is always more powerful than darkness and more powerful in darkness. You can't add more darkness to a space and hope to extinguish a light. The fact that we can see stars billions of miles away proves that light always wins. Travel down tunnels into the deepest caves of the earth, and all you have to do is strike a match to drive darkness out. Light pierces even the heaviest darkness.

Jesus came to our dark world as light. Enough said. He is our glorious Light and our salvation. Light wins and darkness can't prevail against Him. And yet the world is still dark in so many places. Could I be wrong? Is it possible darkness is strong enough to shroud light? Absolutely not. A million times no. The only way darkness can withstand light is when the light decides to cover itself.

We know God will not force people to receive His light, so if they cloak their hearts in rejection of God, then darkness is allowed to continue. But it is even more tragic that so many who have glimpsed and embraced light choose to slide back into darkness. Darkness is allowed to prevail based on the choice of people to not let their light shine.

John, a kind and gentle apostle of Christ, announces that light has appeared and we now have a choice to reflect it or reject it. What will we choose?

I choose light! I want no darkness in my life, dear God. I want the light within me
to grow that I may drive out darkness wherever I am in the world.

FOOLING OURSELVES

If we say we have no sin, we are fooling ourselves, and the truth is not in us.
But if we confess our sins, he will forgive our sins, because we can trust God
to do what is right. He will cleanse us from all the wrongs we have done.

1 JOHN 1:8–9, NCV

No one is perfect but Jesus. Only He lived a pure and sinless life. The rest of us have fallen in our words, deeds, and attitudes, and in our humanness; undoubtedly, despite our best intentions and growth in grace, we will fall again.

What seems to be worse than any sin we might commit is our refusal to acknowledge it. We've all witnessed situations where someone makes a mess of things by sinning but then compounds the mess by trying to cover it up. When we lie to others and ourselves about sin, we create the only condition possible for the power of grace and forgiveness to be blocked from our lives.

If you were to drive along in your car and get a flat tire, surely you wouldn't abandon the car in frustration—and surely you wouldn't continue to drive it until you ruined more than a rubber tire. You would get out and change the tire. That's what confession is and does. It doesn't abandon the faith in anger or discouragement. It doesn't pretend things are okay when they aren't. It changes the tire. And the wonderful news is that when we come to Jesus with a repentant heart, all our sins are forgiven, even ones we aren't aware of.

Let's not fool ourselves and let's certainly not think we can fool God. Confess and move on with full forgiveness and grace in life!

I bring my sin before you, God, thanking you for
forgiving and restoring me completely and victoriously.

SO YOU WILL NOT SIN

My dear children, I write this letter to you so you will not sin.
But if anyone does sin, we have a helper in the presence of the Father—Jesus Christ,
the One who does what is right. He died in our place to take away our sins,
and not only our sins but the sins of all people.

1 JOHN 2:1–2, NCV

As parents, we love our children dearly and deeply. We raise them to know God and live for Him. We raise them to make good decisions and work hard. We want them to be successful in all their endeavors. But when they make wrong decisions and stumble, we don't kick them out of the home and disown them. We don't make excuses for them, but neither do we batter them with our words until they feel like a complete failure. We talk to them. We ask questions. We listen. We help them think through what happened. We pray with them. Bottom line, we still love them. Love covers, protects, waits, and believes in till the very end.

It is a false perception to think that our sins don't matter to God and others. But it's also a false perception to think that sin will cause God not to love us any longer. Some have perceived God as an angry parent or judge, just waiting for us to get out of line so He can squash us like a bug. Nothing could be further from the truth.

He so wants you in grow in grace and walk in light. His will is that you not sin. But He is so faithful in His love for us, to redeem us and reestablish us on our Christian walk. Jesus Christ took our place on the cross to take away our sins and the sins of the world. That event reaches backward and forward to meet our need of forgiveness just when we need it. He is a loving Father who wants only your best. Talk to Him now about any sin or problems you have in your life.

Thank you for your kindness, God. You provide a way for me to experience fellowship
with you, no matter what I've done. I am so grateful for your love.

HATE

Anyone who says, "I am in the light," but hates a brother or sister,
is still in the darkness. Whoever loves a brother or sister lives in the light
and will not cause anyone to stumble in his faith.

1 JOHN 2:9–10, NCV

*H*ave you ever been told—or have you ever told someone—"I hate you"? *Hate* is such a harsh and hurtful word and emotion. Jesus says that hate is the same as murder, because murder springs from a heart that hates.

Now, I'm sure there have been times when the word *hate* has been used when it was really an expression of extreme frustration. But we know that words matter and can take on a life of their own. Speaking hatefully can easily turn into hatred as it fans the flame of a negative emotion.

There are many ways to hurt someone, including ignoring them. But hatred is an active and attentive attitude that needs to be addressed before it causes hurt that is deep and extremely damaging. Even if your hate feels justified, in the end the hatred becomes like a cancer to your soul.

Friends, don't let anger toward anyone take root in your heart. Paul says, "'In your anger do not sin': Do not let the sun go down while you are still angry" (Ephesians 4:26, NIV). Nip even the slightest sign of anger and hatred in the bud. Take it to God in confession and humility. Refuse to live in such darkness!

Righteous God, I don't want to cause anyone to stumble due to
bad attitudes in my life—especially not anger. Give me a heart
of love around everyone I meet.

WHY I WRITE YOU

I remind you, my dear children:
Your sins are forgiven in Jesus' name.

1 JOHN 2:12, THE MESSAGE

*E*ach book has a different purpose. I wrote this book to reveal Jesus, the One I love and serve. John wrote his first letter to reveal Jesus and give a word of encouragement to those whom he loved so dearly. The power and simplicity of the following words is such a perfect expression of those two things:

I write to you, little children, because your sins are forgiven you for His name's sake. I write to you, fathers, because you have known Him who is from the beginning. I write to you, young men, because you have overcome the wicked one. I write to you, little children, because you have known the Father. I have written to you, fathers, because you have known Him who is from the beginning. I have written to you, young men, because you are strong, and the word of God abides in you, and you have overcome the wicked one.

I John 2:12–14, NKJV

Heavenly Father, thank you for letting me know
how much you love and care for me.
Thank you for your words of encouragement and life expressed in Scripture.

DON'T LOVE THE WORLD

Do not love the world or the things in the world. If you love the world,
the love of the Father is not in you. These are the ways of the world:
wanting to please our sinful selves, wanting the sinful things we see,
and being too proud of what we have. None of these come from the Father,
but all of them come from the world. The world and everything that people want
in it are passing away, but the person who does what God wants lives forever.

1 JOHN 2:15–17, NCV

Not love the world? How can this be? The world is our home. Didn't God create the world, after all? Isn't this too severe of a teaching?

First, let's remember that when John says "the world," he is not talking about God's creation. When God created the world He declared that it was both "good" and "very good" (see Genesis 1–2). John is warning us not to love something that is quite different. The culture he lived in was so wicked that when he warned against not loving the world, he was referring to the common and casual immorality of the day—and even more so, the spirit of demanding what we want above what the Father wants for us.

Why should he even have to warn us of this? Simple. Sin can be alluring and seductive, even the sin that destroys relationships and reputations. We already know that the pride of demanding our way over God's way is at the root of all other sins and can be seen since the dawn of time in the garden of Eden.

My friends, God doesn't want to take anything good away from us. When He calls us to separate ourselves from sin, it is because He loves us and only wants what's best for us. Heed His warning today!

Father, protect my spirit and my life from all temptation and sin.
I renew my prayer that I desire your will more than anything else in the world.

CHILDREN OF GOD

*The Father has loved us so much that we are called children of God.
And we really are his children. The reason the people in the world
do not know us is that they have not known Him.*

1 JOHN 3:1, NCV

Have you ever been told, "You wouldn't understand"? Whether they are right or wrong, the person speaking those words believes they have had a unique experience that others can't comprehend.

"You wouldn't understand." Out of caution to not be offensive, we would never put it like that to nonbelievers, but it really is true—you can't understand the joy and purpose found in the Christian life until you have met Jesus for yourself. The world might say good things or bad things about us as Christians based on their assumptions of what our life is like. But it's the opposite of the adage "I'll believe it when I see it." That's not how it works. You'll see it when you believe it. That's when the Christian life makes sense.

The joy of knowing God begins with His love for us. We're not servants or employees. We're not club members. We're not distant relatives. We're not good neighbors. We're children. His children. The Creator of the universe is our Father. He knows us and loves us. What else could give life more meaning and purpose?

---

*You have called me your child, and I am so humbled and moved by that.
Thank you that when I felt like an outcast and an orphan in this world,
you loved me so much you made me part of your family.*

DESTROY THE DEVIL'S WORKS

Dear children, do not let anyone lead you the wrong way. Christ is righteous.
So to be like Christ a person must do what is right. The devil has been sinning
since the beginning, so anyone who continues to sin belongs to the devil.
The Son of God came for this purpose: to destroy the devil's work.

1 JOHN 3:7–8, NCV

John understands that none of us have or will live the perfect life. He reveals God's kindness in forgiving and restoring us when we do sin. Yet he also reveals God's righteousness and that sin will never be taken lightly by Him.

God is loving and patient. He is there for us when we stumble. He knows that we don't have the willpower to always choose the right way. But He does want us to always come back to dependence on Him. If the prayer you pray more than any other is "Forgive me, Father. Thank you for your grace to live your way," then so be it.

Even if it seems you are stuck in a pattern of defeat in your Christian walk, don't give up. Don't stop believing in God and yourself. If He loves you and knows you can live with power and victory, then you must believe the same thing.

Don't forget you really are being transformed into Christlikeness. Earlier in chapter 3 John says, "Dear friends, now we are children of God, and we have not yet been shown what we will be in the future. But we know that when Christ comes again, we will be like him, because we will see him as he really is" (v. 2).

"We will be like him." What a hope. What a future!

Gracious heavenly Father, thank you for your patience and love that forgives
me as many times as I need forgiveness. Thank you that even now you are transforming
me into Christlikeness that I may live pure and victorious.

LOVE EACH OTHER

This is the teaching you have heard from the beginning:
We must love each other.

1 JOHN 3:11, NCV

Whenever we read about sin and unrighteousness in Scripture, the topic of love for one another is sure to follow. For if we think of the Christian life as a long book filled with thousands of rules that must be kept, it makes it sound like a joyless religion that is impossible to live. But when we understand that what God really wants from us is love for Him and love for others, then we gain a vision of how sweet and wonderful our faith really is. It's not a burden of remembering a shopping list of rights and wrongs. It is a lifestyle of worship and kindness that comes naturally from transformed hearts. Our purpose and drive become focused on the question "How can I better love God and others?"

Do you want to love others more? Then love God more. Do you want to love God more? Then love others more. These two loves fit together so perfectly.

If you are struggling to express love to someone today, then reaffirm your love of God and do what you can, all the time saying, "I really do love you, God." Love for that brother or sister is sure to follow. If your relationship with God feels a little stale today, then express love to others in your world as an act of worship, saying, "I love you so much, God."

Thank you that living a pure life for you
is grounded in loving you, my Father, and loving all your children.
Nothing makes life so sweet and true.

GREATER THAN FEELINGS

This is the way we know that we belong to the way of truth.
When our hearts make us feel guilty, we can still have peace before God.
God is greater than our hearts, and he knows everything.

1 JOHN 3:19–20, NCV

*G*uilt is not always a bad thing. Guilt can point out where we are doing wrong. But guilt does have the ability to choke us in the very foundation of who we are. And God certainly does not want our lives dominated by guilt.

The devil is an accuser and loves to throw guilt at us like flaming arrows. He would love to see us bogged down in the misery of feeling too guilty to do anything; guilt can actually paralyze us. My friends, if your life is weighed down by a mountain of guilt, realize that this is not from God but straight from the pit of hell. Claim the forgiveness and new life that God freely offers you in Jesus Christ right now.

But I still feel guilty. If you have asked God for forgiveness and still feel guilty, that means the enemy, the accuser of the brethren, is just trying to play havoc with God's promises over your life. John tells us that God is greater than our hearts. Our feelings can't be trusted. I have learned over many many years that even though I am created an emotional being, my emotions can lie to me. If I allow them to rule me, I will definitely fall short of what God says about me. The joy of the Lord is my strength. Fruit of the Spirit is not dependent on my circumstances.

The devil accuses but God forgives. Believe that, no matter what your feelings tell you today.

❧

God, you are the One who forgives us and makes us new.
Thank you for releasing me from my bondage of guilt and shame.
Thank you for doing a work in my life that cannot be tainted even by my feelings.

NO FEAR

Every spirit who refuses to say this about Jesus is not from God. It is the spirit of the enemy of Christ, which you have heard is coming, and now he is already in the world. My dear children, you belong to God and have defeated them; because God's Spirit, who is in you, is greater than the devil, who is in the world.

1 JOHN 4:3–4, NCV

We have nothing to fear in this world—no matter how dark the valleys seem to be. We are conquerors in Christ because the Spirit that lives within us is greater than any spirits in this world. You are protected and able to fulfill all that God has planned for you to do for Him. How? His Holy Spirit is in you. The devil is not an equal and opposite power to God. He is already defeated.

Fear keeps us from doing what God would have us to do. Perhaps that's why John tells us that fear and love go so closely together: "Where God's love is, there is no fear, because God's perfect love drives out fear. It is punishment that makes a person fear, so love is not made perfect in the person who fears" (v. 18).

Are you feeling fearful today? Ask yourself this question: Do I know and believe how much God, the Creator and Sustainer of the universe, really loves me? If you still feel fearful, keep praying. Keep asking God for the assurance that you truly are His beloved child. Don't stop until His Spirit gives you that assurance deep in your heart.

Only one thing can drive fear out of your life and give you freedom to be who God created you to be. That's full assurance of the love of God.

<hr />

Jesus loves me, this I know, for the Bible tells me so. I do believe you love me, my Lord God. Thank you for driving fear out of my heart and life. Thank you that the Holy Spirit is greater than any other power or force in the world. Thank you that you have not given me a spirit of fear, but of love, power, and a sound mind.

HE FIRST LOVED US

We love because God first loved us.

1 JOHN 4:19, NCV

This single sentence expresses the heart of salvation. No, we aren't saved because we went out and found God and initiated a relationship with Him. We are saved because He loved us first. He spoke to us before we were even thinking about Him. In the same way, we won't love Him, live for Him, honor and worship Him, or obey Him because of our determination and strength to do the right thing. No, once again, our love is our rightful response, from the first day of our salvation until we see Him face-to-face in glory.

Have you thanked God for reaching out to you in love today? Have you thanked Him for the grace to walk in life without fear? Have you thanked Him for taking your sins upon himself in Jesus Christ? Have you thanked Him for delivering you from the destructive force of hatred? Have you thanked Him for the motivation and power to love others? Have you thanked Him for protecting you and your family? Have you thanked Him for calling you His child? Have you thanked Him for the plan of salvation that was present before the beginning of time? Have you thanked Him for the ongoing provision of forgiveness from sin?

We have so much to be grateful for, as John has shown us throughout this powerful little letter. And it all began because God loved us first.

Words cannot express my gratitude for all you have given me, O God.
I ask for nothing other than the privilege of telling you how much I love you today.
I enter your courts with thanksgiving in my heart.

ETERNAL LIFE

*I write this letter to you who believe in the Son of God
so you will know you have eternal life.*

1 JOHN 5:13, NCV

There is a strange notion in the world that if we think beyond this world and into eternity, then we probably don't take this world seriously enough—that maybe we are not even supposed to make the current world a better place.

I don't think anything could be further from the truth. When God plants the seeds of eternity in our hearts, when God offers and bestows to us eternal life, the hope of glory we receive makes us so much more inclined to do the very best with all that God has entrusted to us. We are designed to passionately hope for heaven and to live life fully, loving God and loving others, but remaining mindful that this world is not our home. Heaven awaits.

Have you heard the good news, my friends? When we receive Jesus into our hearts, we get the experience of knowing Him today—and forever. What could be better than that?

I know there are disappointments and setbacks in the world we live in. Things don't always go the way we hope. But Jesus says that we can trust Him as the Lord of our lives today and forevermore. Jesus has shown us the way and gone before us.

If you need a genuine word of encouragement, I am so pleased to echo John's words: "I write this letter to you who believe in the Son of God so you will know you have eternal life."

*Beautiful God, I praise you for the joy of your presence now and forever,
my eternal and all-powerful God.*

WHATEVER WE ASK

And this is the boldness we have in God's presence:
that if we ask God for anything that agrees with what he wants,
he hears us. If we know he hears us every time we ask him,
we know we have what we ask from him.

1 JOHN 5:14–15, NCV

*G*od is not a magician. He is a father, a builder, our Creator. It is incredible that we are asked to go before Him with our requests and expect Him to answer. So what's the key to getting whatever we want in prayer? I believe it's all about desiring what God wants. Just as Jesus prayed, "Not my will but yours," when we pray first and foremost for God's will in our lives, when we enter His presence with thanksgiving and invite the Spirit of God to change us, we can have confidence that God is at work bringing about His good plans into fruition in our lives.

We are asked to bring all our needs and requests before God. Don't hesitate to do so. Realize you are God's child and the delight of His heart. But don't stop there. Pray that you would be part of bringing about His will and His plans in and through you. The plans He has for you are greater and bigger than anything you could ever imagine.

I come before you boldly today, my God.
I want and ask for nothing but your will to be done.
Thank you that I already have what I ask for.

RESTORE US

If my people, who are called by my name, will humble themselves and
pray and seek my face and turn from their wicked ways, then I will hear
from heaven, and I will forgive their sin and will heal their land.

2 CHRONICLES 7:14, NIV

Solomon calls the people of Israel together at his coronation. Though he is not the oldest son, his father, David—the youngest of seven brothers—hands the throne to him with kind and stern words of counsel. Solomon starts right with a beautiful prayer and leads the people to say together, "He is good; His love endures forever" (v. 3). Solomon's reign did not end like it started. He fell into the sins of pride, lust, and idolatry—he worshiped other gods. His sins destabilized the country, and it split in two upon his death.

God had seen the infidelity of His people. He was angry and saddened to know that few of the kings would be true to their promises. The pattern of idolatry led to destruction, which then led to a cry for help, which led to revival and renewal . . . and then back down the slippery slope of not acknowledging God as the one true God, the only source of help and hope.

God is sad and angry with His people, but even if they are not true to their promises, He will be true to His. So the faithful God offers a simple way to return to Him: "Humble yourself; pray and seek my face; turn from your wicked ways." When they do that, He will hear them, forgive them, and heal the land.

This is an instruction to Solomon for national renewal, but the commands for humility, prayer, and repentance are just as powerful for a church or an individual. Have you lost your way? Humble yourself and pray. God will hear!

I ask that you keep me from wicked ways, O God of deliverance.
Thank you that you never turn your face from us when we call to you for help.

RESISTING TEMPTATION

A Classic Devotion by Thomas à Kempis

But the end of all things is at hand:
be ye therefore sober, and watch unto prayer.

1 PETER 4:7, KJV

So long as we live in this world, we cannot remain without trial and temptation: as Job says, "Man's life on earth is a warfare" (Job 7:1). We must therefore be on guard against temptations, and watchful in prayer (I Pet. 4:7), that the Devil find no means of deceiving us. . . .

Although temptations are so troublesome and grievous, yet they are often profitable to us, for by them we are humbled, cleansed, and instructed. All the Saints endured many trials and temptations (Acts 14:22), and profited by them.

No man can be entirely free from temptation so long as he lives; for the source of temptation lies within our own nature, since we are born with an inclination towards evil (James 1:14) when one temptation or trial draws to a close, another takes its place; and we shall always have something to fight, for man has lost the blessing of original happiness.

We must not despair, therefore, when we are tempted, but earnestly pray God to grant us his help in every need. For, as Saint Paul says, 'With the temptation, God will provide a way to overcome it, that we may be able to bear it' (I Cor. 10:13). So, let us humble ourselves under the hand of God (I Peter 5:6), in every trial or trouble, for He will save and raise up the humble in spirit in all these trials.

I humble myself before you, my Lord and Savior.
Strengthen me whenever I face trials and temptations of any kind.

MESSIAH

JESUS IS THE SAVIOR BORN TO US.
HE IS MESSIAH, THE LORD.

DECEMBER

You are ever interceding
    As the lost become the found
You can _never_ be defeated
    For You wear the VICTOR'S crown
You are JESUS the MESSIAH
    You're the HOPE of all the world
By Your grace I live & breathe
To worship You

Glory!

Jesus, you have
overcome the world!
Amen! Amen!

NEVER ASHAMED

*For I am not ashamed of this Good News about Christ. It is the power
of God at work, saving everyone who believes—the Jew first and also the Gentile.*

ROMANS 1:16, NLT

My grandparents began taking me to church when I was a little girl, and I remember that as my parents found faith, they started taking us as well. But it wasn't until our family had gone through a crisis that I found myself as a fifteen-year-old searching for more of God than I had ever known before. I went searching, and He found me. Jesus came into my life and radically transformed my heart, and He has been changing me ever since!

It was after this miraculous encounter that I found a fire of conviction to share my faith. Not out of compulsion, but out of a desperation to see people find the same freedom I had found. A love like no other.

Friends, it's from this place of revelation that we find the confidence to share our faith, to share this great love of God that has saved us with those who are in our world. We have no reason to be afraid, for it is the kindness of God that draws people to himself. I am so glad someone shared this great loving Savior with me.

Let's proclaim with Paul that we are never ashamed of that which saved us, even in the face of opposition. And let's pray for open and receptive hearts so we can have opportunity share this glorious gift with others.

St. Francis of Assisi is quoted as saying, "Preach the gospel at all times, and if necessary, use words." Let's share this gospel of grace with our words and our actions: one message, one hope . . . Jesus.

*Lord Jesus, I pray that my life is a reflection of declaring the gospel
with everything I say and everything I do.*

NO THANKS

*For ever since the world was created, people have seen the earth and sky.
Through everything God made, they can clearly see his invisible qualities—his eternal
power and divine nature. So they have no excuse for not knowing God.
Yes, they knew God, but they wouldn't worship him as God or even give him thanks.*

ROMANS 1:20–21, NIV

Even those who have never heard the name of Jesus Christ are aware of the creator God. Too often, those who don't know God worship the creation rather than the Creator. People see the splendors of all God has done but refuse to give Him honor.

Even today, I find it completely mind-blowing that the Creator of heaven and earth not only created and cares about each one of us but actually desires relationship with us. Take a moment to think about this today.

In every generation, every culture, every society, the same question is eventually posed: Will you worship the creation or the Creator? We worship things like sports, comfort, our own efforts. . . . Unfortunately, it doesn't take long for truthful worship to be corrupted by our own weaknesses. But beautifully, when we are weak, He is strong!

It is when we recognize God as the Creator that we recognize ourselves as created—in His image, perfectly put together, designed for relationship with Him. As the psalmist declares, it is He who has made us. Ultimately, worshiping anything other than the Creator means we have set ourselves up as our own lord and god.

We are so blessed to have heard the name of Jesus, to accept His love and power in our lives, and to receive the revelation of His eternal power and divine nature.

I bow before you in praise today, O God, my Creator, my Designer, and my Deliverer.

GOD'S CHOSEN

A true Jew is one whose heart is right with God. And true circumcision is not merely obeying the letter of the law; rather, it is a change of heart produced by God's Spirit. And a person with a changed heart seeks praise from God, not from people.

ROMANS 2:29, NLT

There are two amazing thoughts in this verse. First, when the Spirit of God enters our life, our hearts are changed. Actually, Ezekiel 36:26 says, "I will give you a new heart and put a new spirit in you; I will remove from you your heart of stone and give you a heart of flesh" (NIV). How grateful I am for this miracle.

Throughout the Old Testament we read how God established His kingdom through the children of Abraham, the Israelites. They were not always faithful, but they were always chosen. Though an obscure tribe in an obscure part of the world, they preserved God's teaching for all generations to come. What an honor to tell and retell the story of the great Yahweh.

A second thought that jumps out at me is that last sentence: "A person with a changed heart seeks praise from God, not from people." Who do you live to please? Who do I live to please? Is it an audience of man, or God Almighty himself? I want to please Him! Think about this today, that the One who is worthy of all our praise and honor also delights in lavishing His love on us. I know I am unworthy, but I am so grateful and humbled that He would do that.

We have been chosen as God's people. We are given a new heart. Even as we praise God, He praises us. These are deep and humbling thoughts indeed!

Thank you for a new heart through the presence of the Holy Spirit in my life.
I put my life in your Hands O God, and live to please you.

UNDESERVED KINDNESS

For everyone has sinned; we all fall short of God's glorious standard.
Yet God, with undeserved kindness, declares that we are righteous.
He did this through Christ Jesus when he freed us from the penalty for our sins.

ROMANS 3:23–24, NIV

*I*f you had been a member of the early church, what would you have thought of Paul? I am sure we would have been tempted to dislike and distrust him. He was there as Stephen was stoned to death. He poured all his considerable energies into hunting down Christians and becoming the chief persecutor of the church. But then while on a mission to expand the persecution of Jesus' followers, he met Jesus face-to-face and his life was changed forever.

If anyone understood that God's kindness was undeserved, it was Paul. Many of us who follow Jesus today know just how broken our lives were before we had our own encounter with the risen Christ. We know just how under served His kindness to us was and is. But even if we grew up in a godly home that taught us from the earliest age to love and honor God—and oh what a blessing that is—we still don't deserve His kindness. All of us have sinned and fallen short of His glory. None of us merit salvation through our own efforts. All of us are absolutely dependent on the love and grace of Jesus Christ and all He has done for us.

No, we don't dwell on the past and our failings. God says He forgets our sins, remembers them no more. But we never forget that salvation and all God's blessings come to us out of His kindness. When He declares us as righteous, our only response can be profound gratitude and all our praise.

I come to you with such a grateful heart, and I believe you declare me righteous, O God,
through your Son, Jesus Christ. I am so undeserving. Yet through faith, I receive with
praise and thanksgiving the gift you have given me. I am always and forever yours.

RIGHT WITH GOD

He was handed over to die because of our sins,
and he was raised to life to make us right with God.

ROMANS 4:25, NLT

The book of Romans has been at the center of revivals throughout history. Even though he had served God as a missionary to the American colony of Georgia, John Wesley still was filled with doubts about his faith, until as he describes, "One was reading Luther's preface to the Epistle to the Romans. About a quarter before nine, while he was describing the change which God works in the heart through faith in Christ, I felt my heart strangely warmed. I felt I did trust in Christ, Christ alone, for salvation; and an assurance was given me that He had taken away my sins, even mine, and saved me from the law of sin and death."

Following this experience, Wesley testifies he went from misery to conqueror: "After my return home, I was much buffeted with temptations, but I cried out, and they fled away. . . . He 'sent me help from his holy place.' And herein I found the difference between this and my former state chiefly consisted. I was striving, yea, fighting with all my might under the law, as well as under grace. But then I was sometimes, if not often, conquered; now, I was always conqueror."

Wesley became one of the greatest evangelists and reformers the church has ever known. It all began when he let the precious words of this precious book sink deep in his heart. His life was changed forever through the Holy Spirit at work. If you are experiencing doubts in your Christian walk, read again—and again—the truth of Romans 4:25. Your heart will be strangely warmed! I am praying for you today.

I do trust in Christ, Christ alone, for salvation. Thank you, God, that you have taken away all my sins, yes, even mine! My heart will trust in you, my God.

AT JUST THE RIGHT TIME

When we were utterly helpless,
Christ came at just the right time and died for us sinners.

ROMANS 5:6, NLT

There is a temptation before and after we experience Christ that we must get our act together to experience God's fullness and favor. It sounds honorable. It seems like a good mind-set. I will please God so that He will love me and call me His child. The problem is that it just doesn't work. In fact, it is one of the most dangerous and confusing teachings that has risen up over centuries, fueling a performance-based Christianity, enabling us to take some of the credit for the change in our lives. As long as the enemy can convince us that there's something we can do to earn God's favor, he knows he can keep us in a state of confusion and defeat and pride. It's not our sinfulness that blocks God's grace and love; it's that nagging and persistent belief that we can do something about it in our own power.

No, my friends, it is Christ who saves us. He comes at just the right time. He saves us when we are utterly helpless—and know we are utterly helpless. Salvation comes through our faith in God—and our victorious living comes in the very same way.

We are called to be bold in our faith. But boldness always begins with humility—the full knowledge that it is by grace, not works, lest any of us boast. My cherished friends, let's dig in and live fully for God, always acknowledging Him as the Source of our victory.

The Bible is a "come as you are" book. You can come today before the Father, just as you are. Welcome Him into your life. You will never be the same.

Dear God, I live boldly for you, always grateful and humble
that I am utterly helpless to do your will without your strength and love.

FRIENDS WITH GOD

*So now we can rejoice in our wonderful new relationship with God
because our Lord Jesus Christ has made us friends of God.*

ROMANS 5:11, NIV

*F*riendship is one of God's great gifts to us. There is the richness of strength and joy that comes from friendship with the people He has put into our lives. We need the love and support of others so much. But what makes our life complete is that God himself becomes our greatest Friend. No one understands and loves us more than the Creator of the universe.

What is our response to this marvelous verse? Do we believe it? Do we cultivate friendship with God? Do we live with the constant thought in mind that God is our best friend? In *The Purpose Driven Life*, Rick Warren says, "You are as close to God as you choose to be. Intimate friendship with God is a choice, not an accident. You must intentionally seek it."

What a gift and blessing is ours that God should call us His friend—that He desires intimate fellowship with us. But as is the case with all His gifts to us, He asks us to respond, to lean in toward Him, not out of compulsion but out of a deep desire for more of Him. He will never force us to receive all He has for us but asks us to make a choice in our heart and mind.

The offer is there. God says, "I have made you my friend through Jesus Christ." Will you walk in that knowledge that God is beside you as your God, your Creator, your Deliverer . . . and your friend?

*You are so great and mighty that I am sometimes afraid to call you my Friend.
I pray that I will let your affection and kindness to me sink deep into my spirit, O God.*

DEAD TO SIN

*For the wages of sin is death, but the free gift of God
is eternal life through Christ Jesus our Lord.*

ROMANS 6:23, NLT

Through this magnificent gospel of grace that we read in Romans, Paul reminds us that God still takes sin seriously. Apparently there were believers in Paul's day—and our day—who formed an opinion that how we live, righteously or sinfully, just doesn't matter. One cult in history that had a famous member—the Russian monk Rasputin—believed that they should sin even more than they did before meeting Christ so that more of His grace would flow. To such nonsense Paul challenges any who would embrace such heresy with the question: "Well then, should we keep on sinning so that God can show us more and more of his wonderful grace? Of course not! Since we have died to sin, how can we continue to live in it?" (vv. 1–2).

Salvation is not by works. Your righteousness is not based on your acts of righteousness. But how you live matters to God. It matters because God is a lover of truth, not living one way and talking another way. The Father is seeking those who will worship Him in spirit and in truth. I truly pray today that you don't feel like you have to hide areas of your life. If there is an area of temptation that continually leads to defeat in your life, please don't ignore it and hope it is of no concern to God, to your own life, and to those around you. Come back to God and ask for deliverance, with a humble and contrite heart but also the full assurance that "the free gift of God is eternal life through Christ Jesus our Lord." What freedom awaits you.

Don't give up. Don't settle. The God who saves you will also deliver you from the power of sin that would destroy your life.

*God, I need your mercy and kindness every day. I am tempted and sometimes fall.
But I know that your victory is mine through the victory of Jesus over sin and death.*

WHO WILL FREE ME?

Oh, what a miserable person I am! Who will free me from this life
that is dominated by sin and death? Thank God! The answer is
in Jesus Christ our Lord. So you see how it is: In my mind I really want
to obey God's law, but because of my sinful nature I am a slave to sin.

ROMANS 7:24–25, NLT

f Paul, a great lion of God, knew the sting of defeat from the pull of his sinful nature, then be assured we will feel this pull too. All honest believers have cried out with a testimony similar to Paul's: "In my mind I really want to obey God's law, but because of my sinful nature I am a slave to sin."

But even before he speaks those words, Paul gives us the way of escape. He already knows the answer: "The answer is in Jesus Christ our Lord."

Paul is describing the futility of trying to please God in our own strength. Embedded in our sinful nature is the desire to do things our own way. We might even do great for a little while, but eventually we fail. So we try harder next time.

Paul was at the end of his rope. He had tried to please God through keeping the law. But despite his tremendous efforts, he had finally discovered what God so patiently and graciously was trying to teach him. You can't do it in your own strength.

Are you at the end of your rope? Have you discovered you just aren't able to get everything done on your own? That's marvelous news. For it's at that point that you and I can escape the misery of believing we can do what only God can do for us. Be joyful—you are now ready to live as God wants you to live!

Forgive me for the pride of my heart that says I can live a righteous life in my own
strength and power. I am broken before you. But you lift me up and show me once again
to depend on the strength of the gift of Christ Jesus my Lord.

NO CONDEMNATION

So now there is no condemnation for those who belong to Christ Jesus.
And because you belong to him, the power of the life-giving Spirit
has freed you from the power of sin that leads to death.

ROMANS 8:1–2, NLT

I will always think of myself as a Bible student, not a Bible scholar. The miracle that God will speak directly to me through His Word is something that I treasure more than anything. And I also treasure the words of great godly men and women who have gone before me. These words from Martin Luther are so profound—yet so clear on the message of Romans:

"Faith is a work of God in us, which changes us and brings us to birth anew from God. It kills the old Adam, makes us completely different people in heart, mind, senses, and all our powers, and brings the Holy Spirit with it. What a living, creative, active powerful thing is faith! . . . Faith doesn't ask whether good works are to be done, but, before it is asked, it has done them. It is always active. Whoever doesn't do such works is without faith; he gropes and searches about him for faith and good works but doesn't know what faith or good works are. . . .

"Faith is a living, unshakeable confidence in God's grace; it is so certain, that someone would die a thousand times for it. This kind of trust in and knowledge of God's grace makes a person joyful, confident, and happy with regard to God and all creatures. This is what the Holy Spirit does by faith."

What a testimony! "And because you belong to him, the power of the life-giving Spirit has freed you from the power of sin that leads to death."

Your life-giving power is at work in me through the Holy Spirit. I thank you and praise
you, God. Thank you that my life is no longer condemned because I belong to Jesus!

FUTURE GLORY

Yet what we suffer now is nothing compared to the glory he will reveal to us later. For all creation is waiting eagerly for that future day when God will reveal who his children really are.

ROMANS 8:18–19, NLT

God created a beautiful world for us. He put us in a garden where our every need was met and our every joy was found. He put us in a place of love, where He himself would walk and talk with us. He gave us the gift of companionship. He gave us a world of beauty and delight. But through sin, oh what a mess we have made of things. Since the fall of Adam and Eve our world has been filled with strife and lack. Paul tells us that not only has sin put burdens on us, but all of creation has suffered and groans under the effects of sin. Earthquakes and hurricanes; famine, drought, and floods; wars and murder . . . all are evidences of a fallen world.

In *Paradise Lost* by John Milton, the Archangel Michael says to Adam: "Since you committed your original sin, there is really no true liberty anymore. Liberty is linked to wisdom, so when a man is unwise or ignores what he should know, that's when unhealthy desires take over. Then his mind becomes a slave to his desires."

Even as we see the loss of our freedom, we catch a glimpse of the future glory that awaits us when we are truly free again. Don't give up hope. A day is coming soon when God will restore all that is lost! "The One on the Throne will pitch his tent there for them: no more hunger, no more thirst, no more scorching heat. The Lamb on the Throne will shepherd them, will lead them to spring waters of Life. And God will wipe every last tear from their eyes" (Revelation 7:15-17, THE MESSAGE).

I eagerly await the day when we will be free from all the ravages of sin and your new heaven and new earth are established!

NOTHING CAN SEPARATE US

And I am convinced that nothing can ever separate us from God's love. Neither death nor life, neither angels nor demons, neither our fears for today nor our worries about tomorrow—not even the powers of hell can separate us from God's love. No power in the sky above or in the earth below—indeed, nothing in all creation will ever be able to separate us from the love of God that is revealed in Christ Jesus our Lord.

ROMANS 8:38–39, NLT

*L*et's not give in to fear and uncertainty. We don't know how every detail of life will work out. We will be faced with an array of threats. Life will include struggles on a grand scale and even in the everyday moments of each day.

But we are more than conquerors. Our foundation is sure. Nothing can drag us away from our place in eternity. No matter how precarious and ferocious the forces against us may seem, nothing, absolutely nothing can separate us from God's love.

Never forget that the devil is a liar that seeks to sidetrack us with fear and worry. What if you are threatened with death? We may not want to leave this world, but we already know in our hearts that we will be in God's presence forever. So that holds no real threat to us. Worries about tomorrow will plague our emotions and make life seem very uncertain—but only if we let them. Fear and worry aren't from God. The Word of God says that perfect love casts out all fear—not just some fear but all fear. Nothing can snatch us from God's arms of protection.

Today is a day to rejoice and worship. Today is a day to affirm that God is all powerful and will work out everything in our lives for His glory. Praise and worship God. And as we focus on His love, our fears and worries are put back into true perspective.

You hold me in your arms, O God. I will not give fear and worry a foothold in my life. I worship you with all my love and faith!

O HOLY NIGHT

Glory to God in the highest heaven, and on earth peace
to those on whom his favor rests.

LUKE 2:14, NIV

Angels and shepherds gave glory at our Savior's birth. Let's join the chorus and sing our praise!

O holy night! The stars are brightly shining,
It is the night of the dear Savior's birth.
Long lay the world in sin and error pining.
Till He appeared and the soul felt its worth.
A thrill of hope the weary world rejoices,
For yonder breaks a new and glorious morn.
Fall on your knees! Oh, hear the angel voices!
O night divine, the night when Christ was born;
O night, O holy night, O night divine!

Truly He taught us to love one another,
His law is love and His gospel is peace.
Chains he shall break, for the slave is our brother.
And in his name all oppression shall cease.
Sweet hymns of joy in grateful chorus raise we,
With all our hearts we praise His holy name.
Christ is the Lord! Then ever, ever praise we,
His power and glory ever more proclaim!

I bow before you, God my King.
I proclaim your power and glory to the world.

THE POWER OF THE MOST HIGH

The angel answered, "The Holy Spirit will come on you, and the power of the Most High will overshadow you. So the holy one to be born will be called the Son of God.

LUKE 1:35, NIV

An angel visited Mary to let her know she was "favored of God." The angel told her, "Do not be afraid, Mary; you have found favor with God" (v. 30). He has repeated that she has found God's favor. None of us will be given Mary's unique and miraculous task, but all of us should note that we too have found God's favor. It is in His loving nature to redeem our lives and give us a supernatural purpose in life. My dear friends, when we realize deep in our hearts that God favors us, there is no longer any room for fear.

But she was so young. And this pregnancy would raise questions about her morals. We know from Matthew's gospel that Joseph thought of ways that he could break his engagement from Mary without causing her shame and humiliation in their hometown. But God visited Joseph as well, and the proclamation of our verse is "the power of the Most High will overshadow you." Her response? "I am the Lord's servant. Let everything you've said happen to me" (v. 38, GOD'S WORD).

God's power was all the protection Mary needed in her obedience to Him. Oh to walk in Mary's humble obedience. Has God whispered in your ear? Has He given you an assignment that seems too great, too grand for your abilities? Then celebrate. You have found God's favor—His power and great love for you will protect and empower you each step of the journey.

*God of power, there are times I have not felt strong enough
to do what you have laid on my heart to do. Give me the simple and humble
confidence and faith that Mary showed!*

JUST AS HE PROMISED

He has helped his servant Israel, remembering to be merciful to Abraham and his descendants forever, just as he promised our ancestors.

LUKE 1:54–55, NIV

One of the amazing things about people of great faith is that they not only celebrate God's faithfulness to His promises after they have come to pass in their lives, but recognize His promises as something complete and finished—even before there is seen evidence.

When Mary went to visit her cousin, Elizabeth was filled with the Holy Spirit and prophesied over Mary's Son: "You are the most blessed of all women, and blessed is the child that you will have. I feel blessed that the mother of my Lord is visiting me. As soon as I heard your greeting, I felt the baby jump for joy. You are blessed for believing that the Lord would keep his promise to you" (vv. 42–45, GOD'S WORD).

To receive such affirmation from a loved one made Mary feel like she was hearing words of encouragement and blessing directly from God—and I believe she was. Mary's heart was so filled with the wonder of God's goodness that her love and gratitude spilled over into a song of praise, blessing those around her. I have wondered if she sang her song of praise to Jesus. Babies need to be held, and nothing comforts them like the soft voice of their mother singing. If so, Mary's song blessed the heart of our Savior. Oh, to write and sing songs that bring joy to God. May it be so.

The theme of her song was praise for God's mercy and faithfulness, that He helped His servants "just as He promised."

Heavenly Father, you have always been true to me. I praise you and thank you for your favor and your promises in my life. We are truly blessed.

PREPARE THE WAY

*And you, my child, will be called a prophet of the Most High; for you will
go on before the Lord to prepare the way for him, to give his people the knowledge of
salvation through the forgiveness of their sins, because of the tender mercy of our God,
by which the rising sun will come to us from heaven to shine on those living in darkness
and in the shadow of death, to guide our feet into the path of peace.*

LUKE 1:76–79, NIV

*M*ary's cousin Elizabeth was called by God to carry a son as well. The
great sorrow of her and Zechariah's life was that they had not been able
to bear children and they assumed she was past the age of childbearing. While doing
his priestly duty, Zechariah received word that he and Elizabeth were to have a child.
Because this faithful man didn't believe God, the Lord made him mute until the birth
of his son. I think Zechariah needed a reminder of who was in charge. But oh how his
mouth was opened up in praise and worship on that eventful day—and just a taste of
his joyful song is noted above.

Her dream of a son fulfilled, Elizabeth still found the time and energy to comfort
and celebrate with her young cousin Mary. Elizabeth's son was not the one who would
bring salvation, but he was born to "prepare the way" for the Messiah—and this he
did until the day of his death. This tenderhearted mother would easily understand
God's plan for his life, for in the same way, her kindness and comfort to Mary also
helped to prepare the way for the birth of the Savior of the world.

How do we prepare the way for people to receive the Savior? Our faithful obedience, a steadfast belief in God's goodness, and our tender love for others will open the
hearts of those God brings into our lives to the reality of God's love.

*O God, I want to proclaim my Savior through my words—but may my everyday life
and love show people that the Savior is truly near.*

DON'T BE AFRAID

But the angel said to them, "Do not be afraid.
I bring you good news that will cause great joy for all the people."

LUKE 2:10, NIV

*I*f you wanted to broadcast the news of an amazing event, where would you go to announce it? Probably a big city. Who would you invite? Undoubtedly the most influential media networks you could gather.

God doesn't do things the way we do them. His ways are not our ways and His thoughts are not our thoughts. God entered the world as a baby in a small town nestled in a small country far from the crossroads of the Roman Empire. The first press release of the birth went to shepherds, everyday laborers who worked far from the bright lights of the city. But God's ways are always perfect, and from this humble beginning the name of Jesus was taken to the four corners of the world.

The first words the angel spoke were "Fear not." Many artistic images of angels are of chubby little babies, cute and harmless. But angels like Michael were mighty warriors. To have one of God's angels appear late one night in a remote landscape would strike terror in the heart of a shepherd armed only with a staff.

As this Christmas season draws near, I pray, my friends, that you will remember two things: First, the message of God's salvation is grand and magnificent—but most often appears in humble, everyday circumstances. Keep your eyes open to see Jesus meet you in a quiet, remote place. He will be looking for you! Second, whatever makes you fearful, be assured that God's messengers always speak to you with the simple command "Fear not." If God is with you and for you, what do you have to fear?

Thank you, glorious Father, for bringing word of salvation
to us through everyday people just like us.

A SAVIOR IS BORN

Today in the town of David a Savior has been born to you;
he is the Messiah, the Lord.

LUKE 2:11, NIV

This verse is the culmination of God's promise: "For to us a child is born, to us a son is given, and the government will be on his shoulders. And he will be called Wonderful Counselor, Mighty God, Everlasting Father, Prince of Peace" (Isaiah 9:6).

Oh what a Savior Jesus is. He doesn't become a Savior over time—even as a baby in the manger He is our Savior. The word for *Savior* tells us that the One has appeared who completely frees us from all evil and danger. Jesus was sent to give us victory, even over death. Nothing can separate us from the love of this Savior!

The Hebrew people had long awaited the Messiah, but many completely missed His appearance due to their preconceptions of how God should do His work. How tragic. But our world isn't so different today. The "arrogance of man" is to tell God how to do His business, when our spiritual response needs to be the very opposite: an attitude of openness and obedience to His will and His ways. In our striving to be strong and get ahead, to have our way, we miss the Wonderful Counselor, the Mighty God, the Everlasting Father, the Prince of Peace.

My dear friends, humble your spirit and open your heart to the birth of the Anointed One. We already know full well our plans, our schemes, doing things in our way and our own power doesn't bring salvation and peace to our souls or to our world. Only a true Savior can do that. He is here. He was born to me, to you, to all of us.

Father, your love and generosity are beyond my ability to comprehend.
I stand in awe that you would come to me with the gift of yourself. Glory to your name!

SPREAD THE WORD

When they had seen him, they spread the word
concerning what had been told them about this child,
and all who heard it were amazed at what
the shepherds said to them.

LUKE 2:17–18, NIV

How wonderful it is to receive a gift. But how much greater it is to share a gift with others. The gift of a Savior is absolutely for you, for your heart and soul. But God's gift of love is given to you to share with others! That's when the joy of receiving such a marvelous gift explodes inside us. When was the last time you shared what God has done in your life with such conviction that others were impacted?

Simple shepherds, going about their business, could not help but run back to their towns to let others know they had been visited by angels proclaiming the long awaited Messiah. They didn't stop to worry that people might think they were a bit crazy or were just seeing things. They didn't worry about whether they had all the right words and could speak with eloquence—they just told what happened to them. That's all God asks. He uses us just as we are. Our testimony of meeting the Savior is powerful and exactly what someone in your life needs to hear.

Study is great. A class might be beneficial. But don't hesitate in the meantime to run back to your village. Tell your friends and loved ones about what you've seen and heard. Share your gift and spread the word—the Savior is born!

Father, the gift of your Son, my Savior, the Savior of the world,
is something I cannot keep to myself. Give me a joyful urgency
to share Jesus with my world.

TREASURED IN THE HEART

But Mary treasured up all these things and pondered them in her heart.

LUKE 2:19, NIV

*M*ary pondered all that had happened to her—from the visit of an angel to a miraculous conception to the fear of losing her betrothed to a long and arduous journey to the birth of her son, the Savior of the world—not just in her mind, but in her heart. She let all that had happened to her—all that God had done in and through her—sink deep into her heart. I am reminded of David's response to God's Word when he declared, "I have hidden your word in my heart that I might not sin against you" (Psalm 119:11).

Life comes at us fast. It is busy and noisy. All the squares in our calendar are filled with appointments and activities—most important and good. But I want to stop, to embrace Sabbath, to slow down, let the world swirl around me, and just think on God: His goodness, mercy, faithfulness, and love. I want to do nothing but ponder the gift of His Son, the Savior of the world. Another meaning for *ponder* is "to weigh"—she gave each moment and memory its true weight and importance in her own life and for the very life of the world.

Do you remember when Martha scolded Mary for not helping with cleaning up after guests and household work? Jesus spoke firmly and lovingly to Martha and said, "Martha, Martha! you worry and fuss about a lot of things. There's only one thing you need. Mary has made the right choice, and that one thing will not be taken away from her" (Luke 10:41-42, GOD'S WORD).

This Christmas season, stop from the work and treasure the gift of Jesus. That is something that can never be taken away from you.

I treasure the gift of Jesus, my Savior, above all other activities and joys. Thank you, God, for the greatest gift of all—something that can never be taken away from me.

AS YOU HAVE PROMISED

Sovereign Lord, as you have promised, you may now dismiss your servant in peace.
For my eyes have seen your salvation, which you have prepared in the sight of all nations:
a light for revelation to the Gentiles, and the glory of your people Israel.

LUKE 2:29–32, NIV

othing stirs my soul like being around God's children who have served him faithfully into their old age. My own grandparents are stirred with great faith even at 98 and 101 years of age. Tears well in my eyes when I think of their faithfulness in both good times and bad. Much like joining the celebration of an elderly couple celebrating a special anniversary—seeing that their love for one another is as real as it was on their wedding day—we just know in our hearts we are in the presence of something beautiful and special.

This precious man Simeon lived a devout and honorable life. He had received a promise from God that gave all his days a divine purpose and meaning: "The Holy Spirit was with Simeon and had told him that he wouldn't die until he had seen the Messiah, whom the Lord would send" (vv. 25–26, GOD'S WORD). Simeon was so attuned to God's voice that he was led to the temple courts on the day that Joseph and Mary brought Jesus to be circumcised. In the midst of the crowd, this saint of God recognized that the Messiah was present—that God was faithful to His promises.

A devout Jew, he knew that the Messiah was for all mankind, for Gentiles and Israel alike. My friends, let us have that same kind of faith, filled with a joyful anticipation that is absolutely confident God will do exactly as He promised. What a powerful statement he makes: "Dismiss your servant in peace." He had no fear of death. He knew he had met the Savior and his life was in the hands of a loving God.

Speak to me, O God, and give me ears to listen to your encouragement and guidance.
When my life on earth is finished, may I express the same confidence as Simeon.

AN HONORABLE MAN

When Joseph woke up, he did what the angel of the Lord had commanded him to do. He took Mary to be his wife.

MATTHEW 1:24, GOD'S WORD

When Joseph learned his fiancée was already pregnant, he made plans to cancel the wedding—even though he and Mary were already husband and wife at the moment of their engagement in that society. Joseph, who had never slept with Mary, was not willing to accept that, but he was not harsh and unkind. "Joseph was an honorable man and did not want to disgrace her publicly" (v. 19). I think there's a lesson for all of us in that simple verse. Even when we don't agree with the actions of others—and in Joseph's case his first assumptions were very wrong—our response should never be to trumpet the wrongdoing of others.

Not only was Joseph honorable, but he was spiritual too. After making his plans, he was visited by an angel in a dream and trusted this was a word from God: "Joseph, descendant of David, don't be afraid to take Mary as your wife. She is pregnant by the Holy Spirit. She will give birth to a son, and you will name him Jesus [He Saves], because he will save his people from their sins" (vv. 20–21).

Not everyone in Nazareth was visited in a dream. Some would whisper behind Joseph's back over the circumstances of Mary's pregnancy. Some men might have conveniently concluded that what happened in the middle of the night was only a dream. But not Joseph. He was, after all, honorable. His instant obedience meant that he was blessed with the indescribable honor of being Jesus' earthly father.

My dear friends, let's not miss the blessing of obedience. Who knows what God has planned for you and me? When God speaks to you, trust Him and obey Him.

Father God, thank you for models of faith and obedience in your Word.

THE LORD'S GREATNESS

My soul praises the Lord's greatness!
My spirit finds its joy in God, my Savior, because
he has looked favorably on me, his humble servant.

LUKE 1:46–48, GOD'S WORD

*E*very mother knows that the birth of a child is a moment of indescribable joy. Even after a long day or night of pain, holding the precious, tiny bundle in your arms is a spiritual moment when you know that God has looked favorably on you.

For Mary there were so many extraordinary events swirling around her life when she carried Jesus in her womb. "I'm a virgin. How can I be pregnant?" The visit of an angel. Wondering if her betrothed would leave her. Her cousin Elizabeth prophesying over her son. The arduous journey to Bethlehem on the back of a donkey. A heavenly host to herald her son's birth.

What a nine-month journey to the birth of her baby, and then to find that the only accommodation available was a lowly stable, not a warm room with a comfortable bed. What carried her through that time? Was she tempted to feel sorry for herself? Did she wonder if God was good?

In Luke 1:46–55, Mary showed us what was in her heart and soul. She lifted her voice in joyful praise at the greatness of God.

On this coming Christmas morning, no matter what my natural circumstances may present, I will treasure the time I share with my family and friends. But most of all, I want to lift my heart in praise of my Savior. Glory to God in the highest.

Thank you, God my Savior, for looking favorably
at me and showering my life with blessings.

JOY TO THE WORLD

Shout for joy to the Lord, all the earth, burst into jubilant song with music.

PSALM 98:4, NIV

I pray your Christmas season has been a time of joy and laughter. But I pray it has also been a season to shout your praise to the Lord!

Joy to the world, the Lord is come!
Let earth receive her King;
Let every heart prepare Him room,
And heaven and nature sing,
And heaven and nature sing,
And heaven, and heaven, and nature sing.

No more let sins and sorrows grow,
Nor thorns infest the ground;
He comes to make His blessings flow
Far as the curse is found,
Far as the curse is found,
Far as, far as, the curse is found.

He rules the world with truth and grace,
And makes the nations prove
The glories of His righteousness,
And wonders of His love,
And wonders of His love,
And wonders, wonders, of His love.

I am in awe at the wonders of your love,
O Lord, that have come to us through the birth and life of Jesus.

A PRAYER FOR CHRISTMAS MORNING

A Classic Devotion by Henry Van Dyke

Glory to God in the highest,
and on earth peace, good will toward men.

LUKE 2:14, KJV

The day of joy returns, Father in Heaven,
and crowns another year with peace and good will.
Help us rightly to remember the birth of Jesus,
that we may share in the song of the angels,
the gladness of the shepherds, and the worship of the wise men.
Close the doors of hate and open the doors of love all over the world.
Let kindness come with every gift and good desires with every greeting.
Deliver us from evil, by the blessing that Christ brings,
and teach us to be merry with clean hearts.
May the Christmas morning make us happy to be thy children,
and the Christmas evening bring us to our bed with grateful thoughts,
forgiving and forgiven, for Jesus' sake.

Amen.

WISE GIFTS

When they entered the house, they saw the child with his mother Mary.
So they bowed down and worshiped him. Then they opened their treasure chests
and offered him gifts of gold, frankincense, and myrrh.

MATTHEW 2:11, GOD'S WORD

There is much we don't know about the wise men—the magi—who visited Jesus. They came from the East bearing gifts befitting of a king. They quite probably studied a number of subjects, including astronomy and religion.

I believe they were sincere in their seeking. They listened attentively to Herod's scholars as they spoke of biblical prophecy and why the Messiah was to be born in Bethlehem. When they arrived at Joseph and Mary's house and saw the baby, their every action was touched by reverence and awe. Spiritually sensitive, they left Bethlehem by a different path that took them far from Herod's scheming.

In that moment of worship, did they understand Jesus was the Savior of the world? We really don't know, but I suspect they never forgot that journey and continued to seek Jesus.

One of the gifts they brought Jesus was gold. Most Bible teachers believe those coins funded Joseph and Mary's trip to Egypt when Herod went on his murderous rampage. The grand message to me is that God used these wise men as part of His wondrous plan of salvation. They worshiped the Savior—and through their gifts were part of God's providence in protecting His Son.

Diligence. Respect. Generosity. Spiritual sensitivity. Perhaps these are the greatest gifts of the wise men for us today in our faith.

Father, I stand in awe at your providence throughout history. I confess I don't always
know what you are doing, but I thank you that you can use me for your work.

THE FULL ARMOR OF GOD

Finally, be strong in the Lord and in his mighty power.
Put on the full armor of God, so that you can take your stand against
the devil's schemes. For our struggle is not against flesh and blood,
but against the rulers, against the authorities, against the powers of this
dark world and against the spiritual forces of evil in the heavenly realms.

EPHESIANS 6:10–12, NIV

There may be evil forces arrayed against us, but we can prevail. We don't even have to be a good warrior. The key is to be strong in the Lord—Jesus is our protector and will fight on our behalf—so that we can take our stand. Notice, it is not our power but Jesus' mighty power. Though the battle is the Lord's to fight for us, we still wear the full armor of God.

What makes up the armor of God? What do we wear into the battle that Jesus will win on our behalf? The belt of truth, the breastplate of righteousness, the gospel of peace, the shield of faith, the helmet of salvation, and the sword of the Spirit. Each part of armor is a way we signify our complete trust in and dependence upon God.

One explanation Paul offers is that the sword of the Spirit is God's Word. The writer to the Hebrews tells us God's Word is alive and sharper than a two-edged sword. Friends, let's always carry that weapon with us. The devil may act like he's not afraid, but watch him keep a safe distance when he sees you wield that lethal weapon! As Jesus said to the enemy in Matthew 4: "It is written." He pushed back with the Word of God, our ultimate authority.

Stand on the Word of God, in Jesus' name. This is where we place all our hopes.

I depend on your mighty power. My strength is in you and nowhere else.
I put on your full armor that I may stand faithful before you and my world.

GENTLY RESTORE

Brothers and sisters, if someone is caught in a sin,
you who live by the Spirit should restore that person gently.
But watch yourselves, or you also may be tempted.

GALATIANS 6:1, NIV

We all know people we love and admire who have really messed up in life. They have blown it, and their sins have caused damage in and around their lives. Usually they already know they've made mistakes, they are embarrassed, and they really don't need the bright spotlight of condemnation. They are probably more disappointed in themselves than anyone else is. They don't need to be berated—and they don't need to be kicked out of our lives. Too often we have severed relationships with those who fall into sin rather than love them back into fellowship with God and the church. Just imagine if God treated us like that in our own sin!

Paul's simple counsel is to help restore the one caught in sin gently, not with a holier-than-thou attitude but with humility and kindness, knowing full well we have the same need for a Savior.

Paul does give one word of warning. If the person we are reaching out to in love is really not serious about being restored, watch out. Don't let them become a temptation to you to fall into sin.

We reveal Jesus to the person we help restore—and to those who witness the return of a prodigal into the family of Christ. Don't ever cut people off because they've made mistakes. We all have. We are all in need of a Savior.

You know my friend who is trapped in sin, O God. You know how much
I care about them and I know how great your love is for them. Give me a gentle spirit
and wise words to help restore them.

HEAVY BURDENS

Carry each other's burdens,
and in this way you will fulfill the law of Christ.

GALATIANS 6:2, NIV

The "burdens" Paul is speaking about are not the everyday challenges and trials we all face. This word describes an excessive weight no one person can pick up by himself. Later on in verse 5 of this chapter Paul says, "For each one should carry their own load." The word for load can be translated "backpack."

Every person needs to take responsibility for their own actions in life. Remember that every action has an outcome. Choose your behavior wisely.

But for the person who has had a weight they did not choose dropped into their life, a weight that is impossible for them to pick up—maybe a crippling illness, the loss of home and livelihood, a terrible loss of relationship, imprisonment that might be physical or psychological—we need to be there. We fulfill the law of Christ by being the friend who helps lift.

We live in a culture where many people don't like to make commitments to others. It might mess up their lives of ease or delay some entertainment they were wanting to watch. Friends, we are to be different from the world, and nowhere will that be more evident than in how we help others bear the excessive weights of life. Are you prepared to be inconvenienced for the sake of another?

Give me a heart of love for everyone I encounter, O God.
Give me a supernatural love for those who are carrying burdens
they can't handle on their own. I want to be more like you, Jesus.

A BLESSED BLESSING

"I will make you into a great nation, and I will bless you; I will make your name great, and you will be a blessing. I will bless those who bless you, and whoever curses you I will curse; and all peoples on earth will be blessed through you."

GENESIS 12:2–3, NIV

God chose Abraham to be the father of our faith. He asked him to leave his father's land—Ur was actually quite prosperous and cultured, so I'm sure it was not an easy place to leave—to travel to an unknown land and destination. He wanted Abraham to separate himself from the godless forces at work in his world. He challenged Abraham to leave his comfort zone. Abraham obeyed.

God promised to bless him, to make his name great, and to make him a blessing to others. He promised to bless those who blessed him and curse those who cursed him. He promised to bless all peoples on earth through him.

God still chooses people today. In fact, God chooses you. Don't look around. I'm talking directly to you. You are chosen. And the promises He makes to you are very similar to the promises He made to Abraham. He chooses you to step out of your comfort zone and obey Him in order that your life is both blessed and a blessing. I pray today that you will sense the great blessing that God is over your world, and that you would in turn live with your heart and hands open to share His greatness with all.

Your call is sealed with the giving of Jesus. He will reveal His Son to you continually—that you may reveal Jesus to your world.

Thank you for choosing me, O God. Thank you for meeting me where I was—lost in my sins. Thank you for loving me and believing in me and giving me a purpose in life.

VICTOR'S CROWN

Words and Music by Darlene Zschech, Israel Houghton, & Kari Jobe

You are always fighting for us
Heavens angels all around
My delight is found in knowing
That You wear the victor's crown
You're my help and my defender
You're my Savior and my friend
By Your grace I live and breathe
To worship You

At the mention of Your greatness
In Your Name I will bow down
In Your presence fear is silent
For You wear the victor's crown
Let Your glory fill this temple
Let Your power overflow
By Your grace I live and breathe
To worship You

Chorus
Hallelujah
You have overcome
You have overcome
Hallelujah
Jesus, You have overcome the world

You are ever interceding
As the lost become the found
You can never be defeated
For You wear the victor's crown
You are Jesus the Messiah
You're the Hope of all the world
By Your grace I live and breathe
To worship You

Bridge
Every high thing must come down
Every stronghold shall be broken
You wear the victor's crown
You overcome
You overcome

At the cross the work was finished
You were buried in the ground
But the grave could not contain You
For You wear the victor's crown

THANK YOU...

*Mark Gilroy for all your help, Danny McGuffey, and my longtime friends
at Bethany/Baker. Thank you to my best friend, Mark Zschech, who as my husband and
my pastor inspires me in my pursuit to follow Christ with all I am. My heart also
belongs to my children and grandchildren. I live to bless them. And thank you to our
Hope UC family. What an honor it is to do life with you all. Greatest days ahead.*

All classic hymn lyrics in the public domain. "Great Is Thy
Faithfulness" by Thomas Obediah Chisholm, 1923. "My Hope
Is Built" ("The Solid Rock") by Edward Mote, 1834. "Amazing
Grace" by John Newton, 1779. "Holy, Holy, Holy!" by Reginald
Heber, 1826. "To God Be the Glory" by Fanny Crosby, 1875.
"Blessed Assurance" by Fanny Crosby, 1873. "Christ the Lord Is
Risen Today" by Charles Wesley, 1739. "Beneath the Cross of
Jesus" by Elizabeth Clephane, 1868. "Breathe on Me, Breath of
God" by Edwin Hatch, 1878. "It Is Well With My Soul" by Horatio
Spafford, 1873. "What a Friend We Have in Jesus" by Joseph
Scriven, 1855. "O Holy Night" by Placide Cappeau, 1847, tr. by
John Dwight, 1855. "Joy to the World" by Isaac Watts, 1719.

"Victor's Crown" copyright © 2013. International Copyright
Secured. All Rights Reserved. Used by Permission.

Scripture quotations identified AMP, and subsequent quotations in the
same devotion unless otherwise indicated, are from the Amplified®
Bible, copyright © 1954, 1958, 1962, 1964, 1965, 1987 by The
Lockman Foundation. Used by permission.

Scripture quotations identified ESV, and subsequent quotations in the
same devotion unless otherwise indicated, are from The Holy Bible,
English Standard Version® (ESV®), copyright © 2001 by Crossway,
a publishing ministry of Good News Publishers. Used by permission.
All rights reserved. ESV Text Edition: 2007

Scripture quotations identified GOD'S WORD, and subsequent
quotations in the same devotion unless otherwise indicated, are from
GOD'S WORD®. © 1995 GOD'S WORD to the Nations. Used by
permission of Baker Publishing Group.

Scripture quotations identified HCSB, and subsequent quotations in
the same devotion unless otherwise indicated, are from the Holman
Christian Standard Bible, copyright 1999, 2000, 2002, 2003 by
Holman Bible Publishers. Used by permission.

Scripture quotations identified THE MESSAGE, and subsequent
quotations in the same devotion unless otherwise indicated, are from

THE MESSAGE by Eugene H. Peterson, copyright © 1993, 1994,
1995, 2000, 2001, 2002. Used by permission of NavPress Publishing
Group. All rights reserved.

Scripture quotations identified NASB, and subsequent quotations
in the same devotion unless otherwise indicated, are from the New
American Standard Bible®, copyright © 1960, 1962, 1963, 1968,
1971, 1972, 1973, 1975, 1977, 1995 by The Lockman Foundation.
Used by permission.

Scripture quotations identified NCV, and subsequent quotations in the
same devotion unless otherwise indicated, are from the New Century
Version®. Copyright © 1987, 1988, 1991 by Word Publishing,
a division of Thomas Nelson, Inc. Used by permission. All rights
reserved.

Scripture quotations identified NIRV, and subsequent quotations
in the same devotion unless otherwise indicated, are from the Holy
Bible, New International Reader's Version®. NIrV®. Copyright
© 1995, 1996, 1998 by Biblica, Inc.™ Used by permission of
Zondervan. All rights reserved worldwide. www.zondervan.com

Scripture quotations identified NIV, and subsequent quotations in the
same devotion unless otherwise indicated, are from the Holy Bible,
New International Version®. NIV®. Copyright © 1973, 1978, 1984,
2011 by Biblica, Inc.™ Used by permission of Zondervan. All rights
reserved worldwide. www.zondervan.com

Scripture identified NIV1984, and subsequent quotations in the same
devotion unless otherwise indicated, taken from the HOLY BIBLE,
NEW INTERNATIONAL VERSION®. Copyright © 1973,
1978, 1984 Biblica. Used by permission of Zondervan. All rights
reserved.

Scripture quotations identified NKJV, and subsequent quotations in
the same devotion unless otherwise indicated, are from the New King
James Version. Copyright © 1982 by Thomas Nelson, Inc. Used by
permission. All rights reserved.

Scripture quotations identified NLT, and subsequent quotations in the
same devotion unless otherwise indicated, are from the Holy Bible,
New Living Translation, copyright © 1996, 2004, 2007 by Tyndale
House Foundation. Used by permission of Tyndale House Publishers,
Inc., Carol Stream, Illinois 60188. All rights reserved.

Scripture quotations identified TNIV, and subsequent quotations
in the same devotion unless otherwise indicated, are from the Holy
Bible, Today's New International Version®. TNIV®. Copyright
© 2001, 2005 by Biblica, Inc.™ Used by permission of Zondervan.
All rights reserved worldwide. www.zondervan.com

Scripture quotations identified KJV, and subsequent quotations in the
same devotion unless otherwise indicated, are from the King James
Version of the Bible.

Art direction by Paul Higdon & LaVonne Downing

Design by Lookout Design, Inc.

Manuscript prepared by Mark Gilroy.